Practice Papers for SQA Exams

Intermediate 2

English

ISBN 978-1-84372-777-4

Published by
Leckie & Leckie Ltd,
an imprint of HarperCollins*Publishers*
Westerhill Road, Bishopbriggs, Glasgow, G64 2QT
Tel: 0870 460 7662 Fax: 0870 787 1720
enquiries@leckieandleckie.co.uk   www.leckieandleckie.co.uk

A CIP Catalogue record for this book is available from the British Library.

Leckie & Leckie is grateful to the following companies for permission to reproduce their material. The following companies have very generously given permission to reproduce their copyright material free of charge:

HarperCollins Publishers Ltd for the extract from 'Toast: The Story of a Boy's Hunger' by Nigel Slater (Practice Exam A, pages 10-11)

Every effort has been made to trace the copyright holders and to obtain their permission for the use of copyright material. Leckie & Leckie will gladly receive information enabling them to rectify any error or omission in subsequent editions.

Questions and answers in this book do not emanate from SQA. All of our entirely new and original Practice Papers have been written by experienced authors working directly for the publisher.

MIX
Paper from
responsible sources
FSC™ C007454

FSC™ is a non-profit international organisation established to promote the responsible management of the world's forests. Products carrying the FSC label are independently certified to assure consumers that they come from forests that are managed to meet the social, economic and ecological needs of present and future generations, and other controlled sources.

Find out more about HarperCollins and the environment at
www.harpercollins.co.uk/green

Introduction

Layout of the Book

This book contains practice exam papers, which mirror the actual SQA exam as much as possible. The layout, paper colour and question level are all similar to the actual exam that you will sit, so that you are familiar with what the exam paper will look like.

The answer section is at the back of the book. Each answer contains a worked out answer or solution so that you can see how the right answer has been arrived at. The answers also include practical tips on how to tackle certain types of questions, details of how marks are awarded and advice on just what the examiners will be looking for.

Revision advice is provided in this introductory section of the book, so please read on!

How To Use This Book

The Practice Papers can be used in two main ways:

1. You can complete an entire practice paper as preparation for the final exam. If you would like to use the book in this way, you can either complete the practice paper under exam style conditions by setting yourself a time for each paper and answering it as well as possible without using any references or notes. Alternatively, you can answer the practice paper questions as a revision exercise, using your notes to produce a model answer. Your teacher may mark these for you.

2. You can use the Topic Index at the front of this book to find all the questions within the book that deal with a specific topic. This allows you to focus specifically on areas that you particularly want to revise or, if you are mid-way through your course, it lets you practise answering exam-style questions for just those topics that you have studied.

Revision Advice

Work out a revision timetable for each week's work in advance – remember to cover all of your subjects and to leave time for homework and breaks. For example:

Day	6pm-6.45pm	7pm-8pm	8.15pm-9pm	9.15pm-10pm
Monday	Homework	Homework	English revision	Chemistry Revision
Tuesday	Maths Revision	Physics revision	Homework	Free
Wednesday	Geography Revision	Modern Studies Revision	English Revision	French Revision
Thursday	Homework	Maths Revision	Chemistry Revision	Free
Friday	Geography Revision	French Revision	Free	Free
Saturday	Free	Free	Free	Free
Sunday	Modern Studies Revision	Maths Revision	Modern Studies	Homework

Make sure that you have at least one evening free a week to relax, socialise and re-charge your batteries. It also gives your brain a chance to process the information that you have been feeding it all week.

Arrange your study time into one hour or 30 minutes sessions, with a break between sessions e.g. 6pm-7pm, 7.15pm-7.45pm, 8pm-9pm. Try to start studying as early as possible in the evening when your brain is still alert.

Study a different subject in each session, except for the day before an exam.

Do something different during your breaks between study sessions – have a cup of tea, or listen to some music.

Have your class notes and any textbooks available for your revision to hand as well as plenty of blank paper, a pen, etc. You may like to make keyword sheets like the example below:

Keyword	Meaning
tone	The way somebody says or writes something as an indicator of what that person is feeling or thinking
theme	Topic or recurring idea in a piece of writing
plot	The story or sequence of events in a novel, play or film

Finally forget or ignore all or some of the advice in this section if you are happy with your present way of studying. Everyone revises differently, so find a way that works for you!

Transfer Your Knowledge

As well as using your class notes and textbooks to revise, these practice papers will also be a useful revision tool as they will help you to get used to answering exam style questions. You may find as you work through the questions that they refer to an example that you haven't come across before. Don't worry! You should be able to transfer your knowledge of a topic or theme to a new example. The enhanced answer section at the back will demonstrate how to read and interpret the question to identify the topic being examined and how to apply your course knowledge in order to answer the question successfully.

Command Words

In the practice papers and in the exam itself, a number of command words will be used in the questions. These command words are used to show you how you should answer a question – some words indicate that you should write more than others. If you familiarise yourself with these command words, it will help you to structure your answers more effectively.

Command Word	Meaning/Explanation
Identify	Used in Close Reading – it asks you to find something, often a technique used by the writer. Sometimes you have to name the technique; at other times find an example of the technique being used.
Suggest	Give more than just simple information – perhaps a reason or an idea.
Show	A word used in Critical Essay questions. It means demonstrate by analysis.
Describe	Give more detail than you would in a basic outline, and use examples where you can.
Explain	Used in Close Reading. Discuss why an action has been taken or an outcome reached or a word/technique chosen – what are the reasons and/or processes behind it.
Justify	Give reasons for your answer, stating why you have reached a particular conclusion.
Define	Give the meaning of the term.
Compare	Give the key features of 2 different items or ideas and discuss their similarities and/or their differences.

In the Exam

Watch your time and pace yourself carefully. Work out roughly how much time you can spend on each answer and try to stick to this. For example, don't spend more than 45 minutes on each essay in the Critical Essay paper.

Be clear before the exam what the instructions are likely to be e.g. how many questions you should answer in each section. The practice papers will help you to become familiar with the exam's instructions.

Read the question thoroughly before you begin to answer it – make sure you know exactly what the question is asking you to do. If the question is in sections e.g. 2(a), 2(b), etc. make sure that you answer all sections.

For the Critical Essay paper, plan your answer by jotting down keywords, key quotes or references, a mindmap or reminders of the important things to include in your answer.

Don't repeat yourself as you will not get any more marks for saying the same thing twice.

Give proper explanations. A common error is to give descriptions rather than explanations. If you are asked to explain something, you should be giving reasons. Check your answer to an 'explain' question and make sure that you have used plenty of linking words and phrases such as 'because', 'this means that', 'therefore', 'so that', 'due to', 'since' and 'the reason is'.

English Intermediate 2 Practice Papers

This book contains four complete Intermediate 2 English exam papers. The questions featured in both the Close Reading and the Critical Essay sections are the kind of questions that come up every year in the SQA exam. Using this book will help you to become familiar with exam questions. As mentioned above, you could either work through the materials as complete exam papers, or use them to help you revise particular questions. The answer section at the end of the book is designed not just to give you the answers, but, more importantly, to explain the answers, and to give you some help with how to arrive at the answers. In the Critical Essay section of the answers I have tried to give you some guidance about how to approach the questions, and an idea of how to plan your answers. I have mentioned a few texts which you may have studied, but only to help explain a point – there are no set texts in Intermediate 2 English. Prepare for the exam with the texts you have studied, and enjoyed.

The four papers can be tackled in any order, but I have made the first Close Reading paper ("Spaghetti Bolognese") an easier read than the other three. If you are working through the book yourself, or are using the book early in the course, it would be a good idea to start with this one. Close Reading is just as it says: a test of your ability to read a text closely, or carefully. It tests your understanding of a text and your ability to analyse what the writer is trying to do; it also asks you to evaluate the writing. Remember, the best way to prepare yourself for it is not just by doing practice papers like these, but by reading, and thinking about what you are reading. Even if you don't especially enjoy reading novels or long texts, you can improve your reading skills by reading newspapers or magazines. Start by reading what interests you: several newspapers contain high quality sports sections, or have extended interviews with actors, musicians or prominent people in the weekend magazines.

Before your exam it would be a good idea to skim through all of the Critical Essay papers just to make sure you can answer two questions from each paper. The questions are not designed to catch you out, rather to give you the opportunity to write about the texts you have studied throughout the year.

Good luck!

Topic Index

Topic	Exam A Close Reading	Exam A Critical Essay	Exam B Close Reading	Exam B Critical Essay	Exam C Close Reading	Exam C Critical Essay	Exam D Close Reading	Exam D Critical Essay	Knowledge for Prelim Have difficulty	Knowledge for Prelim Still needs work	Knowledge for Prelim OK	Knowledge for SQA exam Have difficulty	Knowledge for SQA exam Still needs work	Knowledge for SQA exam OK
Understanding	2, 6, 7, 10, 11, 12, 13		1(a), 4, 5, 8, 10		5, 6, 7, 10, 11(a), 12		1, 2(b), 3(b), 5, 7, 9							
Analysis	1(b), 3, 4, 5, 8, 12(b)		1(b), 1(c), 2, 3, 6, 7, 11, 12		1, 2, 3, 4, 8, 9, 11(b)		2(b), 3(a), 3(c), 4, 8, 11							
Evaluation	9, 14		9, 13		13		6, 10							
Sentence structure	12(b)		1(c), 2(b), 7, 12		2, 8		2(b), 8(a), 8(b)							
Link question			6		3		4							
Tone	1(b)		11				3(c)							
Character		1, 3, 4		1, 3, 4		1, 3, 4, 8, 11		1, 3, 4, 6, 7						
Opening, turning point, ending		2, 6		6, 10				2, 10, 12						
Issue		5		2, 9, 12										
Conflict				3, 11				1, 4						
Experience		8		7				8						
Emotion/ emotional response		7, 9		7		4, 10		3						
Interesting topic				5, 8		8								
Language (advertising)		13		15		15		13						
Language (groups)		14		14		13		15						

Practice Exam A

Practice Paper A: Intermediate 2 English

Practice Papers
For SQA Exams

ENGLISH
INTERMEDIATE 2

Exam A
Close Reading

Answer all of the questions

You have 1 hour to complete this paper.

Read the following passage and then answer the questions. Remember to use your own words as much as possible.

The questions ask you to demonstrate that you:

understand the ideas and details in the passage – **what the writer has said**
(**U**: Understanding)

can identify the techniques the writer has used to express these ideas – **how it has been said**
(**A**: Analysis)

can comment on how effective the writer has been, using appropriate evidence from the passage
– **how well it has been said**
(**E**: Evaluation)

The code letters (U, A, E) are next to each question to make sure you know the question's purpose. The number of marks per question will give you a good idea as to how long your answer should be.

Leckie×Leckie
Scotland's leading educational publishers

SPAGHETTI BOLOGNESE

In this extract from his autobiography, Nigel Slater writes about the first time he ate Spaghetti Bolognese.

"We...are...going to have...spaghetti, no, SPAGHETTI...just try a bit of it. You don't have to eat it if you DON'T LIKE it." Mum is yelling into Auntie Margaret's "good" ear. Quite why she thinks there is a good one and a bad one is a mystery. Everyone knows the old bat doesn't bother to use either ear.

5   Neither Margaret nor Mum has eaten spaghetti before, and come to think of it neither have I. Dad is waiting for the water to boil on the stove. The sauce is already warm, having been poured from its tin a good half-hour ago and is sitting on the cool plate of the stove, giving just the occasional blip-blop.

When the water finally boils my father shakes the strands of pasta out of the blue
10 sugar paper that looks for all the world like a great long firework, and stands them in the bubbling water. They splay out like one of those fibre-optic lights we saw at the Ideal Home Exhibition on the BBC. As the water comes back to the boil he tries to push the spikes under the water. "They'll never all go in," he snaps, trying to read the packet, which, even when read with his glasses, is in Italian. Some of the brittle sticks
15 break in half and clatter over the hotplate.

"Will I like it, Dad?" I ask, half hoping he'll change his mind and Mum will cook us all some chops.

"Just try it," he says, a somewhat exasperated tone creeping in to his voice. "Just try it."

"I think you should put some salt in," chirps in Mum.

20 Auntie Margaret is looking down at her lap. "Do I have to have some?" I think she is going to cry.

"I think it must be done now," says my father twenty minutes later. He drains the slithery lengths of spaghetti in a colander in the sink. Some are escaping through the holes and curling up in the sink like nests of worms. "Quick, get the plates, they're
25 getting away."

We all sit there staring at our tumbling piles of pasta on our glass Pyrex plates. "Oh, Kathleen, I don't think I can," sobs Auntie Margaret, who then picks up a long sticky strand with her fingers and pops it into her mouth from which it hangs all the way down to her lap.

30 "No, wait for the sauce, Margaret," Mother sighs, and then quite out of character, "Come on, Dad, hurry up." Dad pours the sauce, a slurry of reddy-brown mince that smells strange, over the knots and twirls of pasta. Suddenly it all seems so grown-up, so urbane and sophisticated.

Mum wraps the strands round her fork, "Like this, do it like this," then shovels it
35 towards Margaret's pink, little lips. Most of the pasta falls down Margaret's skirt, a little of the sauce gets caught on her bottom lip, she licks it off and shudders. "It's horrible, it's horrible. He's trying to poison me," she wails. We all know she would

have said the same thing even if it would have been the most delectable thing she had ever eaten.

40 Ignoring Margaret's little tantrum, I do as Mother bids, twirling the pasta round my fork while shovelling the escaping pieces back on with my spoon. I rather like it, the feel of the softly slippery noodles, the rich sauce which is hot, salty and tastes partly of tomato, partly of Bovril. I wouldn't mind eating this every day. Unexpectedly, my father takes out a cardboard drum of grated Parmesan cheese and passes it to me to
45 open.

"What's that you've got there?" asks Mum.

'It's grated cheese. Percy Salt said you have to sprinkle it over the top. It doesn't work if you don't." Now we're talking. I peel away the piece of paper that is covering the holes and shake the white powder over my sauce. I pass it to my father who does the
50 same. Mum declines as she usually does with anything unusual. There is no point in asking Auntie Margaret.

Dad shakes the last of the cheese over his pasta and suddenly everyone goes quiet. I'm looking down but I can see my father out of the corner of my eye; he has stopped, his fork in mid-air, a short strand of spaghetti hanging loose. His eyes have gone
55 glassy and he puts his fork down on his plate.

"Dad, this cheese smells like sick," I tell him.

"I know it does, son, don't eat it. I think it must be off."

We never had spaghetti bolognese or Parmesan cheese again. Or for that matter, ever even talked about it.

From *Toast* by Nigel Slater (Slightly adapted)

QUESTIONS

1. Look again at lines 1-4.

   (*a*) Apart from the word "yelling," how does the writer suggest that "Mum" is shouting?   1A

   (*b*) How does the writer establish a tone of dislike, or disapproval, in the last sentence of paragraph one?   1A

2. By referring to **one** of the examples of descriptive detail given in lines 6-8, show how the writer makes the spaghetti bolognese sound unappetising.   2U

3. Look again at lines 9-12.

   Choose **one** example of imagery, and explain how the writer uses it to demonstrate how unusual the pasta seemed to him at that time. 2A

4. In lines 13-14, how does the writer use humour to suggest his father's difficulty with cooking the pasta? 2A

5. Why is the comparison used to describe the spaghetti in lines 23-24 appropriate here? 2A

6. Explain how another word in line 31 helps us to work out the meaning of "slurry." 2U

7. Look again at lines 30-33.

   In what way is the writer's attitude towards spaghetti bolognese changing? Justify your answer with **one** close reference to the text. 2U

8. How does the writer's contrasting word choice in the sentence beginning "Mum wraps..."(lines 34-35) suggest the fact that Aunt Margaret will not eat the pasta? 2A

9. Look again at lines 36-37.

   Identify by example any **two** techniques used by the writer to convey Aunt Margaret's negative reaction to the taste of the pasta, and comment on their effectiveness. 4E

10. What does the expression "little tantrum" (line 40) suggest about the writer's view of Aunt Margaret's behaviour? 1U

11. Explain, in your own words, **two** reasons the writer gives for saying "I rather like it," (lines 41-43). 2U

12. Look at lines 47-51.

    (a) Quote an expression which shows the writer's initial enthusiasm for trying Parmesan cheese. 1U

    (*b*)   Comment on the effectiveness of the structure **or** the order of the last four
          sentences in this paragraph.   2A

13. Why is the father's answer in line 57 surprising? Give two reasons.   2U

14. Explain fully why the last paragraph (lines 58-59) provides an effective conclusion
to the passage.   2E

Total (30)

[End of Question Paper]

Practice Paper A: Intermediate 2 English

Practice Papers
For SQA Exams

ENGLISH
INTERMEDIATE 2

**Exam A
Critical Essay**

Answer TWO questions from this paper.

You have 1 hour 30 minutes to complete this paper.

Each question must be chosen from a different Section (A-E). You are not allowed to choose two questions from the same Section.

In all Sections you may use Scottish Texts.

Write the number of each question in the margin of your answer booklet and begin each essay on a fresh page.

You should spend about 45 minutes on each essay.

The following will be assessed:

- the relevance of your essays to the questions you have chosen

- your knowledge and understanding of key elements, central concerns and significant details of the chosen texts

- your explanation of ways in which aspects of structure/style/language contribute to the meaning /effect/impact of the chosen texts

- your evaluation of the effectiveness of the chosen texts, supported by detailed and relevant evidence

- the quality and technical accuracy of your writing.

25 marks are allocated to each question. The total for this paper is 50 marks.

Leckie×Leckie
Scotland's leading educational publishers

SECTION A - DRAMA

> Your answer should make reference to your chosen text and to such elements as theme, structure, characterisation, plot, setting, key scene(s), conflict, climax....

1. Choose a play in which a main character achieves success at some point in the play.

   Describe the success and go on to show which aspects of the main character's personality helped him to achieve this success, and/or to lose this success.

2. Choose a play in which one scene marks an important turning point in the play.

   Explain what happens in the scene and show how it is important to the rest of the play.

3. Choose a play in which there is a strong relationship between two characters.

   Describe the relationship and explain how the relationship has an important effect on the events and/or the themes of the play.

SECTION B - PROSE

> Your answer should make reference to your chosen text and to such elements as theme, setting, key incident(s), plot, characterisation, structure, language, ideas, narrative technique, climax/turning point, description....

4. Choose a novel or a short story in which one of the characters has to face a difficulty or difficulties.

   Describe the difficulties faced by the character and explain to what extent he or she is successful in dealing with them.

5. Choose a prose work (fiction or non-fiction) in which an issue is effectively portrayed.

   Show how the writer's portrayal of the issue affects you and explain what you have learned.

6. Choose a novel or a short story which has an unexpected ending.

   Explain what happens in the ending and show how it is unexpected.

SECTION C - POETRY

Your answer should make reference to your chosen text and to such elements as content, structure, theme, rhythm, word choice, sound, tone, ideas, imagery....

7. Choose a poem which makes you feel sympathy for a person or an animal.

   Explain how both the content and the poetic techniques create sympathy for the person or the animal.

8. Choose a poem which describes an everyday incident and then goes on to make a more serious point about life.

   Briefly describe the incident and the serious point and then explain how the use of poetic techniques help your understanding.

9. Choose a poem which deals with a strong human emotion such as love, or hate, or jealousy, etc.

   Explain how the content and the language of the poem help you to understand this strong human emotion.

SECTION D - FILM AND TV DRAMA

Your answer should make reference to your chosen text and to such elements as plot, characterisation, use of camera, editing, mis-en-scene, setting, dialogue, music/sound effects, key sequence....

10. Choose a film or TV drama (including a single play, a serial or a series) which contains exciting action at key points in the film or TV drama.

    Briefly describe the action and explain how the use of media techniques make it interesting.

11. Choose a film or TV drama (including a single play, a serial or a series) which makes **effective** use of special **effects**.

    Explain how the special **effects** were used **effectively**.

12. Choose a film or TV drama (including a single play, a serial or a series) which deals mainly with an unpleasant aspect of life.

    Explain how media techniques are used to increase your understanding of this unpleasant aspect of life.

SECTION E - LANGUAGE

> Your answer should make reference to your chosen text and to such elements as tone, vocabulary, register, slang, abbreviation, accent, jargon, dialect....

13. Consider the language of two advertisements.

    By looking closely at the advertisements explain how effective they are at persuading you to buy the product advertised.

14. Consider the differences in spoken or written language between two groups of people – for example people who live in different areas.

    Explain the main differences in the spoken or written language between the two groups.

15. Consider the specialist language of text messaging.

    By referring to specific examples explain the advantages of using this type of language over more conventional written forms of language.

[End of Question Paper]

Practice Exam B

Practice Paper B: Intermediate 2 English

Practice Papers
For SQA Exams

ENGLISH
INTERMEDIATE 2

Exam B
Close Reading

Answer all of the questions

You have 1 hour to complete this paper.

Read the following passage and then answer the questions. Remember to use your own words as much as possible.

The questions ask you to show that you:

understand the ideas and details in the passage – **what the writer has said**
(**U**: Understanding)

can identify the techniques the writer has used to express these ideas – **how it has been said**
(**A**: Analysis)

can comment on how effective the writer has been, using appropriate evidence from the passage – **how well it has been said**
(**E**: Evaluation)

The code letters (U, A, E) are next to each question to make sure you know the question's purpose. The number of marks per question will give you a good idea as to how long your answer should be.

THE CHILD TRAP

In this article, by Joan Acocella, the writer reflects on the rise of overparenting.

We've all been there – that is, in the living room of friends who invited us to dinner without mentioning that this would include a full-evening performance by their four-year-old son. He sings, he dances, he eats all the hors d'oeuvres. When you try to speak to his parents, he interrupts. Why should they talk to you, about things he's not
5 interested in, when you could all be discussing how his hamster died? His parents seem to agree; they ask him to share his feelings about that event. You yawn. Who cares?

Dinner is finally served, and the child is sent off to some unfortunate person in the kitchen. The house shakes with his screams. Dinner over, he returns, his sword point
10 sharpened. His parents again ask him how he feels. It's ten o'clock. Is he tired? No! he says. You, on the other hand, find yourself exhausted, and you make for the door, swearing never to have kids, or if you already did, never to visit your grandchildren. You'll just send cheques.

This used to be known as "spoiling." Now it is called "overparenting" – or "helicopter
15 parenting" or "hothouse parenting" or "death-grip parenting." The term has changed because the pattern has changed. It still includes spoiling – no rules, many toys – but two other, complicated factors have been added. One is anxiety. Will the child be permanently affected by the fate of the hamster? did he touch the corpse, and get germs? The other new element – at odds, it seems, with such solicitude – is achievement
20 pressure. Forget about the child's feelings. He starts a new nursery tomorrow. Will he do well? If not, how will he ever get into a good university?

Most of us have heard of people who pipe Mozart into their child's room. You can buy a Baby Mozart CD but also a Baby Beethoven. Both are available on DVD as well, with the music supplemented by puppet shows and other imagery. These DVDs
25 are for the three-months-and-older age group. Since, at three months, babies cannot sit up, parents will have to hold them in front of the monitor, and since these infants have only just learned to focus their eyes, it is hard to know what they will make of the material.

The DVDs are intended to provide you with a head start on the academic-achievement
30 front, but there is also the environmental-hazards problem. Hovering parents see lethal bacteria on every surface. To thwart bugs in the supermarket, you can buy a protective pad that you insert into the front of the shopping trolley before you put the child in. According to the manufacturer this will guard against "viruses, bacteria, and bodily fluids" left on the trolley. In a recent survey, a third of parents reported that
35 they sent their offspring to school with antibacterial hand gells. Who trusts soap?

Once the child goes to nursery school, the academic pressure begins. Out go the finger paints, in comes the reading and maths preparation. As the child progresses, the academic load becomes heavier, and his ability to carry it is now regularly measured by tests. Ambitious parents may, at this point, begin hiring tutors. It is said that there
40 is now a four-billion-dollar tutoring industry in the United States, much of it serving primary school children. (Some of the tutors sent out by Princeton Review, a leading tutor provider, charge close to four hundred dollars an hour).

Overparented children typically face not just a heavy academic schedule but also a strenuous programme of extra-curricular activities – tennis lessons, Mandarin classes,
45 ballet. After-school activities are thought to impress universities. At the same time, they keep kids off the street. Extracurricular activities are areas where competition between parents, thought to be a major culprit in this whole business, is likely to surface.

When the student goes off to college or university, overparenting need not stop.
50 Many mothers and fathers edit their children's essays by e-mail. They also give them mobile phones equipped with G.P.S monitors in order to track their movements. The mobile phone, by allowing children to consult with their parents over any problem, any decision, any flicker of experience, has become the foremost technological assistant of overparenting. Some parents are not content with calling. They buy a
55 second home in their child's university town.

Students provided with such benefits may study harder, and upon graduation, land a top job. On the other hand, they may join the ranks of the "boomerang children," who move straight back home. A recent survey found that fifty-five per cent of American men between the ages of eighteen and twenty-four, and fourteen per cent between
60 the ages of twenty-five and thirty-four, live with their parents. Among the reasons given are the high cost of housing, heavy competition for good jobs, and the burden of repaying student loans, but another factor may be sheer habit, even desire. While hovering parents say that their goal is to launch the child into the world successfully, the truth may lie deeper, in some dark dependency, some transfer of the parent's
65 identity to the child.

However, the issue of overparenting raises a number of sticky questions. For example, is it really wrong for us to push our children to excel in areas where they are talented? One parent of a seven-year-old boy was told by an art teacher that his child was a truly gifted artist. So the next morning the parent suggested to the boy that he take
70 an art class after school, and got the following response: "I don't want to go to class and have a teacher tell me what to do – I just want to draw…Why do grown-ups have to take over everything?" The parent backed off, ashamed. If the fathers of Mozart and the Williams sisters had done the same thing, the history of human achievement would have been different.

Adapted from an article in *The New Yorker*

QUESTIONS

1. Look again at lines 1-7.

   (a) Explain how the context of the first paragraph helps you to understand the expression "We've all been there".   2U

   (b) Quote **two** expressions which make the writer's dinner with friends sound a rather unpleasant experience.   2A

    (c) How does the writer use **sentence structure** to show her reluctance to listen to the child's hamster story?   2A

2. Look again at lines 8-13.

    (a) "The house shakes with his screams." (line 9)

        How does the writer's **word choice** in this sentence clearly show her displeasure with the child's behaviour?   2A

    (b) How does the **sentence structure** in the remainder of the paragraph further convey this displeasure?   2A

3. Look again at lines 14-15.

    Choose one of the expressions "overparenting," or "helicopter parenting," or "hothouse parenting," or "death-grip parenting," and explain what this expression suggests about the style of parenting described.   1A

4. Using **your own words** as far as possible, explain what the writer means by the "two other factors" outlined in lines 17-22 which have been added to our ideas about spoiling children.   2U

5. Explain **in your own words** two reasons why the writer concludes that "it is hard to know what they will make of the material" (lines 27-28) after considering Baby Mozart and Baby Beethoven CDs   2U

6. Explain how the sentence "The DVDs are intended...the environmental-hazards problem." (lines 29-30) performs a successful linking function.   2A

7. Look again at the sentence "Out go the finger paints, in comes the reading and maths preparation." (lines 36-37)

    Identify and give an example of one technique the writer uses to achieve the effect of balance or contrast.   2A

8. Using **your own words**, explain why the writer believes that "the mobile phone... has become the foremost technological assistant of overparenting." (lines 51-55)   2U

9. Comment on the effectiveness of the expression "boomerang children" (line 57) in describing one of the possible consequences of overparenting.　　2E

10. Look again at lines 60-65.

   (a) What reason is given by "hovering parents" to explain their behaviour? Use **your own words** as far as possible.　　1U

   (b) What does the writer suggest is the true explanation for their behaviour, as suggested by the expression "dark dependency"? (line 64)　　1U

11. How does the writer suggest a tone of anger in the seven-year-old boy's response to his parent? (lines 70-72)　　2A

12. What is the parent's reaction to this anger, and how does the **sentence structure** help to convey it in line 72?　　2A

13. In what ways might "The Child Trap" be considered a particularly appropriate title for this article?　　2E

Total (30)

[End of Question Paper]

Practice Paper B: Intermediate 2 English

Practice Papers
For SQA Exams

ENGLISH
INTERMEDIATE 2

Exam B
Critical Essay

Answer TWO questions from this paper.

You have 1 hour 30 minutes to complete this paper.

Each question must be chosen from a different Section (A-E). You are not allowed to choose two questions from the same Section.

In all Sections you may use Scottish Texts.

Write the number of each question in the margin of your answer booklet and begin each essay on a fresh page.

You should spend about 45 minutes on each essay.

The following will be assessed:

• the relevance of your essays to the questions you have chosen

• your knowledge and understanding of key elements, central concerns and significant details of the chosen texts

• your explanation of ways in which aspects of structure/style/language contribute to the meaning /effect/impact of the chosen texts

• your evaluation of the effectiveness of the chosen texts, supported by detailed and relevant evidence

• the quality and technical accuracy of your writing.

25 marks are allocated to each question. The total for this paper is 50 marks.

Leckie ✕ Leckie
Scotland's leading educational publishers

SECTION A - DRAMA

Your answer should make reference to your chosen text and to such elements as theme, structure, characterisation, plot, setting, key scene(s), conflict, climax....

1. Choose a play in which a character makes an important decision.

   Explain why he/she made that decision and go on to show how the decision affects him or her in the rest of the play.

2. Choose a play which deals with an issue which is important to the world today.

   State what the issue is and explain how the plot and the characters increase your understanding of the issue.

3. Choose a play in which there is significant conflict between two characters.

   Show how the conflict is significant and explain whether or not it is resolved later in the play.

SECTION B - PROSE

Your answer should make reference to your chosen text and to such elements as theme, setting, key incident(s), plot, characterisation, structure, language, ideas, narrative technique, climax/turning point, description....

4. Choose a novel or a short story which deals with a relationship or relationships within a family.

   Describe the relationship(s) and explain how they change or develop throughout the story or novel.

5. Choose a prose work (fiction or non-fiction) which deals with an interesting topic.

   Show how the writer portrays this topic and explain how it is made interesting for you.

6. Choose a novel or a short story in which there is a significant incident which affects the outcome of the story.

   Briefly describe the incident and go on to show how significant it is for the characters and the plot of the story.

SECTION C - POETRY

> Your answer should make reference to your chosen text and to such elements as content, structure, theme, rhythm, word choice, sound, tone, ideas, imagery....

7. Choose a poem which describes a happy or a positive experience.

Briefly describe the experience and explain how the poet has used poetic techniques to suggest happy or positive feelings.

8. Choose a poem which tells an interesting story.

Briefly explain the story and show how the poetic techniques make the story interesting.

9. Choose a poem which helps you to think about an important aspect of life.

Explain how the content and the language of the poem help you to think about this important aspect of life.

SECTION D - FILM AND TV DRAMA

> Your answer should make reference to your chosen text and to such elements as plot, characterisation, use of camera, editing, mis-en-scene, setting, dialogue, music/sound effects, key sequence....

10. Choose a film or TV drama (including a single play, a serial or a series) which has an interesting opening sequence which establishes important elements of the film or TV drama.

Briefly describe the opening sequence and explain how it establishes important elements of the film or TV drama.

11. Choose a film or TV drama (including a single play, a serial or a series) which deals with conflict in family life.

Briefly describe the conflict and explain how media techniques are used to highlight the conflict.

12. Choose a film or TV drama (including a single play, a serial or a series) which deals with an important issue.

Explain how media techniques are used effectively to portray this issue.

SECTION E - LANGUAGE

Your answer should make reference to your chosen text and to such elements as tone, vocabulary, register, slang, abbreviation, accent, jargon, dialect....

13. Consider the language of television programmes aimed at young people.

    By referring to specific examples explain how this use of language is distinctive and appropriate to the audience.

14. Consider the particular type of language used in connection with a job or a sport or an interest.

    Explain with reference to selected examples what is recognisable about this particular use of language and how effective it is.

15. Consider the language of two advertisements which you have found persuasive.

    By examining the advertisements closely explain how they were persuasive.

[End of Question Paper]

THE CHECKOUT GIRL: ABUSED, IGNORED AND ON A TILL NEAR YOU

The witty observations of a French checkout girl have become an international bestseller

Notice anything the last time you went to a supermarket? An irritatingly long queue, perhaps? Or a mispriced product? But what about the woman – it was almost certainly a woman – at the checkout, performing one of the most thankless tasks in modern society? Did you return her greeting or ignore her as you hurried to put away the debit card and pack the shopping? Few would blame you if you did. After all, how many of us bother to pay attention to the silent workers scanning bar codes for low pay and little thanks.

But soon we may have to because the checkout girls of Europe have found a figurehead. Her name is Anna Sam and she worked in a French supermarket for almost a decade, smiling at shoppers but receiving little besides insults and disdain in return. She witnessed behaviour ranging from the loathsome to the loving – queue-jumping, cheating, thieving, moaning and sometimes a quick kiss between the meat and cheese counter.

She put up with self-important managers watching the staff from behind a one-way mirror, a salary of £680 (£605) a month and the orange polyester jacket that she had to wear. She would often joke with other checkout girls that someday someone should write a book about their plight.

Last summer, Sam did. "The Tribulations of a Checkout Girl" proved a monumental success and has sold 100,000 copies in France. It is to be made into a film. Sam's status has been transformed. She used to be part of the modern proletariat – the untrained disposable female supermarket workers who take your money while dreaming of a better life. Now she is the voice of the voiceless, and the witty observer of a place that seems to bring out the worst in us all.

She used to say "bonjour" 250 times a day; few shoppers bothered to reply. She squirmed on her swivel chair waiting for authorisation to go to the toilet; managers kept her waiting. She greeted families at her till; parents frowned and warned their children: "If you don't work hard at school, you'll end up like that lady." Her account has struck a chord not only in France but across Europe and beyond. Her book has been translated into ten languages.

"I'd like to think that I could help to change the way people look at checkout workers," she says, standing outside the hypermarket in Brittany, where she used to work. "It would be a start if they were just a little more polite to them."

Anna Sam is a dark-haired 29-year-old who spent five years at Rennes University studying literature. On graduating she was articulate, cultured and unable to find work in publishing, her chosen field. So she went back to the hypermarket where she had been working for 12 hours a week to finance her studies.

"I meant to spend six months or so in the job while I looked for something else," she says. By her late twenties she was still there. "There are an awful lot of people like me," she says. "They have studied hard, got a degree and found that it leads to a job that they don't want." It is a problem throughout Europe, but particularly acute in France. Here, 63.4 per cent of young people leave school with a Baccalaureat, which gives them an automatic right to the course and university of their choice.

Practice Paper C: Intermediate 2 English

Practice Papers
For SQA Exams

ENGLI
INTERMEDIAT

Exar
Close Read

Answer all of the questions

You have 1 hour to complete this paper.

Read the following passage and then answer the questions. Remember to use your own words
much as possible.

The questions ask you to show that you:

understand the ideas and details in the passage – **what the writer has said**
(**U**: Understanding)

can identify the techniques the writer has used to express these ideas – **how it has
been said**
(**A**: Analysis)

can comment on how effective the writer has been, using appropriate evidence from the passag
– **how well it has been said**
(**E**: Evaluation)

The code letters (U, A, E) are next to each question to make sure you know the question's
purpose. The number of marks per question will give you a good idea as to how long your ans
should be.

The result is great confusion. Take Rennes, for example. "Something like 400 students graduate with literature degrees every year in Rennes and they pretty much all want to become teachers," says Sam. "But there aren't that many teaching jobs." Some
45 become postmen, others live off welfare benefit. Many – mainly women – join France's 170,000 checkout workers.

"Are you in prison?" a six-year-old girl, peering over the till, asked Sam one day.

Not quite. A typical shift would be six hours with a 16-minute break. She would scan up to 21,000 products a week, lift 800 kg an hour and ask the customers for their
50 loyalty cards 200 times a day. At night the beeping of her till filled her dreams.

"There are a lot of health problems in this job – tendonitis, lumbago, that sort of thing. There is a lot of depression as well because you're completely ignored by everyone: by your managers and by the customers. After a while you become convinced that you're less than nothing."

55 Our conversation is interrupted by an irate shopper wondering whether "there's anyone working at the till today." He had been kept waiting for less than a minute.

In 2007, Sam began to exercise her frustrations in a blog. She wrote about the bosses who criticised her for not smiling enough; about her biceps bulging under the weight of beer, soft drinks and mineral water; about the clientele.

60 There were the shoppers who sneakily took 11 or 12 products to the ten-items-or-fewer express checkout; who tried to get out with CDs hidden in boxes of camembert. Then there were those who vented their anger on Sam because they thought – mistakenly – that she was overcharging them; or who ignored her as they marched past her till while talking on their mobile phones.

65 With a million visits to date, the blog has been a triumph – largely because it has provided an outlet for supermarket staff throughout France, who write in with tales that are sometimes poignant, sometimes funny.

Sam's opinion has been sought by politicians and business leaders. When the French Parliament debated Sunday opening, Sam was called in to explain why she opposed it.
70 At a retail conference in Luxembourg, Sam suggested to executives that they should greet checkout staff every day. "It was as if they had never thought of it. Oh, yes, that's a good idea, they said. They all made a note – "Say hello in the morning" – to remind themselves."

Sam's next venture is to organise a conference for supermarket managers, where she
75 will insist on the need for checkout workers to receive training. She says that staff need to know how to deal with conflict, and should be taught how to placate shoppers who blow a fuse because they have been kept waiting by a faulty till, or who hurl insults because they think they are entitled to a reduction.

"You can't educate shoppers to behave better but you can train employees to handle
80 them," says Sam. She pauses, then adds: "But what checkout girls would really like is a hammer to hit them over the head."

From *The Times*, March, 6, 2009 (Slightly adapted)

QUESTIONS

1. Look again at lines 1-7.

   (a) Quote **two** expressions which suggest that checkout workers are not well treated.   2A

   (b) How does the punctuation help to convey the writer's sympathy for checkout workers?   2A

2. Comment on the effectiveness of the structure of the sentence in lines 10-12.   2A

3. Show how the sentence "Last summer, Sam did." (line 17) is a successful link between paragraphs 3 and 4.   2A

4. Explain with clear reference to the whole sentence why the writer uses a dash in line 19.   2A

5. Using **your own words as far as possible** give **two** reasons the writer uses in lines 23-26 to show that supermarkets seem "to bring out the worst in us all." (line 22)   2U

6. Apart from the word "graduating," pick another **word** from lines 32-35 which shows that Anna Sam did well at university.   1U

7. Look again at lines 40-46.

   Explain **in your own words** one reason **or** one example given to support Sam's statement that "There are an awful lot of people like me."   2U

8. Explain fully how the sentence "Not quite." (line 48) achieves its impact.   2A

9. Look again at lines 60-64.

   Explain fully how **two** examples of the writer's **word choice** make clear that Sam was critical of the supermarket customers.   2A

10. (*a*) Look again at lines 65-67.

Explain fully how other words in the paragraph make clear the meaning of the word "outlet" as it is used here. 2U

(*b*) In what other way is the word "outlet" appropriate here? 1U

11. Look again at lines 68-73.

(*a*) Identify **two** examples the writer gives to show how successful Sam has become. 2U

(*b*) Identify and briefly explain the writer's use of humour at the end of this paragraph. 2A

12. Look again at lines 74-78.

(*a*) **Using your own words as far as possible** explain why Sam believes that there is a "need for checkout workers to receive training." (line 75) 1U

(*b*) Which word in this paragraph means the same as "calm down"? 1U

13. "But what checkout girls would really like is a hammer to hit them over the head." (lines 80-81)

Comment on the effectiveness of this sentence as a conclusion to the whole passage. 2E

Total (30)

[End of Question Paper]

Practice Paper C: Intermediate 2 English

Practice Papers
For SQA Exams

ENGLISH
INTERMEDIATE 2

Exam C
Critical Essay

Answer TWO questions from this paper.

You have 1 hour 30 minutes to complete this paper.

Each question must be chosen from a different Section (A-E). You are not allowed to choose two questions from the same Section.

In all Sections you may use Scottish Texts.

Write the number of each question in the margin of your answer booklet and begin each essay on a fresh page.

You should spend about 45 minutes on each essay.

The following will be assessed:

- the relevance of your essays to the questions you have chosen

- your knowledge and understanding of key elements, central concerns and significant details of the chosen texts

- your explanation of ways in which aspects of structure/style/language contribute to the meaning /effect/impact of the chosen texts

- your evaluation of the effectiveness of the chosen texts, supported by detailed and relevant evidence

- the quality and technical accuracy of your writing.

25 marks are allocated to each question. The total for this paper is 50 marks.

Leckie×Leckie
Scotland's leading educational publishers

SECTION A - DRAMA

> Your answer should make reference to your chosen text and to such elements as theme, structure, characterisation, plot, setting, key scene(s), conflict, climax....

1. Choose a play in which a main character has a human weakness, such as ambition, jealousy, arrogance, self-doubt, etc.

   Explain how the character's human weakness affects the events of the play and the other characters in the play.

2. Choose a play which has a memorable ending.

   Explain how the ending is effective in terms of the characters and/or the themes of the play.

3. Choose a play which deals with conflict within a family or a group of people.

   Describe the conflict and explain what effects the conflict has on the characters and the events of the play.

SECTION B - PROSE

> Your answer should make reference to your chosen text and to such elements as theme, setting, key incident(s), plot, characterisation, structure, language, ideas, narrative technique, climax/turning point, description....

4. Choose a novel or a short story in which you felt sympathy for one of the characters because of the problems he or she has to face.

   Describe the character's problems and explain why you felt sympathy for him or her.

5. Choose a prose work (fiction or non-fiction) in which setting in place and/or time is effectively portrayed.

   Describe the setting in place and/or time and explain why you enjoyed it or what you have learned from it.

6. Choose a novel or a short story in which there is a clear turning point.

   Briefly describe what leads up to the turning point and explain the effect it has on the rest of the novel or the short story.

SECTION C - POETRY

> Your answer should make reference to your chosen text and to such elements as content, structure, theme, rhythm, word choice, sound, tone, ideas, imagery....

7. Choose a poem which deals with an unpleasant aspect of life.

   Explain how the content of the poem and the poet's use of poetic techniques has increased your understanding of this unpleasant aspect of life.

8. Choose a poem which describes a person or a place in an interesting way.

   Show how the poet describes the person or the place and explain how the poet's use of poetic techniques makes the person or the place interesting.

9. Choose a poem which has an interesting or an unexpected ending.

   Explain why the ending makes an interesting or unexpected conclusion to the whole poem.

SECTION D - FILM AND TV DRAMA

> Your answer should make reference to your chosen text and to such elements as plot, characterisation, use of camera, editing, mis-en-scene, setting, dialogue, music/sound effects, key sequence....

10. Choose **one** scene from a film or a TV drama (including a single play, a serial or a series) in which a powerful human emotion (eg love, hate, fear, etc.) is shown.

    Briefly describe the scene and explain how this emotional scene is important to the film or TV drama as a whole.

11. Choose a film or TV drama (including a single play, a serial or a series) which contains conflict between two people or two groups of people.

    Briefly describe the conflict and explain how media techniques are used to highlight the conflict.

12. Choose a film or TV drama (including a single play, a serial or a series) which has an effective closing sequence.

    Briefly describe the closing sequence and explain how media techniques are used to make the closing squence effective as an ending to the film or TV drama.

SECTION E - LANGUAGE

Your answer should make reference to your chosen text and to such elements as tone, vocabulary, register, slang, abbreviation, accent, jargon, dialect....

13. Consider the language of two groups of people who are different in an important way. For example they may be different in age or from different places.

   By referring to examples describe the language differences and evaluate their effectiveness.

14. Consider the language used by two newspapers.

   By referring to specific examples explain and evaluate the differences in language use.

15. Consider the use of persuasive language in advertising.

   By referring to specific examples from two advertisements explain how language is used effectively.

[End of Question Paper]

Practice Exam D

Practice Paper D: Intermediate 2 English

Practice Papers
For SQA Exams

ENGLISH
INTERMEDIATE 2
Exam D
Close Reading

Answer all of the questions

You have 1 hour to complete this paper.

Read the following passage and then answer the questions. Remember to use your own words as much as possible.

The questions ask you to show that you:

understand the ideas and details in the passage – **what the writer has said**
(**U**: Understanding)

can identify the techniques the writer has used to express these ideas – **how it has been said**
(**A**: Analysis)

can comment on how effective the writer has been, using appropriate evidence from the passage
– **how well it has been said**
(**E**: Evaluation)

The code letters (U, A, E) are next to each question to make sure you know the question's purpose. The number of marks per question will give you a good idea as to how long your answer should be.

Scotland's leading educational publishers

CARAVAGGIO: PAINTING GETS PHYSICAL

In this extract from his book, Power of Art, Simon Schama reflects on an incident which took place during the filming of a TV programme about the Italian painter, Caravaggio (1571-1610).

From the start, there are only two things you need to know about Caravaggio: that he made the most powerful Christian art that has ever been painted, and that he killed someone. Do these facts have the slightest connection? I should hope not, the art historians will tell you, horrified by the question. The fact of the painter's crime, they

5 will say, is merely a sensationalist footnote to his career as maker of pictures. Beware reading the art from the life, or for that matter vice versa; the one has nothing to do with the other.

But then you look at Caravaggio's shocking painting of himself as the severed head of the giant Goliath in the painting *David with the Head of Goliath*. And you see

10 something that had never been painted before and would never be painted again: a portrait of the artist as ogre, his face a grotesque mask of bad behaviour. It's an unsparing image of self-accusation and it certainly makes you wonder.

It's often said about Caravaggio's pictures that, more than those of any other artist, the viewer responds to his figures physically. All the same, I wasn't ready to hold in

15 my hand something that Caravaggio had held in his.

"Please," said the wizened church official with the beaky nose and the black cassock, nudging me in the ribs. "Please take." I wasn't in the mood to be nudged. It had been yet another embarrassing day with Caravaggio, attempting to say something that illuminated his story while painfully conscious that he did his own lighting, thanks

20 very much; and that words were feeble fluttering things beside the muscular bulk of his painting. In the cathedral chapel at Valletta in Malta, my back to Caravaggio's painting *The Beheading of St John the Baptist*, face to the camera, speech had never been so redundant. I wanted to be out of the musty dimness of that church. I had had my fill of art.

25 Still, courtesies were called for. Rule number one of location filming is to show proper gratitude to those whose premises you have occupied with the self-important baggage of cable, lights, camera. Besides, the small man in the cassock was giving me a wry grin as he did his prodding: "Please, take." So, I sighed, looked and took.

In my hand was an ancient iron key about five inches long. The looped handle

30 end had got furry in the way very old pieces of metalwork do, but the entry end sported massive squared-off teeth. I had used keys like this before when I had taught at Cambridge University and occasionally had to open doors with 17th-century locks. But why was I getting this key in the cathedral of the Knights of St John? I smiled uncomprehendingly back at the caretaker, now vaguely aware

35 that I had seen this particular key somewhere before. The gnomic figure in black now tightly grasped my free hand, as if I were a child and he a schoolteacher, and turned me round to face Caravaggio's painting. And of course, there it was: one of three keys hanging from the belt of the grimly handsome prison officer who was pointing to the basket in which the head of John the Baptist was about to be

40 deposited.

Caravaggio almost always used live models, and since the figures in the Beheading of St John the Baptist are life-sized, and he had painted it in this cathedral, there could be little doubt that he had done so in the space in which we were now all standing. He needed the keys – emblems of incarceration – to ramp up the nightmarish
45 claustrophobia that manages to pervade even this huge painting. So he had posed his model and then, perhaps, asked for a set of keys to hang from the man's belt. The cathedral clergy were probably as accommodating to him as they had been to us, lending whatever was to hand. The key in my hand matched precisely, tooth for tooth, the one in the painting. "See, yes see," said the caretaker. "His." I palmed the
50 blackened thing, then I wrapped my fingers around its worn shaft. I was nervously shaking hands with a 400-year-old-genius-killer.

Caravaggio, the jailbird, was haunting me at the scene of my own crime – cutting him down to television size. But then Caravaggio is the most confrontational of painters, with everything calculated to be too close for comfort. His big paintings get in our face
55 like no others. A blaze of light catches the figures, but around them is utter blackness swallowing up the comfort zone of art-gazing: frame, wall, gallery. Looking at the outflung arms of Christ in Caravaggio's *Supper at Emmaus*, you almost duck to avoid the impact. Caravaggio's paintings shamelessly come out and accost us, as if he were crossing the street and, oh no, coming our way:

60 "You *looking* at me?"

Adapted from *Power of Art* by Simon Schama

QUESTIONS

1. Look again at lines 1-7

   (*a*) What is surprising about the "two things you need to know about Caravaggio" when considered together?   1U

   (*b*) Explain **in your own words as far as possible** the concerns of the art historians.   2U

2. Look again at lines 8-12.

   (*a*) Explain with clear reference to the whole sentence why the writer uses a colon in line 10.   2A

   (*b*) Explain how other words in this paragraph help you to understand what the writer means by "unsparing image of self-accusation." (line 12)   2U

3. Look again at lines 16-24.

   (a) How does the writer's contrasting word choice in lines 20-21 convey his difficulty in describing Caravaggio's painting for the television programme?

   2A

   (b) Quote **one** expression from this paragraph which suggests that the writer feels he may never be able to give a proper description of Caravaggio's painting. 1U

   (c) How does the writer create a weary, tired tone at times in this paragraph? 1A

4. Explain how the sentence "In my hand was an ancient iron key about five inches long" (line 29) is an effective link between the paragraphs contained in lines 25-40. 2A

5. Which **word** in lines 29-40 makes it clear that, at first, the writer did not realise the significance of the key? 1U

6. Identify by example **one** technique used by the writer to convey his stupidity in lines 35-37, and comment on its effectiveness. 2E

7. Using you own words as far as possible explain why the writer is convinced that Caravaggio's painting The Beheading of St John the Baptist had been painted where "we were now all standing" (line 43). 2U

8. Look again at the sentence contained in lines 44-45 ("He needed the keys...huge painting).

   (a) Identify a feature of sentence structure the writer uses effectively here.

   1A

   (b) Explain how this feature helps to clarify or support the point being made by the writer. 2A

   (c) Explain fully the appropriateness of the word choice of "nightmarish claustrophobia." 2A

9. Using your own words as far as possible summarise the three reasons the writer gives in lines 45-49 to support his claim that the keys in his hand were the same as the keys in the painting. 3U

10. "I was nervously shaking hands with a 400-year-old-genius killer."

   Comment on the effectiveness of this sentence as a conclusion to the paragraph contained in lines 41-51. 2E

11. Explain how the short final paragraph (line 60) achieves its impact. 2A

Total (30)

[End of Question Paper]

Practice Paper D: Intermediate 2 English

Practice Papers
For SQA Exams

ENGLISH
INTERMEDIATE 2

**Exam D
Critical Essay**

Answer TWO questions from this paper.

You have 1 hour 30 minutes to complete this paper.

Each question must be chosen from a different Section (A-E). You are not allowed to choose two questions from the same Section.

In all Sections you may use Scottish Texts.

Write the number of each question in the margin of your answer booklet and begin each essay on a fresh page.

You should spend about 45 minutes on each essay.

The following will be assessed:

- the relevance of your essays to the questions you have chosen

- your knowledge and understanding of key elements, central concerns and significant details of the chosen texts

- your explanation of ways in which aspects of structure/style/language contribute to the meaning /effect/impact of the chosen texts

- your evaluation of the effectiveness of the chosen texts, supported by detailed and relevant evidence

- the quality and technical accuracy of your writing.

25 marks are allocated to each question. The total for this paper is 50 marks.

Scotland's leading educational publishers

SECTION A - DRAMA

> Your answer should make reference to your chosen text and to such elements as theme, structure, characterisation, plot, setting, key scene(s), conflict, climax....

1. Choose a play in which a main character suffers failure in his relationships with other characters.

   Show what caused this failure and explain how it is important in the play as a whole.

2. Choose a play which has an effective opening.

   Explain how the opening is effective in terms of the characters, the plot, and the themes of the play.

3. Choose a play in which one of the main characters displays a strong emotion such as love, hatred or jealousy.

   Show why the character displays this emotion and explain what effect this display of emotion has on the other characters and the events of the play.

SECTION B - PROSE

> Your answer should make reference to your chosen text and to such elements as theme, setting, key incident(s), plot, characterisation, structure, language, ideas, narrative technique, climax/turning point, description....

4. Choose a novel or a short story in which two of the characters find themselves in conflict.

   Explain the reasons for the conflict and show how the conflict affects the rest of the novel or the short story.

5. Choose a prose work (fiction or non-fiction) which deals with an unpleasant aspect of life.

   Show how this unpleasant aspect of life is described and explain how it is made real for you.

6. Choose a novel or a short story in which a character clearly changes throughout the story.

   Show the causes of this change and explain the effects of this change on the characters and the events of the story.

SECTION C - POETRY

> Your answer should make reference to your chosen text and to such elements as content, structure, theme, rhythm, word choice, sound, tone, ideas, imagery....

7. Choose a poem in which an incident or a character is effectively described.

   Explain how the content of the poem and the poet's use of poetic techniques make the description effective.

8. Choose a poem which deals with an unhappy experience.

   Briefly describe the experience and explain how the poet has used poetic techniques to express a feeling of unhappiness.

9. Choose a poem which deals with a certain time in a person's life, eg childhood, old age, etc.

   Explain how the poet uses poetic techniques to create a clear picture of that time of life.

SECTION D - FILM AND TV DRAMA

> Your answer should make reference to your chosen text and to such elements as plot, characterisation, use of camera, editing, mis-en-scene, setting, dialogue, music/sound effects, key sequence....

10. Choose a film or TV drama (including a single play, a serial or a series) in which one sequence concentrates on a turning point for a character or the action.

    Briefly describe the sequence and explain its importance for the character and/or the action.

11. Choose a film or TV drama (including a single play, a serial or a series) which makes effective use of humour.

    Briefly describe the use of humour and explain how media techniques are used to make the use of humour successful.

12. Choose a film or TV drama (including a single play, a serial or a series) which makes use of suspense or tension either in one scene or in the film or TV drama as a whole.

    Explain how media techniques are used effectively to create suspense or tension in the film or TV drama.

SECTION E - LANGUAGE

Your answer should make reference to your chosen text and to such elements as tone, vocabulary, register, slang, abbreviation, accent, jargon, dialect....

13. Consider the language of advertisements which aim to persuade you to buy something or to persuade you to change your behaviour.

    By referring to examples explain how successful the persuasive language is.

14. Consider the written language of email or text messaging.

    Explain with reference to specific examples how this differs from more conventional forms of writing and evaluate its effectiveness.

15. Consider the differences in spoken language between two groups of people who are from different places or are different in significant ways.

    By referring to specific examples explain and evaluate the differences in spoken language between the two groups.

[End of Question Paper]

Worked Answers

PRACTICE PAPER A   CLOSE READING WORKED ANSWERS

Note: alternative answers are shown by /. Words that may be used in an answer, but are not essential, are enclosed in brackets

1. (*a*) Use of ellipsis/or dots (1 mark) OR Use of capital letters (1 mark)

> **HINT** With a question like this you have to look at the selected lines from the passage, and see if you notice anything distinctive, or unusual, about the language. In this case there are two fairly obvious things. You just have to write down one to gain one mark.

(*b*) Reference to "old bat"/"doesn't bother" (1 mark)

> **HINT** Questions about "tone" are often thought to be quite difficult. At Intermediate 2 level, you are often given the "tone" before being asked to show how it is established. It is often enough just to pick out a word, or words, which suggest the tone given, then simply write them down.

2. Reference to:

("poured from its") "tin" (1 mark) + comment (eg tin suggests ready made/mass produced therefore lacking in taste) (1 mark)

("a good") "half-hour ago" (1 mark) + comment (eg food has been sitting there for some time/cooling down) (1 mark)

("sitting on the") "cool plate"("of the stove") (1 mark) + comment (eg suggests it is cold and therefore unappetising) (1 mark)

("the occasional") "blip-blop" (1 mark) + comment (eg onomatopoeia suggests unappealing substance) (1 mark)
(Total 2 marks)

> **HINT** The words "By referring to" mean you must **quote** an example from lines 6-8. Then you must make a comment on your example showing how it suggests that the spaghetti is unappetising.

3. Reference to the wrapped spaghetti looking like a firework (1 mark) + comment (eg a firework is very different to spaghetti/food) (1 mark) OR Reference to the fibre-optic lights (1 mark) + comment (eg these lights were very modern/different/ seen on the TV, etc) (1 mark)
(Total 2 marks)

> **HINT** This question asks you, first of all, to find an example of imagery (in this case where the spaghetti is compared to something else, as in a metaphor or a simile), and comment on how this comparison makes the spaghetti seem unusual.

4. He uses his glasses to read the instructions (1 mark) which are in a foreign language (1 mark)
(Total 2 marks)

> **HINT** Questions on humour are often found to be tricky. In this example the humour comes from the writer poking fun at his dad's failure to read the instructions.

5. The spaghetti is compared to escaping worms (1 mark) + comment (the fact that they are escaping suggests the whole process is out of control/they can't control the situation) (1 mark)
(Total 2 marks)

> **HINT** As in Question 3, you are asked here to think about why one thing is compared to another, and why this comparison is effective: that is, why this comparison fits in with the writer's meaning at this point in the passage.

6. "Slurry" means liquid/semi-liquid mixture (1 mark) + reference to "poured." (1 mark)
(Total 2 marks)

> **HINT** As with all questions of this type, first of all look at what the word identified is doing in the sentence. Here it is describing the sauce. How does the mince appear to you here? The writer makes it clear that "Dad" has to "pour" the sauce, not spoon it; this perhaps suggests it is "runny", or "liquid."

7. Changing attitude – starts to appeal to him because it now seems adult/advanced/modern (1 mark) + reference to any **one** of "suddenly," "grown-up," "urbane," "sophisticated" (1 mark)
(Total 2 marks)

> **HINT** Up to this point in the passage the writer has made the spaghetti bolognese seem unattractive. After the word "suddenly" his attitude towards it seems to change. To answer this question you have to make a comment about the way in which his attitude changes, and then pick a word, or words, from the passage to support this.

8. Answer: Reference to "shovels (it towards)" which suggests a large amount/dealt with roughly (1 mark), and "(pink), little (lips)" which suggests the dainty/small nature of Aunt Margaret's mouth (1 mark)
(Total 2 marks)

> **HINT** In a question about contrast, make sure you refer to both sides of the contrast. Remember, a contrast is a striking difference between two things.

TOP EXAM TIP

In the English Intermediate 2 Close Reading paper, it is usual for questions to be worth a maximum of 2 marks; however, it is possible that you will have a question worth more. Look out for this as writing too little for a question like this will mean you lose a large number of marks. You may have to make 4 points, or as in this next question, 2 references and 2 comments.

9. Word choice – "shudders" (1 mark) effective because it suggests a reaction of disgust (1 mark)

"(trying to) poison (me)" (1 mark) effective because it suggests that she will die if she eats it (1 mark)

"(she) wails" (1 mark) effective because it suggests misery at the thought of eating it (1 mark)

Repetition – "It's horrible, it's horrible." (1 mark) is effective because it emphasises the extent of her dislike (1 mark)
(Total 2 marks)

10. He thinks she is being childish/immature (1 mark)

11. Any two from

Reference to texture (gloss of "the feel of the softly slippery noodles") (1 mark)

Reference to taste (gloss of sauce being "hot"/ "salty"/"tastes partly of tomato")/ reminds him of Bovril (1 mark)
(Total 2 marks)

12. (a) "Now we're talking." (1 mark)

(b) Sentence structure – balance of "I peel..." and "I pass..." (1 mark) reflects the initial enthusiasm of the writer and his father (1 mark)

Sentence order – Sentences relating to father and writer come first/and together (1 mark) separating them from mother and Margaret who are less enthusiastic (1 mark)

OR

Sentence dealing with Auntie Margaret comes last (1 mark) highlighting her reluctance to try anything (1 mark).

13. Father was initially in favour of the cheese/thought the cheese necessary (1 mark).

A parent would not normally agree with this kind of statement (1 mark)
(Total 2 marks)

14. Reference to "We never had spaghetti bolognese/Parmesan cheese again" (1 mark) + reference to earlier mentions of either in the passage (in a positive or negative way) (1 mark)

Reference to ("Or for that matter,") "ever even talked about it" (1 mark) + comment (eg contradiction with much discussion here/some enthusiasm here/ OR is appropriate because it clearly didn't go down well) (1 mark)
(Total 2 marks)

> **HINT**
>
> A common type of question. In this passage the last paragraph only consists of two sentences. Try to consider how the ideas of the last paragraph fit in with ideas elsewhere in the passage. Do they repeat earlier ideas? Do they expand on, or contrast with, earlier ideas?

PRACTICE PAPER A   CRITICAL ESSAY WORKED ANSWERS

EXAM ANSWER ADVICE

You have to choose two essays from five sections. There is not much time to do this as you will need close to 45 minutes to plan and write each essay. Under the pressure of exam conditions it is hard not to make a quick, and perhaps panicked choice, but try to choose your essay questions calmly. You need to pick questions which suit the texts you know and will allow you to demonstrate your knowledge. Try to scan the questions and circle the ones which look possible. Then have another look at your circled questions before making a final choice.

Note that the questions are made up of two lines. The first line asks you to make a selection from the texts you have studied. The second line gives you a task. This task often asks you to do **two** things.

Remember the main piece of advice to keep in mind when writing a Critical Essay: answer the question. Have the question in your mind all the way through your essay and try to develop a line of thought which is relevant to the question. Try to make your essay more than just a list of techniques that the writer has used.

Section A - Drama

EXAM ANSWER ADVICE

Read the information in the box given at the start of each section of questions. This is a guide to some of the things you could cover or include in your essay. Words from this text box are also a reminder of the kind of technical terms that would be appropriate for you to use.

Remember that when answering on a play you are trying to write about quite a large piece of literature. Your answer should focus on elements like character, conflict between characters, setting, plot, themes, etc. It is not appropriate to attempt the kind of micro-analysis you would do when writing about a poem or a short story.

1.

> **HINT**
>
> This question asks you to think about a play in which a character achieves "success at some point in the play." You have to think about whether or not the play you have studied would fit this question. Does a character achieve a goal, or an aim, or an ambition? Note that the question says: "at some point in the play." The success does not have to be achieved at the end of the action, or maintained until the end. To take two examples: Macbeth does achieve success - he becomes King of Scotland; Romeo and Juliet do achieve their dream of being together (if only for a short time).

If you decide that the play you have studied would fit this question, you then have to think carefully about the structure. You would have to identify the character and the success achieved at the beginning of the essay. Then deal with the aspects of the character's personality that helped him or her to achieve this success. Finally, you would look at whether or not the success was maintained. Did aspects of the character's personality cause him or her to lose the success? (Macbeth's excessive ambition or growing paranoia?) Or was loss of success down to factors outwith the character's control? (The conflict between families in Romeo and Juliet?)

2.

> **HINT**
>
> When preparing for the exam, it is perhaps useful to revise and to know well three scenes from the play you have studied: an opening scene which sets up the characters and concerns of the play, the ending of the play, and, as in this question, a scene which marks some kind of turning point in the action.

In your answer make it clear at the outset which scene you have chosen, what happens in it and why it is important, then deal with what leads up to it, and finally how the consequences following on from this scene have an impact on the ending of the play.

3.

> **HINT**
>
> This question asks you to think about a play in which there is a "strong relationship" between two characters. Your first reaction to this question might be to consider a play in which there is a close, loving relationship, for example Romeo and Juliet, or Othello. An answer to a play like this would work very well. You would begin your essay by describing the relationship, and then go on to say how the relationship affected the events and/or themes of the play.

However, note the word "strong" in the question. You are asked to consider a "strong relationship." This does not just mean a positive relationship – it could include a relationship in which there is a lot of conflict: Willy and his sons in Death of a Salesman, for example. You would treat this essay in exactly the same way: first of all describe the relationship (drawing on references to the play), then explain the effects of the relationship on the events and/or the themes of the play.

Section B - Prose

> ### EXAM ANSWER ADVICE
>
> At Intermediate 2 level most questions will allow you to answer on either a novel or a short story. Watch out, however, for a question which asks for a "non-fiction text." A novel or a short story would not be appropriate here, and you would lose marks if you answered using this type of text. A question asking for "a prose work" allows you to answer on any kind of prose writing (fiction or non-fiction).
>
> Read the information in the box given at the start of each section of questions. This is a guide to some of the things you could cover or include in your essay. Words from this text box are also a reminder of the kind of technical terms that would be appropriate for you to use.
>
> Remember that when answering on a **novel** you are trying to write about quite a large piece of literature. Your answer should focus on elements like character, conflict between characters, setting, plot/narrative, themes, etc. It is not appropriate to attempt the kind of micro-analysis you would do when writing about a short story.

4. This question asks you to really narrow down your focus onto a difficulty (or dificulties) faced by a character in the novel or story you have read. In some ways, this may be easier to do with a short story: the difficulty might be the main part of the story. In Father and Son, by Bernard McLaverty the father has a clear difficulty in that he finds it hard to communicate with his son. However, there may be more of a decision to make, more to choose from in a novel. The important thing is to focus clearly on a difficulty (or a series of difficulties) faced by a character. For example, in To Kill a Mockingbird Atticus Finch has to face a difficult task: defending the black man Tom Robinson in a largely racist town. You could make the decision to focus on that particular difficulty. But a novel could present you with choices. For the same novel you could write about the difficulty Scout has in making sense of the town in which she lives. (This option could allow you to discuss many aspects of the novel: the trial, Boo Radley, etc.)

5. This question allows you to answer on any kind of prose writing (fiction or non-fiction, novel or short story). Often non-fiction writing will deal with an issue, such as the environment, or bullying. This would work well with this question. However, a work of fiction equally could be concerned with an issue: it could be said that Of Mice and Men, by John Steinbeck is about the issue of loneliness.

> **HINT**
>
> To answer this question the approach would be the same for fiction or non-fiction: make it clear from the start of your essay which issue you are going to write about. Keep your essay relevant to a discussion of this issue. Think of all the ways that the writer makes you think about this issue – key incidents, descriptions, the words or actions of a character, the observations of a witness, etc.

6. Here you have to select a novel or a short story which has an unexpected ending. That is, something must happen at the end of the novel or short story which the reader might consider surprising. An example could be the shooting of Lennie by his friend George at the end of the novel, Of Mice and Men.

> **HINT**
>
> Again, with this question you have to be careful to make your essay relevant. It would be a good idea to deal with the unexpected ending first (perhaps after a short summary of the novel or short story), and then go on to write about the factors which lead up to this ending.

Section C - Poetry

> **EXAM ANSWER ADVICE**
>
> Read the information in the box given at the start of each section of questions. This is a guide to some of the things you could cover or include in your essay. Words from this text box are also a reminder of the kind of technical terms that would be appropriate for you to use.
>
> Remember that if you are writing about a fairly short poem you will be expected to analyse it in some detail. In your programme of revision it may be worth trying to memorise the whole poem. This would give you access to all of the poem's words and phrases, and would remind you of techniques, in the exam. Quickly writing out sections of the poem on your exam paper would give you something to work from as you plan and write your essay.

7. This question asks you to choose one poem which is about a person or an animal, and which gives you reason to feel sympathy (or feel in some way sorry for) that person or animal. To begin an answer to this question, you would need to state

clearly the reasons for your sympathy, and then go on to show how the poet's portrayal of the person or the animal caused you to feel sympathy. You would be expected to go on to refer to quite a bit of detail here – the poet's choice of words, use of imagery/metaphors/similes, maybe the title, use of rhythm or rhyme, etc.

8. The key phrase in this question is "unhappy experience." Many poems are about experiences which the poet has had, and which have had an effect on the poet. An example from the poems you have studied might be Visiting Hour by Norman McCaig. In this poem, McCaig describes an unhappy experience common to most people – a hospital visit.

HINT In your answer you must clearly state at the beginning what the experience is, and then go on to select from the poem key words, phrases, comparisons, use of rhythm, rhyme, punctuation, etc. which go together to make an effective description of an unhappy experience.

9. Here you are asked to choose a poem which deals with a certain time of life. Note the use of "etc." in the question. This means that you do not have to restrict your answer to the two examples given (childhood and old age). You could answer on a poem which is about another time of life – being a teenager, or a new mother, for example. The main thing is to make clear at the start of your essay which time of life the poem you have selected is concerned with.

Section D - Film and TV Drama

EXAM ANSWER ADVICE

Critical Essays for Film and TV Drama are marked in just the same way as those for Drama, Prose, Poetry. You should be concerned with many of the same things as you would if writing an essay on a play or a novel – plot, character, theme. However, it may be appropriate to use other more specific media techniques in your answer (refer to the box at the start of the questions).

Read the information in the box given at the start of each section of questions. This is a guide to some of the things you could cover or include in your essay. Words from this text box are also a reminder of the kind of technical terms that would be appropriate for you to use.

10. This question asks you to consider a film or TV drama which contains "exciting action at key points." Your first reaction to this question might be to think first of all of the "action film" genre. This would be an appropriate choice, but notice also the words in the question "at key points." These words allow you to choose almost any film or TV drama which makes some use of exciting action. The main challenge in this question is selection – you must attempt to select key scenes involving action and then describe their use and significance. The danger is that you write a summary of the story of the film and nothing else.

11. Again the main thing to keep in mind here is selection. Start your essay with a very brief summary of the film or TV drama which you have studied. Choose a

few examples of the use of special effects from the film or TV drama which you have studied and describe them. As you are doing this, try to think of why they are used – how do they fit into the film or TV drama as a whole? What do they add to character or theme?

12. The question asks you to choose a film or TV drama which deals with an unpleasant aspect of life. State clearly what the aspect is at the outset of your essay, and then select key scenes, portrayal of character, and any use of media techniques which highlight or develop this aspect throughout the film or TV drama. As you proceed with your essay try to maintain a line of thought in which you explain how the film or TV drama has affected you – how it has increased your understanding of this particular unpleasant aspect of life.

Section E - Language

EXAM ANSWER ADVICE

If you have used a Language text (or texts) for your Personal Study, or made a close study in class of the language of different groups, or the language of advertising you might want to consider this section. You must be sure that you have plenty of detailed examples if your essay is to be successful.

Read the information in the box given at the start of each section of questions. This is a guide to some of the things you could cover or include in your essay. Words from this text box are also a reminder of the kind of technical terms that would be appropriate for you to use.

PRACTICE PAPER B   CLOSE READING WORKED ANSWERS

Note: in the answers section alternative answers are shown by /. Words that may be used in an answer, but are not essential, are enclosed in brackets

1. (*a*)   The writer gives examples of the behaviour of spoilt children (1 mark) which we have all experienced (1 mark)

OR

Reference to an example from the text plus an appropriate explanation, e.g. "a full-evening performance by their four-year-old-son" (1 mark) clearly conveys a sense of irritation we can easily relate to (1 mark).
(Total 2 marks)

> **HINT** This type of question asks you to understand what the writer means by "We've all been there." As well as writing down what she means by this, you have to look for an example from the first paragraph which helped you to find this meaning. The marks would be awarded as 1 plus 1 (1 mark for the correct meaning, and 1 mark for the example).

(*b*)   Reference to any two of:

"full-evening performance"

"he sings, he dances"

"he eats all the hors d'oeuvres"

"he interrupts"

"they ask him to share his feelings" etc
(Any 2 for 2 marks)

> **HINT** This question simply asks you to go back into the passage and find two expressions which suggest an unpleasant experience. Remember, do not write down long chunks of the passage, an expression is a few words only. Also, you are still looking only at lines 1-7.

(*c*)   Reference to short/two-word sentence "You yawn." (1 mark)
Comment – this emphasises the writer's boredom (1 mark)

Reference to question/rhetorical question "Who cares?" (1 mark)
Comment – this indicates that the writer is not interested (1 mark).

[Identification of feature(1) Comment(1) = 2 marks]

> **HINT** Sentence structure questions are often thought to be difficult, but what you are asked is not complicated. You should aim to identify one feature of the sentence structure in the relevant area, and then say how it emphasises the writer's reluctance to listen to the hamster story.

> **TOP EXAM TIP**
>
> Remember that the key words of a question are in bold. These are words the examiner wants you to pay special attention to, e.g. **word choice**, **sentence structure, tone,** or, very importantly, **in your own words.**

2. (*a*)   Reference to "(house) shakes" (1 mark) suggests excessive noise (1 mark)

OR

"screams" (1 mark) suggests spoilt behaviour/ a tantrum(1 mark)
(Total 2 marks)

(b) Any one from:

Balance/brevity of "Dinner over, he returns." (1 mark) This suggests the writer's dread/unwelcome nature of the child's return. (1 mark)

Brevity of "It's ten o'clock." (1 mark) This emphasises the writer's disapproval of the child still being up. (1 mark)

Question/answer "Is he tired? No! he says." (1 mark) Suggests child's bad behaviour/ cheek/answering back (1 mark).

Short final sentence "You'll just send cheques."/Short final sentence contrasting with longer preceeding sentence (1 mark) sums up writer's displeasure with this child/children in general (1 mark).
(Total 2 marks)

3. Any **one** from

"overparenting" suggests excess/too much parenting (1 mark)

"helicopter parenting" suggests hovering above (or around) the child/very quick to respond to child's wishes (1 mark)

"hothouse parenting" suggests protectiveness/very close nurture (1 mark)

"death-grip parenting" suggests extreme hold on the child (1 mark)

4. Gloss of

"anxiety" eg worry, concern, nervousness (1 mark)

and

"achievement pressure" eg feeling forced to succeed (1 mark)
(Total 2 marks)

> **HINT**
>
> First of all, look for where the writer introduces the idea of there being "two factors" in the passage. It is in line 17. Read on from this point, and you will be able to identify what the two factors are.
>
> The first one is "anxiety." Having identified it, you will have to get it into your own words. If you recognise right away that "anxiety" means worry, then you have your answer. If not, then look for clues from the words around it. There are clues to help you, such as: "will the child be permanently affected by the fate of the hamster?" Or: "did he touch the corpse, and get germs?" Both of these suggest worry.
>
> The second factor is "achievement pressure." When attempting to put a phrase into your own words, it is sometimes a good idea to try to find substitutes for each word. In this case, you might look at the word "achievement" and think that it means "to do well." If you are looking for clues in the passage, you will see that these words are near by ("Will he do well?"). Now, remember that the question asks you to "use your own words as far as possible." This means that you will have to try to find a word of your own, such as "success." The word "pressure" is a little easier; you might go for a word like "force" or "stress." Putting them together, you might come up with the answer "forced to succeed."

5. Babies at that age are lying down/ can't support themselves in front of the TV (1 mark)

   Babies can only just see/their eyes don't work very well (1 mark), etc.
   (Total 2 marks)

> **HINT**
>
> Again, here you have to find the small area in the passage which this question is concerned with, work out what it means, then try to find your own words for it. The question gives you: "it is hard to know what they will make of the material." (lines 27-28) The answer is found in the rest of the sentence – the words which come before this: "Since, at three months, babies cannot sit up, parents will have to hold them in front of the monitor, and since these infants have only just learned to focus their eyes." This is the section you have to show your understanding of, in your own words.

6. "The DVDs" links back to the ideas (about "achievement" and child development) mentioned in the previous paragraph. (1 mark)

   "the environmental-hazards problem" leads on to what will be dealt with in the rest of this paragraph ("bugs", "bacteria", etc). (1 mark)
   (Total 2 marks)

> **HINT**
>
> 'Link' questions are common, and will vary a little depending on the passage, but there is a basic similarity in what you have to do. You have to explain how this sentence joins two pieces of the writer's argument together. If you look at the sentence, you will see that it begins with "The DVDs." Now, from answering Question 5, you will remember that DVDs were the subject of the previous paragraph. If you read to the end of the linking sentence you will come to the expression "environmental-hazards problem." Reading on, you will note that the rest of the paragraph expands on the idea of "the environmental- hazards problem."

7. Any one of:
   Word choice (1 mark) + reference to balance/contrast of "finger paints" and "reading and maths preparation." (1 mark)

   Sentence structure (1 mark) + reference to use of comma to balance the two parts of the sentence (1 mark)
   (Total 2 marks)

> **HINT**
>
> This question asks you to **identify,** and then give **an example** of a technique which creates balance or contrast. For one mark you must identify (and name) a technique used; for the second mark you must quote an example of it.

8. It enables young people (1 mark) to ask their parents about anything/eveything (1 mark)

    (Total 2 marks)

> **HINT**
>
> The answer to this question comes from the rest of the sentence, which comes just before the quote selected. The clue is the word "by," and your answer comes just after it: "by allowing children to consult with their parents over any problem, any decision, any flicker of experience..." To get the marks you have to show an understanding of this; you do so by putting it in your own words.

9. It is appropriate/effective (1 mark) as many children/young adults return home/ move back (1 mark)

    (Total 2 marks)

> **HINT**
>
> An evaluation question (note the letter "E" at the side of the page), asks you "how appropriate" or "effective" something is. It is often a good idea to use these words in your answer.

10. (*a*) They aim to give the child a good start in life (1 mark)

> **HINT**
>
> Again, if you look carefully at the section of the passage which the question directs you to (lines 60-65), you will notice that "hovering parents" appears near the beginning. The expression is followed by the word "say." The words which follow "say" give you your answer: "that their goal is to launch the child into the world successfully." Having found the reason, you then have to write it down, using your own words as far as possible.

    (*b*) A need to hang onto the child/keep close control of the child (1 mark)

> **HINT**
>
> This is a more difficult question, asking you to work out what is implied by the expression "dark dependency." (What are its connotations?) To answer this, you could try to look at the connotations of each word in this context: "dark" suggests secret, hidden; "dependency" suggests a need to hang onto something. A further clue is given in the words which follow this expression: "some transfer of the parent's identity to the child." This too suggests a dependency, a need for close control.

11. The "I don't want to...I just want to" construction (1 mark)

    OR

    The use of a question ("Why do grown-ups have to take over everything?")
    (1mark)

    (Total 1 mark)

> **HINT**
>
> A tone is created by the language used (word choice, sentence structure, punctuation, etc.) In this question you are given the tone ("anger.") What you have to do is find **one** language feature (it is only worth one mark) which suggests the boy's anger.

12. Reference to: The comma isolates the word "ashamed" (1 mark), and suggests the parent is feeling guilty (1 mark)

    OR

    The short sentence (1 mark) emphasises the parent's guilty reaction (1 mark)
    (Total 2 marks)

> **HINT** Here you are asked to look at just one sentence. What is the reaction of the parent to the boy's anger? How is this reaction conveyed by the sentence structure? What do you notice about the sentence? Is there any punctuation? Does this punctuation highlight any of the words?

13. Answers should deal with:

The relevance/effectiveness of "The Child Trap" [eg children are controlled/imprisoned (1 mark) by their (over protective) parents (1 mark)]

OR

The connotations of the expression [eg "Child Trap" suggests the pitfalls/errors (1 mark) of some kinds of (overprotective) parenting (1 mark)]

> **HINT** With a question like this you should try to do two things: firstly, think of a way (or ways) in which the title is relevant to the writer's ideas in the passage; secondly, try to think of the connotations (or suggestions) of the words in the title. How do these suggestions fit in with the writer's ideas?

PRACTICE PAPER B   CRITICAL ESSAY WORKED ANSWERS

EXAM ANSWER ADVICE

You have to choose two essays from five sections. There is not much time to do this as you will need close to 45 minutes to plan and write each essay. Under the pressure of exam conditions it is hard not to make a quick, and perhaps panicked choice, but try to choose your essay questions calmly. You need to pick questions which suit the texts you know and will allow you to demonstrate your knowledge. Try to scan the questions and circle the ones which look possible. Then have another look at your circled questions before making a final choice.

Note that the questions are made up of two lines. The first line asks you to make a selection from the texts you have studied. The second line gives you a task. This task often asks you to do **two** things.

Remember the main piece of advice to keep in mind when writing a Critical Essay: answer the question. Have the question in your mind all the way through your essay and try to develop a line of thought which is relevant to the question. Try to make your essay more than just a list of techniques that the writer has used.

Section A - Drama

EXAM ANSWER ADVICE

Read the information in the box given at the start of each section of questions. This is a guide to some of the things you could cover or include in your essay. Words from this text box are also a reminder of the kind of technical terms that would be appropriate for you to use.

Remember that when answering on a play you are trying to write about quite a large piece of literature. Your answer should focus on elements like character, conflict between characters, setting, plot, themes, etc. It is not appropriate to attempt the kind of micro-analysis you would do when writing about a poem or a short story.

1. To answer this question you have to identify a moment in the play you have studied when a character makes a decision which has an important effect on him or her or the events of the play. For instance in Shakespeare's Macbeth, Macbeth makes a decision to kill King Duncan. The taking of this decision changes everything for Macbeth, for his wife, and for Scotland. It would be a good approach to make the taking of the decision the starting point of your essay.

Then to write about the factors which contributed to the taking of this decision (in this example, Macbeth's own ambitions, the influence of Lady Macbeth, the predictions made by the witches). This would be followed by a section on the effects of the decision: the changes in Macbeth's relationship with his wife, further murders, Macbeth's own mental deterioration.

2. This is quite a wide question which hopefully would let you write about almost any play you have studied. The term "issue" could cover a range of ideas contained in a play which are relevant to today's world – war, jealousy, love, responsibility, etc. Again, the requirement is to identify the issue and keep your essay relevant to a discussion of it.

3. Conflict is an essential element of drama and it is a good idea to refer to it no matter what play you are writing about. Here, conflict is the central subject of the essay. You are asked to identify and focus on conflict between two characters. In some plays there may be conflict between several characters (eg An Inspector Calls), but for this question you need to select two characters. You should identify these two characters at the beginning of your essay, and select which key scenes or moments in the play best highlight the conflict between them. Note also that the question requires you to comment on whether or not the conflict is resolved, or sorted out.

Section B - Prose

EXAM ANSWER ADVICE

At Intermediate 2 level most questions will allow you to answer on either a novel or a short story. Watch out, however, for a question which asks for a "non-fiction text." A novel or a short story would not be appropriate here, and you would lose marks if you answered using this type of text. A question asking for "a prose work" allows you to answer on any kind of prose writing (fiction or non-fiction).

Read the information in the box given at the start of each section of questions. This is a guide to some of the things you could cover or include in your essay. Words from this text box are also a reminder of the kind of technical terms that would be appropriate for you to use.

Remember that when answering on a **novel** you are trying to write about quite a large piece of literature. Your answer should focus on elements like character, conflict between characters, setting, plot/narrative, themes, etc. It is not appropriate to attempt the kind of micro-analysis you would do when writing about a short story.

4. This question asks you to consider a novel or a short story which deals with relationships within a family. Note that you are not restricted to discussion of one relationship, you could deal with several – this is an approach you could take with a novel like To Kill A Mockingbird which is concerned with various relationships within the Finch family. On the other hand, a short story may concentrate on one relationship within a family – A Time to Dance by Bernard MacLaverty focuses on a mother/son relationship.

Again, identify the relationships at the start of your essay and try to map the development of the relationships (how they change) from the beginning through the middle to the end of the story.

5. This question gives you the opportunity to write about a non-fiction text; however, it also allows you to write about a novel or a short story. In the opening paragraph of your essay state the text you have chosen, and also state the topic that you have found interesting. You then have to show how the writer deals with the topic and how it is made interesting for you (what techniques the writer has used to make the topic interesting). For non-fiction writing this may include the writer's use of description and descriptive detail, anecdotes, dialogue, facts, statistics, etc. For an essay on fiction you would look to analyse plot, character, key incidents, etc.

6. This question asks you to choose a novel or a short story which contains a significant incident which affects the outcome of the story. This is a fairly open question which would allow you to write about most novels or stories that you have studied. The main requirement is to identify an important incident which changes things for the characters involved. This is also known as a turning point. Plan your essay by identifying the significant incident, and then dealing with how it came about, and how it affected the characters afterwards.

Section C - Poetry

> ### EXAM ANSWER ADVICE
>
> Read the information in the box given at the start of each section of questions. This is a guide to some of the things you could cover or include in your essay. Words from this text box are also a reminder of the kind of technical terms that would be appropriate for you to use.
>
> Remember that if you are writing about a fairly short poem you will be expected to analyse it in some detail. In your programme of revision it may be worth trying to memorise the whole poem. This would give you access to all of the poem's words and phrases, and would remind you of techniques, in the exam. Quickly writing out sections of the poem on your exam paper would give you something to work from as you plan and write your essay.

7. For this question you need to choose a poem which simply describes a happy experience, or one which seems to take a "positive" view of an experience, or perhaps is in some way inspiring or uplifting. Your selection of material to use from the poem should be words and phrases, comparisons, etc. which convey this kind of mood or feelings.

8. This question asks you to deal with a poem which tells an interesting story. This could be a narrative poem which has as its main business the telling of a substantial story, or it could be, perhaps, a shorter poem which tells the story of a more concise, or brief experience (eg Robert Frost's "Out Out," or one of many poems by Edwin Morgan or Norman McCaig). Be careful in your answer not to just re-tell the story. The question asks you to "show how the poetic techniques make the story interesting." You must, of course, devote some of your essay to the story told, but you must also look at the poet's interesting use of language.

9. Question 7 from this paper offers a limited choice of options; question 8 again offers a restricted choice; but this question is pretty open. The "important aspect

of life" could be almost anything that people consider to be important in their lives: birth, death, illness, love, hate, loss, etc. Most poems which you have studied could be said to deal with an important aspect of life. After making your selection, the main thing to remember is to concentrate on language techniques used by the poet as well as the content. You should also try to include some evaluation, your own reaction to the words and ideas of the poem – this is addressed by the final words of the question "help(s) you to think about this important aspect of life."

Section D - Film and TV Drama

EXAM ANSWER ADVICE

Critical Essays for Film and TV Drama are marked in just the same way as those for Drama, Prose, Poetry. You should be concerned with many of the same things as you would if writing an essay on a play or a novel – plot, character, theme. However, it may be appropriate to use other more specific media techniques in your answer (refer to the box at the start of the questions).

Read the information in the box given at the start of each section of questions. This is a guide to some of the things you could cover or include in your essay. Words from this text box are also a reminder of the kind of technical terms that would be appropriate for you to use.

10. Many films or TV dramas are known for their interesting or arresting opening sequences which make use of interesting special effects or unusual sound and camera work in addition to giving clear indications of what the main (or later) concerns will be. If this has been a focus of your study, you may well have an opportunity here to write convincingly about the use of media techniques. However, you must also explain how the opening sequence relates to later events, concerns or character developments.

11. A fairly specific question which may well suit TV drama. Remember that you should deal with the same kind of elements as in a Drama or Prose response here (character development, plot, theme), in addition to the use of more specific media techniques which may have been used to highlight aspects of the conflict.

12. A clear identification of the issue involved is needed at the outset of your essay in response to this question. Remember that the definition of "issue" is fairly wide – it could be a specific environmental or health issue, but it could be a wider issue such as prejudice, or poverty, or violence.

Section E - Language

EXAM ANSWER ADVICE

If you have used a Language text (or texts) for your Personal Study, or made a close study in class of the language of different groups, or the language of advertising you might want to consider this section. You must be sure that you have plenty of detailed examples if your essay is to be successful

Read the information in the box given at the start of each section of questions. This is a guide to some of the things you could cover or include in your essay. Words from this text box are also a reminder of the kind of technical terms that would be appropriate for you to use.

PRACTICE PAPER C   CLOSE READING WORKED ANSWERS

Note: in the answers section alternative answers are shown by /. Words that may be used in an answer, but are not essential, are enclosed in brackets

1. (*a*) Any **two** from

    "thankless task"

    "ignore her"

    "low pay"

    "little thanks"
    (Total 2 marks)

> **HINT** For this type of question you simply have to identify two expressions and write them down. You do not need to make any comment. Remember, an expression is just a few words. Do not copy down large chunks of the passage: you will lose marks by doing this.

  (*b*) (Repeated) use questions/question marks (1 mark) shows that the writer wants us to examine our behaviour or attitude towards checkout workers / draws attention to our attitudes towards ckeckout workers (1 mark)
(Total 2 marks)

> **HINT** After a quick scan of the first paragraph, you will see that there is a very obvious repeated use of questions. A closer look at the questions will show you that the writer is asking the reader to examine his or her attitudes towards checkout workers, the implication being that our attitudes are not good.

2. Reference to dash (1 mark) introducing a range of behaviours (observed)/ a list of different behaviours (observed) (1 mark)

    Reference to a list (1 mark) of different behaviours (observed) (1 mark)
    (Total 2 marks)

> **HINT** In this question you are given just one sentence to look at. Do you notice any obvious features?

3. "Last summer" refers back to "someday"/ idea of time (mentioned in previous paragraph (1 mark). "Sam did" refers to what Sam actually did (write a book, as mentioned in rest of this paragraph) (1 mark)
    (Total 2 marks)

> **HINT** This is the common 'link' question in which you have to show how a sentence operates as a link in the writer's argument. If you look at this short sentence you will notice that "Last summer" reminds us of the idea of time (**someday** someone should write a book") mentioned at the end of paragraph 3. The remaining words "Sam did" refer on to what Sam actually did about it: she wrote a book called "The Tribulations of a Checkout Girl" (the subject of the remainder of paragraph 4).

4. "untrained disposable (female supermarket) workers" expands/explains (1 mark) the idea of "the modern proletariat" (1 mark).
(Total 2 marks)

> **HINT** Here the dash performs the same function as a colon: what comes after it explains or expands on what has gone before.

5. She greeted the customers, but they did not answer her (1 mark); when she needed to go to the toilet permission was not given (1 mark); she was friendly to families, but parents were unfriendly in return / used her as a way to lecture their children about their futures (1 mark).
(Any 2 = 2 marks)

> **HINT** Make sure you take your reasons from the correct lines - they are given in the question. Be careful to pick two separate reasons in order to achieve two marks. The key to this type of question is not to lift chunks of text from the passage: you have to use your own words.

6. "articluate" or "cultured" (1 mark)

> **HINT** This type of question is concerned with vocabulary. It is testing how well you have understood the words in this paragraph (lines 32-35). Remember, the question is just asking for one word: you only have to write down that one word, nothing else. If you look at the sentence which contains the word "graduating," you will see that it goes on to explain what Anna was like after graduating (leaving / achieving her qualifications). It says she was "articulate" and "cultured." These words mean that she is able to express herself clearly, and that she is knowledgeable about culture. Both are qualities you would expect from an education at university.

7. Reason: many young people in France leave school with qualifications (1 mark) which allow them to go to university (1 mark).

OR

Example: (in Rennes) many students gain qualifications (as teachers) (1 mark), but there are not enough teaching jobs / they have to take other jobs (1 mark).
(Total 2 marks)

> **HINT** As is usual with Close Reading questions, you are directed to a small section of the passage. After reading it again quickly, you have to decide which part contains the reason, and which part contains the example. (The reason comes first, then the example). Remember, you only have to deal with one of them.

8. It is very short (1 mark) and therefore stands out (1 mark); it answers the question ("Are you in prison?") (1 mark) from the previous paragraph (1 mark); it introduces (1 mark) the content of the rest of the paragraph (about how her job is almost like prison) (1 mark).
(Total 2 marks)

> **HINT** Writers often vary the length of sentences in order to achieve impact (to draw attention to something). In this question you are asked to consider why the writer does so here.

9. "sneakily" suggests customers behaved in an underhand way (1 mark); "tried to get out with" suggests that they were devious (1 mark); "vented their anger" suggests aggressiveness (1 mark); "mistakenly" suggests the customers are wrong (1mark); "ignored her" suggests they pay no attention to her (1 mark); "marched past (her)" suggests they take no notice of her (1 mark).
    (Total 2 marks) (Example only = 0 marks)

> **HINT**
> In a question like this you are given an attitude: that Sam is critical of the customers. You have to find **two** examples of how the writer's word choice reflects this. The words "explain fully" tell you that it is not enough just to find examples, the marks will be awarded for your comments.

10. (a) Answer: Something that provides the means / the way for people to express themselves (1 mark); we know this from "who write in (with tales)"/ "sometimes poignant, sometimes funny" (1 mark)
    (Total 2 marks)

    (b) Answer: It means "shop" (1 mark)

> **HINT**
> The use of the word "outlet" is interesting in this paragraph. It can just mean "shop" as in "retail outlet." But here it is referring to Sam's blog. It provides an "outlet" (a way) for people "to write in with tales" (ie tell their stories).

11. (a) "politicians.../ business leaders" ask her advice (1 mark); she spoke at the French Parliament (1 mark); she spoke at a "retail conference (in Luxembourg)" (1 mark).
    (Any two = 2 marks)

> **HINT**
> A straightforward question – you simply have to give two examples. You may quote them.

    (b) Making a note to say hello (1 mark) is absurd / unusual / silly (and therefore funny) (1 mark)

> **HINT**
> Humour is often hard to explain. In this example, the humour comes from the fact that the executives had to make a written note to remind themselves to say hello. Sam is suggesting that saying hello should come automatically, and should not require a note: she is poking fun at them.

12. (a) Checkout workers need to know how to cope with (1 mark) aggressive/angry/ abusive customers (1 mark)
    (Total 2 marks)

> **HINT**
> A straightforward own words question which asks you to demonstrate your understanding of the ideas in the paragraph selected.

    (b) "placate" (1 mark)

> **HINT**
> Try to find a place in the paragraph where the phrase "calm down" would fit.

13. The idea of the checkout girls' frustration (at the shoppers) (1 mark) fits in with other / earlier ideas in the passage / in the title (1 mark)

   Provides a (humorous / ironic) contrast (1 mark) with the content of the previous paragraph (dealing with conflict) (1 mark).

> **HINT**
>
> As is often the case, the last question is an evaluation question which asks you to consider the ending, and how it fits in with other ideas in the passage. You often have to consider the whole passage for your answer to this type of question.

PRACTICE PAPER C   CRITICAL ESSAY WORKED ANSWERS

EXAM ANSWER ADVICE

You have to choose two essays from five sections. There is not much time to do this as you will need close to 45 minutes to plan and write each essay. Under the pressure of exam conditions it is hard not to make a quick, and perhaps panicked choice, but try to choose your essay questions calmly. You need to pick questions which suit the texts you know and will allow you to demonstrate your knowledge. Try to scan the questions and circle the ones which look possible. Then have another look at your circled questions before making a final choice.

Note that the questions are made up of two lines. The first line asks you to make a selection from the texts you have studied. The second line gives you a task. This task often asks you to do **two** things.

Remember the main piece of advice to keep in mind when writing a Critical Essay: answer the question. Have the question in your mind all the way through your essay and try to develop a line of thought which is relevant to the question. Try to make your essay more than just a list of techniques that the writer has used.

Section A- Drama

EXAM ANSWER ADVICE

Read the information in the box given at the start of each section of questions. This is a guide to some of the things you could cover or include in your essay. Words from this text box are also a reminder of the kind of technical terms that would be appropriate for you to use.

Remember that when answering on a play you are trying to write about quite a large piece of literature. Your answer should focus on elements such as character, conflict between characters, setting, plot, themes, etc. It is not appropriate to attempt the kind of micro-analysis you would do when writing about a poem or a short story.

1. This question would suit a play which followed the pattern of a tragedy in which a character suffers a downfall which is at least partly explained by a weakness identified in his or her character. The human weakness in Macbeth, for example, is perhaps over-ambition or arrogance, in Othello perhaps jealousy, in Hamlet self-doubt or hesitation. To answer this question you must make a clear identification of the human weakness at the start of your essay followed by an explanation of how this weakness affects the character you have chosen as well as how it has affected others and the events in the play. In Macbeth his ambition spurs him on to have everything, but it also has serious consequences for himself, for others (Lady Macbeth and Banquo, for example), and for his country.

2.

> **HINT**
>
> This question asks you to focus on the ending of a play. Unfortunately, this type of question is often done poorly in exams. Essays are often unbalanced, concentrating mostly on what leads up to the ending, leaving mention of the ending to the final paragraph of the essay. Perhaps this is because it is natural to think that discussion of the ending should come "at the end."

Maybe it is better to think of this type of question the other way round: deal with the ending of the play at the beginning of your essay; this will give it immediate relevance. Then go on to write about the factors leading up to the ending. Remember to focus on character and/or themes. Identify the character(s) and/or theme(s) right at the start of your essay.

3.

> **HINT**
>
> In the Drama section, questions which ask directly about conflict are common. Here you are asked to write about a play in which there is conflict within a family or a group of people. While this does narrow down your choice to some extent, it should allow you to write about most plays you might have studied. A play such as An Inspector Calls would fit well here, or most Arthur Miller plays.

Again, make sure you clearly identify which characters in the play are in conflict, why they find themselves in conflict, and what are the consequences of this conflict. Keep your essay relevant to the question.

Section B - Prose

> **EXAM ANSWER ADVICE**
>
> At Intermediate 2 level most questions will allow you to answer on either a novel or a short story. Watch out, however, for a question which asks for a "non-fiction text." A novel or a short story would not be appropriate here, and you would lose marks if you answered using this type of text. A question asking for "a prose work" allows you to answer on any kind of prose writing (fiction or non-fiction).
>
> Read the information in the box given at the start of each section of questions. This is a guide to some of the things you could cover or include in your essay. Words from this text box are also a reminder of the kind of technical terms that would be appropriate for you to use.
>
> Remember that when answering on a **novel** you are trying to write about quite a large piece of literature. Your answer should focus on elements like character, conflict between characters, setting, plot/narrative, themes, etc. It is not appropriate to attempt the kind of micro-analysis you would do when writing about a short story.

4. It is one of the main purposes of a writer of fiction to make you care about the characters that he or she has created. This question which asks you to write about a character for whom you felt some kind of sympathy should present you with several options. To answer this question you must make a clear identification of one character. Then you must describe the problems faced by the character in the story and as you do so explain why you felt sympathy for this character.

5. This question widens your choice to include non-fiction. It asks specifically about setting "in place and/or time." This might suit non-fiction very well: perhaps a piece of travel writing in which a certain place is vividly described. The question asks for an explanation of what you have learned or enjoyed, and again these may be appropriate to non-fiction writing, eg a humorous treatment of a place in a piece of travel writing. However, equally it could work with a fiction text: a place or a certain time in history (or in the future) could be at the heart of the story. Make it clear at the start of your essay which aspect you are dealing with – is it fiction or non-fiction? a place or a time?

6. Again, after selecting your text, make clear at the start of your essay what the turning point is. There is no "right answer" about your selection of what the turning point is: it is all about the justification of your selection. Therefore, after clearly stating what you consider the turning point to be, you have to devote the rest of your essay to explaining what leads up to the turning point, and what follows it. As you do so, try to give reasons for its importance in terms of plot, characters and themes.

Section C - Poetry

EXAM ANSWER ADVICE

Read the information in the box given at the start of each section of questions. This is a guide to some of the things you could cover or include in your essay. Words from this text box are also a reminder of the kind of technical terms that would be appropriate for you to use.

Remember that if you are writing about a fairly short poem you will be expected to analyse it in some detail. In your programme of revision it may be worth trying to memorise the whole poem. This would give you access to all of the poem's words and phrases, and would remind you of techniques, in the exam. Quickly writing out sections of the poem on your exam paper would give you something to work from as you plan and write your essay.

7. A poem about war, violence, suffering, death, loss, etc. would be appropriate here, and many poems which you have studied in class would be suitable. The main thing to keep in mind is to make a clear identification of which "unpleasant aspect of life" you are addressing. This will help you to write a relevant essay. Make detailed reference to the poem as you explain what the poem has told you about this unpleasant aspect of life.

8.

HINT

This is a narrower choice than the previous question, but is fairly straightforward if a poem you have studied has as one of its main purposes a description of a person or a place (Norman McCaig's "Aunt Julia" would be a common example here).

9.

HINT

A question about an ending can crop up in any of the Drama, Prose, Poetry or Media sections. It is worth considering it when preparing for the exam. You have to be careful with relevance in questions about endings. Don't leave mention of the ending until the end of your essay – make it clear early in your essay what the ending is, and how it is an interesting or an unexpected conclusion to the whole of the poem.

As you are writing about a poem, remember that the ending does not need to be the conclusion to some kind of story, it can just be a very fitting or appropriate last line, or group of words, or image. An example of this would be Owen's "Dulce et Decorum est."

Section D - Film and TV Drama

EXAM ANSWER ADVICE

Critical Essays for Film and TV Drama are marked in just the same way as those for Drama, Prose, Poetry. You should be concerned with many of the same things as you would if writing an essay on a play or a novel – plot, character, theme. However, it may be appropriate to use other more specific media techniques in your answer (refer to the box at the start of the questions).

Read the information in the box given at the start of each section of questions. This is a guide to some of the things you could cover or include in your essay. Words from this text box are also a reminder of the kind of technical terms that would be appropriate for you to use.

10. This question asks you to focus on one scene in which there is a display of "powerful human emotion." This would suit many films, and would be especially appropriate for TV Drama. Remember that it is appropriate here to make discussion of character, plot and theme in addition to other media techniques which are referred to in the box above. Make a clear identification of one scene at the start of your essay. Then you can refer to other scenes, the opening, the ending, etc. in order to demonstrate how your scene is important to the film or drama as a whole.

11. This question should be tackled in much the same way as a question about conflict in the Drama section. Make a clear identification of the characters or groups of people involved in conflict at the start of your essay. Characterisation and plot will be significant in your explanation of the conflict. Refer to media techniques to explain how the conflict is highlighted.

12. After indicating your text selection and giving a short summary of the plot and main concerns, refer right away to the closing sequence, before explaining in which ways it is effective with reference to the film or TV drama as a whole.

Section E - Language

EXAM ANSWER ADVICE

If you have used a Language text (or texts) for your Personal Study, or made a close study in class of the language of different groups, or the language of advertising you might want to consider this section. You must be sure that you have plenty of detailed examples if your essay is to be successful.

Read the information in the box given at the start of each section of questions. This is a guide to some of the things you could cover or include in your essay. Words from this text box are also a reminder of the kind of technical terms that would be appropriate for you to use.

Note: in the answers section alternative answers are shown by /. Words that may be used in an answer, but are not essential, are enclosed in brackets

1. (*a*) They are contrasting statements / you wouldn't expect an (Christian) artist to be a murderer (1 mark).

> **HINT** The writer highlights the two things he wants you to remember through his use of a colon in line 1. Two statements follow the colon. Have a look at them, and decide what is surprising about them when placed side by side.

(*b*) Caravaggio's crime should be treated separately (1 mark) because it is not important/is just scandal making (1 mark).

It is a mistake to link what an artist does (1 mark) with what he paints (1 mark).
(Total 2 marks)

> **HINT** This question asks you to demonstrate your understanding of the ideas contained in the second half of the paragraph, from lines 4-7.

2. (*a*) "(a portrait) of the artist as ogre" (following the colon) (1 mark) explains or expands the idea of what has "never been painted before (or "again")" (1 mark)
(Total 2 marks)

> **HINT** Note that this question asks you to make "clear reference to the rest of the sentence." This tells you that you have to refer to the words in the sentence while explaining the function of the colon.

(*b*) "shocking painting of himself" / "(a portrait of the) artist as ogre" / "(his face a) grotesque mask" / "of bad behaviour" (1 mark) suggests an image of / sense of guilt (1 mark).
(Total 2 marks)

> **HINT** For this question you have to show some understanding of "an unsparing image of self-accusation." Look at words in the expression that you recognise. An "accusation' is when you claim that someone has done something wrong. A "self-accusation" must mean here that Caravaggio is making that claim about himself. Now, try to find other words from the paragraph which would suggest that kind of guilt, self-hatred.

3. (*a*) Words are described as "feeble" which suggests weak / "fluttering" which suggests lightweight, easily blown away (1 mark). This contrasts with the words used to refer to his paintings: "muscular" which suggests strong / "bulk" which suggests solidity (1 mark).
(Total 2 marks)

> **HINT** The key section in the passage here is: "words were feeble fluttering things beside the muscular bulk of his painting." For a question about contrasting word choice it is important to show that you understand **both** sides of the contrast.

(*b*) "speech had never been so redundant" (1 mark).

> **HINT** All you have to do here is find the most appropriate expression (small group of words), and write it down. No explanation or comment is needed.

(c) Reference to any one of:
"I wasn't in the mood," "(It had been) yet another," "thanks very much," "I wanted to be out," "I had had my fill of art."
(Total 1 mark)

> **HINT**
> At times in this paragraph, the writer's tone makes it clear that he is tired, weary of trying to explain the paintings. The question requires you to find words or expressions which suggest this weariness.

4. "(In my) hand" refers back to "took" / ideas in the previous paragraph (1 mark), while "(an ancient iron) key" introduces a description of the key contained in this paragraph (1 mark).
(Total 2 marks)

> **HINT**
> This is a common type of question. You are asked to explain how the writer's ideas are linked across two paragraphs. In this example, the writer is telling us a story (or *anecdote*). In the previous paragraph, the caretaker is handing the writer something. In this paragraph (line 29), we find out what it is: a key.

5. "uncomprehendingly" (1 mark)

> **HINT**
> Here you have to scan the paragraph quickly, looking for just one word which suggests the writer doesn't realise, or doesn't know, something. There is really just one option. The phrase "vaguely aware" might have done, but that is, of course, two words.

6. **Comparison/metaphor/image** – writer compared to child/caretaker to teacher (1 mark) effectively shows writer's stupidity as he needs to be shown/taught **or** he is made to seem very young/immature (1 mark).

   Word choice – "turned me round" (1 mark) effectively shows writer's stupidity as he needs to be physically shown/ he doesn't get it himself (1 mark).

> **HINT**
> You are helped here by being given a very small section of the passage to look at. Within this section there are really only two possible techniques you could identify which suggest the writer's stupidity: comparison/metaphor/image or word choice. The "E" symbol at the end of the question tells you that you have to make a comment about how effective the technique is.

7. The artist used real people (to paint from/copy) / he painted them actual size / the painting was done in that church. (Any 2 = 2 marks).

> **TOP EXAM TIP**
> Remember that the key words of a question are in bold. These are words the examiner wants you to pay special attention to, e.g. **word choice, sentence structure, tone,** or, very importantly, **in your own words.**

> **HINT**
> To answer this question you have to pinpoint key words or expressions from the passage, and then try to find your own words in order to demonstrate your understanding. The key words and expressions are: "live models," "life-sized," "cathedral."

8. (a) parenthesis / dashes (1 mark).

> **HINT**
> Occasionally, you will be asked simply to identify a language feature. These features will be taken from the Course Arrangements (available on the SQA website).

(b) This feature explains / emphasises the suggestion / point that the keys (1 mark) represent prison / locking up (1 mark).

> **HINT** Parenthesis is a word or phrase inserted by the writer as an explanation, or afterthought (marked here by dashes). In this case the words in parenthesis explain or emphasise the writer's point about a set of keys in the picture.

(c) "nightmarish" suggests awful experience / dream / thought, etc (1 mark)

"claustrophobia" suggests being shut in / enclosed / prison, etc. (1 mark) (Total 2 marks).

> **HINT** With this type of question you have to look directly at the expression quoted and think about what it suggests to you, at this point in the writer's argument. This question is asking you to think about connotations. In this case it is just two words. You could look at each word separately. What does each word suggest to you? "nightmarish" - bad dreams, something unpleasant, a bad experience, "claustrophobia" – being locked up, shut in, enclosed. Or you could look at the whole expression, and consider what it suggests to you - the awful experience of being locked up, perhaps.

9. Caravaggio requested keys (1 mark). The church officials / staff / people give him the keys they used / had available (1 mark). The keys (the writer is holding) are the same (as the ones in the picture) (1 mark). (Total 3 marks).

> **HINT** Questions in this paper are usually 1 or 2 marks; however, you will sometimes see a question for 3 or 4 marks. In this case the approach needed is to identify 3 separate points in the writer's explanation, and attempt to write them down in your own words. (Of course, there is no need to find an alternative for every word, eg "keys").

10. He (finally) realises (1 mark) he is holding the (actual) key from the painting / that Caravaggio had held (1 mark). (Total 2 marks).

> **HINT** This question asks you to think about how well the sentence identified works as a conclusion to a reasonably long paragraph. A conclusion brings something to an end, or it sums up. You have to consider in what ways this sentence does these things.

11. It is a sentence on its own (1 mark).

It is a question (1 mark) which challenges the reader (1 mark).

The italics ("*looking*") (1 mark) suggest a challenge / threat (1 mark).

It is an unusual way to end (1 mark). (2 points = 2 marks).

> **HINT** "Impact" means that it has made an impression on the reader; it has stood out in some ways. How does this paragraph do this? Or, in what ways is it unusual as a paragraph?

PRACTICE PAPER D   CRITICAL ESSAY WORKED ANSWERS

EXAM ANSWER ADVICE

You have to choose two essays from five sections. There is not much time to do this as you will need close to 45 minutes to plan and write each essay. Under the pressure of exam conditions it is hard not to make a quick, and perhaps panicked choice, but try to choose your essay questions calmly. You need to pick questions which suit the texts you know and will allow you to demonstrate your knowlege. Try to scan the questions and circle the ones which look possible. Then have another look at your circled questions before making a final choice.

Note that the questions are made up of two lines. The first line asks you to make a selection from the texts you have studied. The second line gives you a task. This task often asks you to do **two** things.

Remember the main piece of advice to keep in mind when writing a Critical Essay: answer the question. Have the question in your mind all the way through your essay and try to develop a line of thought which is relevant to the question. Try to make your essay more than just a list of techniques that the writer has used.

Section A- Drama

EXAM ANSWER ADVICE

Read the information in the box given at the start of each section of questions. This is a guide to some of the things you could cover or include in your essay. Words from this text box are also a reminder of the kind of technical terms that would be appropriate for you to use.

Remember that when answering on a play you are trying to write about quite a large piece of literature. Your answer should focus on elements like character, conflict between characters, setting, plot, themes, etc. It is not appropriate to attempt the kind of micro-analysis you would do when writing about a poem or a short story.

1. "Failure in his relationships" is, perhaps, another way of saying "conflict;" therefore this question should be suitable for most plays that you may have studied. It would suit several Arthur Miller plays, along with Macbeth, Romeo and Juliet, An Inspector Calls, Educating Rita, Bold Girls, etc. The main thing is to select a character to focus on, and then to explain with reference to key scenes, dialogue, etc. how this character is unsuccessful in his or her relationships with other characters throughout the play. As you do this, you should try to suggest reasons for the causes of the relationship problems.

2. A common question, along with questions about endings or turning points. You will need to demonstrate a fairly detailed knowledge of what happens in terms of plot, character and theme in the opening of the play, and then show how this is all important later in the play (making mention of other key scenes/happenings/ important speeches in the play).

3.

 HINT — This question would suit a play which has a strong emotion as its essential subject matter: for example, love or hate in Romeo and Juliet, or jealousy in Othello.

Again, your essay should begin with a clear statement of the emotion involved, and the character who expresses it. You should go on to explain why this character feels the need to express this emotion (eg the reasons for Othello's jealousy), and the effects this has on the other characters (making mention of other key scenes/ happenings/important speeches in the play).

Section B - Prose

> **EXAM ANSWER ADVICE**
>
> At Intermediate 2 level most questions will allow you to answer on either a novel or a short story. Watch out, however, for a question which asks for a "non-fiction text." A novel or a short story would not be appropriate here, and you would lose marks if you answered using this type of text. A question asking for "a prose work" allows you to answer on any kind of prose writing (fiction or non-fiction).
>
> Read the information in the box given at the start of each section of questions. This is a guide to some of the things you could cover or include in your essay. Words from this text box are also a reminder of the kind of technical terms that would be appropriate for you to use.
>
> Remember that when answering on a **novel** you are trying to write about quite a large piece of literature. Your answer should focus on elements like character, conflict between characters, setting, plot/narrative, themes, etc. It is not appropriate to attempt the kind of micro-analysis you would do when writing about a short story.

4. This should allow you to write about most of the novels or stories which you have studied. Remember to read the wording of the question carefully, though. It asks you to concentrate on two characters. This will probably involve some element of selection on your part. If you have studied a novel, you may have to narrow your choice down to two characters from a fairly long list. (In To Kill A Mockingbird, for example, you might focus on the conflict between Atticus and Bob Ewell). The question does ask you, however, to go on to show how the conflict between these two characters affects the other characters and events in the story. This will allow you to include more material from a longer piece of fiction. (Returning to "Mockingbird," you could go on to show how Atticus' conflict with Ewell affects Scout, Jem, and Boo Radley).

5. This question allows you to write about either fiction or non-fiction. For non-fiction, an "unpleasant aspect of life" might be a human or political issue. But, it could equally be something personal, such as coping with death or loss. For non-fiction, the second half of the task "explain how it is made real for you" could include anecdotes, eye witness accounts, detailed description, question and answer, etc. As always, make a clear statement of which "unpleasant aspect of life" you are dealing with.

6. Remember to focus on one character in your answer to this question. Try to think of your story or novel in terms of a beginning, middle and end, then map the changes undergone by your chosen character. You should refer to changing relationships with other characters, key incidents in the plot, and theme.

Section C - Poetry

7. This question asks for a response on a poem which is concentrated on the description of a person or an incident. The incident or the person will have made a great impact on the poet. Try to get over a sense of this in your essay. Refer to the poet's use of language in as much detail as you can. Try to think about what the poet is saying about the person or the incident.

8. State clearly at the start of your essay what the "unhappy experience" is. Next, spend a bit of time describing the experience itself before attempting an explanation of how the poet has used words and phrases, rhyme, comparisons, etc. to express this feeling of unhappiness.

9. In a question like this, note the use of the "etc." in the question. This means that you are not restricted to the times of life as specified in the question – you can add one which is better suited to a poem which you have studied. Just make sure that you state clearly which time of life you are writing about. The question asks you to explain how the poet has attempted "to create a clear picture of that time of life." This requires you to make detailed reference to the poet's use of language and techniques.

Section D - Film and TV Drama

10. This question should be approached in the same way as a similar question might appear in the Drama or Prose sections. The first thing to do is to make a selection of one particular sequence from the film or TV drama which you have studied. This sequence must mark a clear change in the fortunes of one character, or mark a change in direction of the plot. Make clear your selection at the start of your essay, and then go on to explain what leads up to this sequence (in terms of plot, character, ideas), and what follows on from it.

11. Humour can be tricky to explain. Your essay should concentrate on finding examples from a film or TV drama which you have found amusing. (There will be an element of personal reaction here). In addition to this, you have to attempt to explain how the effect of humour, or amusement, has been created by the use of techniques (plot, character, and more specific media techniques).

12. This question asks you to respond to a film or TV drama which contains a lot of suspense or tension. You have to make a decision right away: to concentrate on one scene only, or to deal with the whole film or TV drama. Make clear at the outset which option you are taking. Again, refer to the box at the start of the section for a list of techniques you should consider for reference.

Section E - Language

> **EXAM ANSWER ADVICE**
>
> If you have used a Language text (or texts) for your Personal Study, or made a close study in class of the language of different groups, or the language of advertising you might want to consider this section. You must be sure that you have plenty of detailed examples if your essay is to be successful.
>
> Read the information in the box given at the start of each section of questions. This is a guide to some of the things you could cover or include in your essay. Words from this text box are also a reminder of the kind of technical terms that would be appropriate for you to use.

pure points™

2002 cookbook

Over 300 recipes low in points

Becky Johnson

SIMON & SCHUSTER
A VIACOM COMPANY

First published in Great Britain by Simon & Schuster UK Ltd, 2002.
A Viacom Company.

Copyright © 2002, Weight Watchers International, Inc.

Simon & Schuster UK Ltd
Africa House
64–78 Kingsway
London
WC2B 6AH

Editorial Project Manager: Anna Hitchin
Photography and styling: Steve Baxter
Food preparation: Joy Skipper
Design: Jane Humphrey
Typesetting: Stylize Digital Artwork
Printed and bound in Singapore

Weight Watchers Product Marketing Manager: Elizabeth Egan
Weight Watchers Product Manager: Corrina Griffin
Weight Watchers Publications Assistant: Celia Whiston

A CIP catalogue for this book is available from the British Library

ISBN 0 85941 998 3

Pictured on the front cover: Sun-drenched Turkey Towers (page 105)
Pictured on the back cover: Little Chocolate Pots (page 151)

Recipe notes:
Egg size is medium, unless otherwise stated.
Fruit and vegetables are medium-sized unless otherwise stated.

Ⓥ denotes a vegetarian recipe and assumes that free-range eggs and
vegetarian cheeses are used.

Virtually fat-free fromage frais and low-fat crème fraîche may contain traces of
gelatine so they are not always vegetarian: please check the labels.

contents

introduction
and healthy tips

Welcome to Weight Watchers® and to *Pure Points*™, the diet with a difference. *Pure Points*™, as you will see, is not about forbidden or special 'diet' foods but about combining a common sense approach to what you eat with a healthy lifestyle where you enjoy looking after yourself.

This book has been written by a home cook for other home cooks as well as for those who may not have cooked often before and now want to start eating more freshly cooked food. Cooking your own meals puts you in control of what goes into your body in a way that leaves you feeling good about yourself. Many people find cooking, with its endless possibilities, very therapeutic and it doesn't have to take up too much of your time. It uses your imagination and concentration and channels your energies creatively to a satisfying end. Cooking for yourself also opens up a range of tastes and textures that living on microwave and pre-prepared suppers denies you.

You will find this book contains many traditional favourite recipes ranging from Chicken Caesar Salad (page 43) to Roast Turkey (page 103), Toad-in-the-Hole (page 143) and Steak, Mushroom and Guinness Pie (page 131). There are recipes galore for those with a sweet-tooth: Jam Roly Poly (page 170) or Chocolate Brownies (page 185), Lemon Meringue Pie (page 172) or Blueberry Muffins (page 193). All the recipes are straightforward to follow with simple cooking techniques combined with readily available ingredients.

Many of the recipes will be familiar, everyday meals which are delicious, nutritious, easy-to-prepare and satisfying. I have been fortunate enough to have travelled extensively

for success...

and experienced food from other cultures. I've also had access to a wide range of exciting ingredients, and I have included some of these more exotic ingredients into a few of the recipes. But every ingredient needed to make the recipes in this book is readily available in the supermarkets. I hope that everyone will find recipes to suit their tastes and from continued use of the book gain the confidence to try new flavours and combinations.

The various food scares that have appeared in the media over the last few years have made us all much more conscious of what we eat, and where our food comes from. At the same time, we are being bombarded by advertising for convenience and junk foods. Unfortunately, good quality food is usually accompanied by a hefty price tag. In order to budget successfully and stay healthy, it is important to reassess our eating habits.

Processed foods are often not of the highest quality; they frequently contain far more fat and sugar and cost more than fresh fruit, vegetables and wholefoods. Meat and dairy products can also be expensive, whilst not always being advantageous to our health so it is a good idea to only include them in part of your diet.

The Weight Watchers philosophy of a healthy mind and body considers exercise as a very important component to boosting weight loss. The health benefits derived from taking regular exercise are undisputed, not to mention the benefits to your figure! But including exercise in your everyday life requires planning. It won't just happen, you have to find the time for it, do it regularly and value yourself sufficiently to put your needs first for a little time every day. Weight Watchers is here to support you in your decision to become fit and healthy. After all, it is very important that you feel well, enthusiastic and beautiful and that you have the energy to cope with life.

Soups are invaluable to Weight Watchers Members; they warm you up, cool you down and fill you up – and all this for so few points. In this chapter there are 5 soups with no points at all and all the others contain 5 or less points per serving!

scrumptious soups

French onion soup

| 4 Points per serving | Points per recipe **16½** |

 if using vegetarian cheese ● Serves 4 ● Preparation time 15 minutes ● Cooking time 1 hour 10 minutes ● Calories per serving 250 ● Freezing not recommended

A very filling soup served with cheesy croûtons that could be a main course for a family supper.

low-fat cooking spray
600 g (1lb 5 oz) onions, sliced very finely
1 teaspoon caster sugar
1 tablespoon plain flour
1.5 litres (2¾ pints) hot stock
150 ml (5 fl oz) dry white wine
8 × 2.5 cm (1-inch) slices of French stick
50 g (1¾ oz) mature Cheddar cheese, grated
salt and freshly ground black pepper

1 Heat a large non-stick saucepan and spray with the low-fat cooking spray then add the onions and stir-fry for 5 minutes, until softened.

2 Season and cover with a piece of baking paper tucked down the sides of the pan, then cover with a lid and leave the onions to sweat on the lowest possible heat for 15 minutes.

3 Remove the lid and paper, stir well to get any caramelised onions off the bottom of the pan and sprinkle with the sugar. Add the flour and cook for a few minutes, stirring.

4 Add the stock and wine, bring to the boil then simmer with the lid off for 45 minutes, removing any froth that comes to the surface.

5 Just before serving, check the seasoning then pour the soup into four warmed bowls. Preheat the grill to high. Float two bread slices on top of each bowl of soup, sprinkle with the grated cheese. Grill for 1–2 minutes until the cheese is bubbling and golden, then serve.

Tomato and rice soup

1½ Points per serving	Points per recipe **6**

 Serves 4 ● Preparation time 5 minutes ● Cooking time 40 minutes ● Calories per serving 155 ● Freezing not recommended *This soup is very quick to make and satisfying to eat. It is low enough in points to serve with a medium crusty roll (2 points) as a filling lunch.*

> low-fat cooking spray
> 1 large onion, chopped
> 2 garlic cloves, crushed
> 2 × 400 g cans chopped tomatoes
> 1 tablespoon clear honey
> 1.2 litres (2 pints) stock
> leaves from a small bunch of parsley, thyme,
>   rosemary or basil, chopped
> 100 g (3½ oz) basmati rice
> salt and freshly ground black pepper

1 Heat a large saucepan and spray with the low-fat cooking spray then fry the onion and garlic for 5 minutes until softened, adding a little water if necessary to stop them sticking. Add the tomatoes, seasoning and honey, bring to the boil and simmer for 10 minutes.
2 Add the stock, herbs and rice and simmer a further 25 minutes, then serve.

Top tip Use 2 teaspoons of garlic purée as a convenient alternative to fresh garlic.
Variation Use 3 teaspoons caster sugar instead of the honey.

Spicy pumpkin soup

0 Points per serving	Points per recipe **0**

 if using vegetable stock ● Serves 4 ● Preparation time 15 minutes ● Cooking time 30–35 minutes ● Calories per serving 45 ● Freezing not recommended. *A hot and spicy autumnal soup with no points!! Perfect as a 'stop-gap' when hunger persists.*

> low-fat cooking spray
> 1 large onion, chopped
> 2 garlic cloves, chopped finely
> 750 g (1 lb 10 oz) pumpkin, peeled, de-seeded and
>   chopped roughly
> 1.2 litres (2 pints) vegetable or chicken stock
> salt and freshly ground black pepper
> 1 teaspoon dried chilli flakes, plus a few extra to garnish
> snipped fresh chives, to garnish (optional)

1 Heat a large saucepan and spray with the low-fat cooking spray. Gently fry the onion and garlic for a few minutes until softened, adding a little water to the pan if necessary to stop them sticking.
2 Add all the other ingredients except the chives and bring to the boil. Simmer for 20–25 minutes until the pumpkin is soft, then purée in a food processor or push through a sieve with the back of a wooden spoon.
3 Just before serving check the seasoning and scatter with the remaining chilli flakes and snipped chives, if using.

Top tip For a finishing touch, scatter 25 g (1 oz) toasted pumpkin seeds over each bowl in step 3 before serving. This adds a ½ point per serving.
Variations Butternut or other squash is equally delicious in this recipe.

Believe in yourself – you can do it –
    and believing this will help to make it come true

Curried parsnip soup

| **2** Points per serving | Points per recipe **9** |

 if using vegetable stock ● Serves 4 ● Preparation time 10 minutes ● Cooking time 40 minutes ● Calories per serving 135 ● Freezing not recommended *A classic recipe for a thick parsnip soup with a mild curry flavour and optional chilli depending on whether you like your food spicy.*

low-fat cooking spray
1 large onion, chopped
1 garlic clove, chopped
½ fresh chilli, de-seeded and chopped finely (optional)
900 g (2 lbs) parsnips, peeled and chopped roughly
2 teaspoons ground coriander seeds
1 teaspoon turmeric
1 teaspoon ground ginger
1.2 litres (2 pints) vegetable or chicken stock
salt and freshly ground black pepper

1 Heat a large saucepan and spray with the low-fat cooking spray then stir-fry the onion, garlic and chilli for about 5 minutes until soft, adding a little water if necessary to stop them sticking.
2 Add the parsnips and spices, cover and heat very gently for 20 minutes, stirring occasionally, until the parsnips are really soft.
3 Add the stock and seasoning. Bring to the boil and simmer for a further 10 minutes, then blend in a liquidiser. Check the seasoning and serve.

Variation Use water if you have no stock. The points per serving would be the same.

Sweetcorn chowder

| **2½** Points per serving | Points per recipe **9½** |

 if using vegetable stock and vegetarian crème fraîche ● Serves 4 ● Preparation time 10 minutes ● Cooking time 35 minutes ● Calories per serving 220 ● Freezing not recommended *This is a luxurious, spicy, creamy-textured soup which is perfect for supper on a chilly, autumnal evening.*

2 medium red peppers, halved and de-seeded
low-fat cooking spray
1 large onion, chopped
2 garlic cloves, chopped
325 g can sweetcorn, drained
1 tablespoon ground cumin
1 tablespoon ground coriander
1 small red chilli, de-seeded and chopped finely (optional)
600 ml (1 pint) skimmed milk
600 ml (1 pint) stock
3 medium potatoes, peeled and diced
1 tablespoon half-fat crème fraîche
salt and freshly ground black pepper
a small bunch chives or parsley, chopped, to garnish

1 Preheat the grill and place the peppers skin-side-up on the grill pan. Grill for 5–10 minutes or until blackened and blistered. Transfer to a plastic bag, wrap and leave to cool.
2 Meanwhile, heat a large saucepan and spray with the low-fat cooking spray. Stir-fry the onion and garlic for 5 minutes until softened, adding a little water if necessary to stop them sticking. Add half the sweetcorn, the spices, chilli, milk and stock, bring to the boil then simmer for 5 minutes.
3 Blend in a liquidiser until smooth and return to the saucepan. Remove the skin from the peppers and dice the flesh finely
4 Add to the blended soup with the remaining half of the sweetcorn, potatoes and seasoning then simmer for a further 20 minutes, until the potatoes are tender. Serve the chowder with a swirl of crème fraîche and sprinkled with chopped chives or parsley.

Variation For a more substantial supper dish try adding 300 g (10½ oz) skinless, boneless smoked haddock fillet, cut into bite-size chunks at step 4. The points per serving will be 3.

Menu plan

Just for Two

~

Hot Red Pepper Soup, page 11
(pictured here)
1 serving ... 0 points

~

Steak au Poivre, page 133
1 serving ... 8 points

~

Cream Hearts, page 162
1 serving ... 2 points

Total points per meal 10 points

Hot red pepper soup

| **0** Points per serving | Points per recipe **0** |

(v) if not using Worcestershire sauce ● Serves 4 ●
Preparation time 15 minutes ● Cooking time 25 minutes
● Calories per serving 120 ● Freezing not recommended
This is a very intense and fiery, deep red soup –
perhaps serve with a little low-fat plain yogurt to
cool things down; a teaspoon adds no extra points.

6 medium red peppers, halved and de-seeded
low-fat cooking spray
2 medium onions, chopped finely
1 tablespoon fennel seeds (optional)
3 garlic cloves, crushed
1 red chilli, de-seeded and chopped finely (optional)
400 g can chopped tomatoes
1.2 litres (2 pints) vegetable stock
2 tablespoons Worcestershire sauce
2 teaspoons Tabasco sauce
salt and freshly ground black pepper
a small bunch of fresh basil, chopped roughly, to garnish

1 Preheat the grill and put the peppers on the grill pan
skin-side-up. Grill for 5–10 minutes, until blistered and
blackened and then place in a plastic bag, wrap and
leave to cool.
2 Meanwhile heat a large non-stick saucepan and spray
with the low-fat cooking spray then stir-fry the onions
with the fennel seeds for 5 minutes, adding some water
if necessary to stop the mixture sticking.
3 When the peppers are cool enough to handle, peel
them and add the flesh to the onions along with all the
other ingredients except the basil. Bring to the boil and
simmer for 10 minutes.
4 Liquidise the soup in batches and then return to the
pan. Reheat gently, check the seasoning then serve
garnished with the basil.

Variation For a less spicy version, just omit the chilli and
Tabasco sauce.

Spinach and potato soup

| **1½** Points per serving | Points per recipe **7** |

(v) if using vegetarian crème fraîche ● Serves 4 ●
Preparation time 10 minutes ● Cooking time 35 minutes
● Calories per serving 130 ● Freezing not recommended
A fresh, green soup which is full of nutrients
and ideal for a winter lunch when you need an
energy boost.

low-fat cooking spray
450 g (1 lb) potatoes, peeled and sliced
1 large onion, sliced
1.2 litres (2 pints) vegetable stock
freshly grated nutmeg
200 g (7 oz) fresh spinach, rinsed, drained and chopped
3 tablespoons half-fat crème fraîche
salt and freshly ground black pepper

1 Heat a large non-stick saucepan and spray with the
low-fat cooking spray then stir-fry the potatoes and
onion for 1 minute. Reduce the heat to the lowest
setting. Add seasoning and cover the pan with a piece
of baking paper tucked down into the sides and then
put on the lid. Leave to 'sweat' for 20 minutes until
soft, stirring occasionally to make sure the mixture
does not stick.
2 Add the stock, a pinch or two of nutmeg and the
spinach and stir together. Bring to the boil then blend in
a liquidiser. Check the seasoning then pour into serving
bowls. Top each serving with a little crème fraîche
swirled on the top.

Variation Use watercress instead of spinach but check
the seasoning carefully before adding extra pepper as
watercress itself can be quite hot.

Mushroom and thyme soup

| ½ Point per serving | Points per recipe **1½** |

 Serves 4 ● Preparation time 10 minutes ● Cooking time 1 hour ● Calories per serving 55 ● Freezing not recommended *A light, full-flavoured mushroom soup which is made extra-special with a touch of brandy.*

low-fat cooking spray
1 large onion, sliced
2 garlic cloves, crushed
400 g (14 oz) mushrooms e.g. field, chestnut or
    brown cap, sliced
3 tablespoons brandy
a small bunch thyme, chopped, plus a few extra sprigs,
    to garnish
600 ml (1 pint) vegetable stock
25 g (1 oz) dried porcini soaked in 600 ml (1 pint) boiling
    water for at least 10 minutes, chopped, soaking liquid
    reserved (optional)
salt and freshly ground black pepper

1 Heat a large non-stick saucepan and spray with the low-fat cooking spray then stir-fry the onion and garlic for about 5 minutes until soft, adding a little water if necessary to prevent the mixture from sticking.
2 Add the mushrooms and stir-fry over a high heat for another 5 minutes then add the brandy and cook, stirring, for 1 minute until the alcohol has evaporated.
3 Reduce the heat, add the thyme, stock, dried mushrooms, if using, seasoning and reserved soaking liquid. Bring to the boil and simmer for 45 minutes.
4 Serve garnished with fresh thyme sprigs.

Top tips Use young thyme, sometimes known as soft thyme, as you can then use the stems as well. In older thyme you have to cut away the woody stems.

Porcini are dried Italian wild mushrooms. They have a very distinctive, earthy taste and need only be used in small quantities. They are now readily available in supermarkets and delicatessans.
Variation Use parsley instead of thyme. If you omit the brandy, the points per serving will be 0!

Minestrone verde

| **3** Points per serving | Points per recipe **12½** |

Serves 4 ● Preparation time 5 minutes ● Cooking time 20 minutes ● Calories per serving 90 ● Freezing recommended *This soup is packed with nutrients and energy and makes a refreshing lunch.*

low-fat cooking spray
2 medium rashers rindless, unsmoked, lean back
    bacon, chopped
2 medium onions, chopped
2 garlic cloves, crushed
2 medium celery sticks, sliced thinly
1.2 litres (2 pints) vegetable stock
50 g (1¾ oz) small pasta shapes
300 g can borlotti beans, rinsed and drained
200 g (7 oz) green beans, fresh or frozen, diced
200 g (7 oz) courgettes, diced finely
100 g (3½ oz) frozen petit pois
salt and freshly ground black pepper
fresh basil, chopped roughly, to garnish (optional)
4 teaspoons pesto sauce

1 Heat a large non-stick saucepan and spray with low-fat cooking spray. Fry the bacon over a high heat until crispy. Reduce the heat, add the onions, garlic, celery and cook for 5 minutes until softened, stirring gently.
2 Pour the stock over and bring to the boil. Add the pasta and cook for 10 minutes then add the vegetables and cook for a further 5 minutes. Finally, check the seasoning, scatter the basil over, if using, and serve with a swirl of pesto sauce on top of each serving.

Variations Any canned cooked beans can be used ranging from haricot blanc to black-eyed beans.

You could use a 500 g bag of frozen mixed vegetables instead of all the fresh vegetables for a quick alternative. The points per serving would be 4.

Satisfying vegetable soup

| **0** Points per serving | Points per recipe **0** |

🆅 Serves 4 ● Preparation time 25 minutes ● Cooking time 40 minutes ● Calories per serving 100 ● Freezing not recommended *As this soup is point-free you can eat it as often as you like to fill you up. It is full of flavour and nutritious so tuck in!*

low-fat cooking spray
1 medium onion
2 medium leeks, chopped finely
2 garlic cloves, crushed
400 g can chopped tomatoes
2 medium carrots, diced finely
175 g (6 oz) white cabbage, shredded thinly
1.2 litres (2 pints) hot vegetable stock
350 g (12 oz) courgettes, diced finely
100 g (3½ oz) green beans, quartered lengthwise
1 tablespoon balsamic vinegar
salt and freshly ground black pepper
chopped flat leafed parsley, to garnish

1 Heat a large saucepan and spray with low-fat cooking spray then sauté the onion and leeks for 5 minutes until softened, adding a little water if necessary to stop the mixture sticking. Add the remaining vegetables except the courgettes, beans and parsley. Mix everything together, pour the hot stock over and simmer for 30 minutes.
2 Add the courgettes, beans, seasoning and vinegar and cook a further 5 minutes. Serve sprinkled with chopped parsley.

Carrot and coriander soup

| **0** Points per serving | Points per recipe **0** |

🆅 if using vegetable stock ● Serves 4 ● Preparation time 10 minutes ● Cooking time 20 minutes ● Calories per serving 230 ● Freezing not recommended *This classic is transformed by the fresh coriander.*

low-fat cooking spray
1 large onion, sliced thinly
1 kg (2 lb 4 oz) carrots, peeled and chopped roughly
1.2 litres (2 pints) chicken or vegetable stock
1 packet of fresh coriander, including roots, rinsed, drained and chopped
salt and freshly ground black pepper

1 Heat a large non-stick pan and spray with the low-fat cooking spray then stir-fry the onion for 5 minutes until softened, adding a little water if necessary to stop the mixture sticking.
2 Add the carrots, stock, the chopped roots and stalks of the coriander and seasoning. Bring to the boil and then simmer for 15 minutes until the carrots are tender. Add the rest of the chopped coriander.
3 Liquidise the soup in batches and return to the pan to warm through. Check the seasoning and serve garnished with the reserved coriander.

Variation This soup is also very good made with parsnips instead of carrots. The points per serving will be 2½.

Mussel and tomato chowder

Serves 4 ● Preparation time 10 minutes ● Cooking time 25 minutes ● Calories per serving 225 ● Freezing not recommended *Delicious and satisfying.*

low-fat cooking spray
4 medium lean back bacon rashers, diced finely
1 large onion, chopped finely
1 celery stalk, chopped finely
1 carrot, chopped finely
2 medium potatoes, peeled and cut into 1 cm (½-inch) dice
2 × 400 g cans chopped tomatoes
1.2 litres (2 pints) fish stock
2 × 205 g jars of mussels, rinsed and drained
a small bunch thyme, chopped
salt and freshly ground black pepper

1 Heat a large non-stick saucepan and spray with the low-fat cooking spray then stir-fry the bacon for 2 minutes until it begins to brown. Add the onion, celery and carrot, season, cover, and cook for about 10 minutes until soft, adding a little of the stock if necessary to prevent the mixture sticking.
2 Add the potatoes, tomatoes and stock and bring to the boil. Simmer for 10 minutes then add the mussels and thyme and simmer gently for 2 minutes more. Check that the potatoes are tender, season to taste then serve.

Variation Fresh mussels (1 kg/2 lb 4 oz) could be used instead of the canned ones but wash very well first. Add with the stock and discard any that have not opened after simmering. (see Top tip for Moules Provençales on page 124)

Hot and sour prawn soup

Serves 4 ● Preparation and cooking time 15 minutes ● Calories per serving 135 ● Freezing not recommended *This soup is very quick to make and has a bite that will refresh the most jaded tastebuds.*

450 g (l b) frozen cooked peeled prawns
juice and zest of 3 limes
4 teaspoons fish sauce
1 small green chilli, de-seeded and chopped finely
grated zest of 2 lemons
1 litre (1¾ pints) chicken stock
a small bunch of coriander, chopped, plus extra to garnish
2 medium shallots, chopped finely
150 g (5½ oz) shiitake or button mushrooms, cleaned and sliced
a medium bunch of spring onions, chopped finely

1 Place the prawns in a bowl with half the lime juice, 2 teaspoons fish sauce, the chilli and a teaspoon of grated lemon zest. Set aside.
2 Meanwhile, heat the chicken stock in a large saucepan with all the other ingredients including the remaining lemon juice, fish sauce and lemon zest. Bring to the boil then add the prawns and their marinade. Cook for 2 minutes then serve garnished with coriander leaves.

Top tip Fish sauce is now available in the Oriental/curry sauce section of many supermarkets. It is a sauce made from dried fish which is used in many Thai and many other south east Asian dishes. A good alternative is Worcestershire sauce.

Always prepare lots of extra vegetables,

which can then be used for making point-free soup

Classic fish soup with rouille

Serves 6 ● Preparation time 30 minutes ● Cooking time 45 minutes ● Calories per serving 250 ● Freezing not recommended Enjoy this soup with a pungent garlic mayonnaise – a popular way to serve fish soup all over the Mediterranean. This soup is quite an elaborate affair and ideal for a special occasion.

1 kg (2 lb 4 oz) mixed fresh white fish, filleted heads and
    trimmings reserved (ask the fishmonger to include them)
250 g (9 oz) frozen uncooked prawns with their shells on,
    defrosted and peeled, shells reserved
a small bunch of parsley
1 bay leaf
2 medium onions, halved
low-fat cooking spray
3 stalks celery, sliced
3 garlic cloves, crushed
400 g can chopped tomatoes
1 strip of orange zest
1 tablespoon fennel seeds
1 tablespoon tomato purée
a pinch of saffron, soaked in 2 tablespoons
    boiling water (optional)
1 kg (2 lb 4 oz) mussels in their shells, washed and prepared
salt and freshly ground black pepper
For the rouille
2 garlic cloves, crushed
2 tablespoons low-fat mayonnaise
juice of ½ lemon

1 Put all the fish trimmings and prawn shells in a large saucepan. Cover with 1.5 litres (2¾ pints) water and add the parsley stalks, bay leaf, one onion half and seasoning. Bring to the boil then simmer for 15 minutes. Strain and set aside, throwing away the shells and trimmings.

2 Meanwhile, slice the remaining 3 onion halves. Heat a large non-stick saucepan, spray with low-fat cooking spray and stir-fry the onion and celery for 5 minutes until softened. Add a little water if necessary to stop the mixture from sticking.

3 Stir in the garlic, tomatoes, orange zest, fennel seeds, tomato purée and saffron with its soaking liquid, if using. Season to taste then add the strained fish stock and bring to the boil, cover and simmer for 20 minutes.

4 Meanwhile, make the rouille by stirring together the garlic and mayonnaise with the lemon juice and seasoning.

5 Add the fish to the pan and cook for 1 minute, then add the mussels and the prawns. Boil for another 4–5 minutes until the fish is opaque, the prawns pink and all the mussels are open, discarding any that remain closed.

6 Chop the remaining parsley and scatter over the soup. Serve with a swirl of rouille on top of each serving.

Top tip Step 1 results in a delicious fish stock which can be used as a base for many fish soups and dishes but you can always use bought fish stock instead.

Moroccan chick-pea soup

2½ Points per serving	Points per recipe 9½

 if using vegetable stock ● Serves 4 ● Preparation time 15–20 minutes ● Cooking time 2½ hours ● Calories per serving 185 ● Freezing not recommended This soup is understandably popular all over the Mediterranean where you'll find many versions of it, each one with a slight variation.

> 200 g (7 oz) chick-peas, soaked overnight, rinsed and drained
> low-fat cooking spray
> 1 celery stalk with leaves, chopped finely
> 4 garlic cloves, crushed
> a small sprig of rosemary, chopped finely
> 6 fresh sage leaves, chopped finely, plus extra to garnish
> 400 g can chopped tomatoes
> 850 ml (1½ pints) stock
> juice of ½ lemon
> salt and freshly ground black pepper

1 Cook the chick-peas in a large non-stick saucepan with plenty of water for 1½ hours until soft.

2 Drain the chick-peas reserving the cooking liquid. Take 2 cupfuls of chick-peas and liquidise with 2 cupfuls of the cooking liquid. Set aside.

3 Heat a saucepan and spray with the low-fat cooking spray and stir-fry the celery, garlic and herbs for 1 minute, then add the tomatoes and cook for a few minutes more.

4 Add the remaining cooked chick-peas and at least 300 ml (½ pint) of the cooking liquid, made up with water if there is not enough, season, cover and simmer for 20 minutes.

5 Stir in the liquidised chick-peas and stock, cover again and simmer a further 15 minutes, stirring occasionally.

6 Add the lemon juice, check the seasoning and serve garnished with sage leaves.

Variation Substitute 2 × 400 g cans chick-peas, rinsed and drained and use 1 litre (1-¾ pints) stock instead of the cooking liquid and stock in the recipe. The points per serving will be the same.

Thai chicken noodle soup

3½ Points per serving	Points per recipe 14½

Serves 4 ● Preparation and cooking time 15 minutes ● Calories per serving 205 ● Freezing not recommended A familiar, soothing soup which is given a new twist with the addition of Thai curry spices and coconut milk.

> low-fat cooking spray
> 1 tablespoon Thai curry paste
> 2 medium onions, sliced thinly
> 2 garlic cloves, crushed
> 1 dried Kaffir lime leaf, or the zest of 1 lime
> 2 litres (3½ pints) chicken stock
> 150 g (5½ oz) cooked chicken, shredded
> 125 g (4½ oz) rice noodles, broken into short lengths
> 100 ml (3½ fl oz) reduced-fat coconut milk
> a small bunch of fresh coriander or basil, chopped
> salt and freshly ground black pepper
> 4 lime wedges, to serve (optional)

1 Heat a large saucepan and spray with low-fat cooking spray then add the curry paste and fry for 30 seconds. Add the onions, garlic and lime leaf and a ladleful of chicken stock and cook for 5 minutes until the onions are softened and the stock has evaporated.

2 Add the chicken and the remaining stock and bring to the boil. Add the noodles and simmer for 2–4 minutes. Remove from the heat, discard the lime leaf then stir in the coconut milk, coriander or basil and season to taste. Serve with the lime wedges, if using

Top tip Dried kaffir lime leaves are now available in the spice sections of supermarkets.

Spiced cauliflower soup

 0 Points per serving   Points per recipe **0**

Ⓥ if using vegetable stock • Serves 4 • Preparation time 10 minutes • Cooking time 30 minutes • Calories per serving 55 • Freezing recommended *A creamy-coloured, warm and sweet, spiced cauliflower soup, especially good on dark wintery evenings.*

1 large cauliflower, broken into florets
2 tablespoons ground cumin
low-fat cooking spray
1 large onion, chopped
2 garlic cloves, crushed
1.2 litres (2 pints) vegetable or chicken stock
salt and freshly ground black pepper
a small bunch of chives, chopped, to garnish (optional)

1 Preheat the oven to Gas Mark 7/220°C/425°F. Place the cauliflower florets in a roasting tin sprinkle with cumin and seasoning and toss to coat. Spray with the low-fat cooking spray then bake for 20 minutes until tender and slightly charred.
2 Meanwhile, heat a large non-stick saucepan and spray with the low-fat cooking spray then stir-fry the onion and garlic for 5 minutes until softened, adding a little water if necessary to stop the mixture sticking.
3 Add the cauliflower to the onion and then pour the stock over. Bring to the boil and simmer for 5 minutes then liquidise in batches and return to the pan to warm through. Check the seasoning then serve garnished with chopped chives.

Chunky potato soup

 3 Points per serving   Points per recipe **11½**

Ⓥ if using vegetable stock • Serves 4 • Preparation time 5 minutes • Cooking time 20 minutes • Calories per serving 225 • Freezing not recommended *This soup is quick and easy to make using only a few inexpensive ingredients yet is delicious and nourishing. You could use any herb, fresh or dried but I've chosen thyme as it goes especially well with potato.*

low-fat cooking spray
2 large onions, chopped finely
2 garlic cloves, crushed
1 kg (2 lb 4 oz) potatoes, peeled and diced into
   2.5 cm (1-inch) cubes
a small bunch of thyme, chopped, plus extra to garnish
700 ml (1¼ pints) vegetable or chicken stock
150 ml (5 fl oz) skimmed milk
salt and freshly ground black pepper

1 Heat a large non-stick saucepan and spray with the low-fat cooking spray then stir-fry the onions and garlic for 5 minutes until softened, adding a little water if necessary to stop the mixture sticking.
2 Add the potatoes, seasoning, chopped thyme, and stock, bring to the boil then simmer for 15 minutes until the potatoes are tender.
3 Remove from the heat and allow to cool a little then add the milk and stir through. Check the seasoning and serve garnished with sprigs of thyme.

Top tip To make your own vegetable stock, reserve all the trimmings and peelings from various vegetables and then boil in a pan with 1.2 litres (2 pints) water, a handful of peppercorns, ½ onion, a bay leaf and a bunch of herbs of your choice. Cook for 1 hour, then remove from the heat and strain. It will keep in a jug in the refrigerator for a few days, or can be frozen for later use.

spicy beef noodle soup

5 Points per serving   Points per recipe **20½**

Serves 4 ● Preparation time 10 minutes + 30 minutes marinating ● Cooking time 35 minutes ● Calories per serving 355 ● Freezing not recommended *This recipe is inspired by the clear, fragrant noodle soups found all over South East Asia, and makes a very filling lunch.*

225 g (8 oz) lean beef steak, sliced thinly
250 g (9 oz) noodles
200 g (7 oz) sugar snap peas, mange-tout peas or green beans, sliced lengthways
a small bunch of fresh coriander, chopped (optional)

For the soup
2 litres (3½ pints) chicken stock
1 garlic clove
1 stick lemongrass, chopped roughly (or 1 tablespoon dried lemongrass, chopped)
1 small red chilli
1 star anise
1 cm (½-inch) piece of fresh root ginger, crushed

For the marinade
1 tablespoon soy sauce
1 garlic clove, crushed
1 cm (½-inch) fresh ginger root, peeled and grated
1 tablespoon honey
1 small red chilli, de-seeded and chopped finely

1 Blend all the marinade ingredients together in a shallow bowl and mix in the beef strips. Leave to marinate for 30 minutes. Place all the soup ingredients in a saucepan, bring to the boil then simmer for 30 minutes.

2 Meanwhile, cook the noodles as instructed on the packet, drain and place in the bottom of four serving bowls.

3 Heat a frying-pan until very hot then brown the marinated beef on all sides. Remove from the pan and set aside.

4 Strain the soup into a clean pan and bring back to a simmer. Add the peas or beans and simmer for 2 minutes.

5 Pile the beef on top of the noodles in the bowls, pour the soup over and serve sprinkled with chopped coriander, if using.

Variation For a fishy version, this soup could be made with raw king or tiger prawns instead of the beef. The points per serving will be 4.

Pasta, pork and bean soup

4½ Points per serving	Points per recipe 18½

Serves 4 ● Preparation time 10 minutes ● Cooking time 20 minutes ● Calories per serving 335 ● Freezing recommended *A thick and tasty soup in which the earthy flavour of the rosemary perfectly complements the beans and the sweetness of the pork.*

  low-fat cooking spray
  250 g (9 oz) lean pork, diced finely
  1 medium red onion, chopped finely
  2 garlic cloves, crushed
  2 sprigs of fresh rosemary, chopped
  2 litres (3½ pints) chicken stock
  400 g can red kidney beans, rinsed and drained
  200 g (7 oz) small pasta shapes
  salt and freshly ground black pepper

1 Heat a large non-stick saucepan and spray with the low-fat cooking spray then fry the pork over a high heat for 5 minutes until golden brown. Add the onion, garlic, rosemary and seasoning and stir-fry for another 5 minutes until the onion has softened.
2 Add the stock and bring to the boil. Add the beans and pasta and simmer for 10 minutes. Check the seasoning then serve.

Variation For an equally satisfying vegetarian version of this soup, omit the pork and use a vegetable stock. The points per serving will be 3½.

Pea, mint and ham soup

2½ Points per serving	Points per recipe 11

Serves 4 ● Preparation time 5 minutes ● Cooking time 15 minutes ● Calories per serving 170 ● Freezing not recommended *A modern version of the classic Pea and Ham Soup, this is a vibrant pea-green soup garnished with crispy curls of grilled Parma ham.*

  low-fat cooking spray
  2 medium onions, chopped finely
  2 garlic cloves, crushed
  1 soft-leaved (i.e. round) lettuce, sliced
  a small bunch of fresh mint
  500 g (1 lb 2 oz) fresh or frozen peas, thawed
  a pinch of sugar
  850 ml (1½ pints) chicken or vegetable stock
  4 thin slices Parma ham
  4 tablespoons half-fat crème fraîche
  salt and freshly ground black pepper
  fresh chives, to garnish (optional)

1 Heat a large non-stick saucepan and spray with the low-fat cooking spray then fry the onions and garlic for 4 minutes until softened. Add all the other ingredients except the crème fraîche and Parma ham. Bring to the boil and simmer for 2 minutes.
2 Meanwhile grill the Parma ham on a foil-covered grill pan until crispy.
3 Liquidise the soup in the food processor, then check the seasoning and stir in the crème fraîche. Serve with the grilled Parma ham, sprinkled with fresh chives, if using.

Variation If you don't have Parma ham, grill two medium rashers of lean back bacon until very crispy then chop and sprinkle over. The points per serving will be 3.

Cold cucumber and mint soup

1½ Points per serving	Points per recipe 5½

Ⓥ if using vegetable stock ● Serves 4 ● Preparation time 10 minutes + minimum 4 hours chilling ● Cooking time 15 minutes ● Calories per serving 100 ● Freezing not recommended *A luxurious, delicate soup to refresh you on a hot summer day.*

>   low-fat cooking spray
>   2 small shallots, chopped finely
>   1 large cucumber, peeled, chopped finely
>   1 tablespoon plain flour
>   850 ml (1½ pints) stock
>   500 ml (18 fl oz) low-fat plain yogurt
>   a small bunch of mint, chopped
>   salt and freshly ground black pepper

1 Heat a large non-stick saucepan and spray with the low-fat cooking spray. Stir-fry the shallots and cucumber for 5 minutes until softened, adding a little water if necessary to stop the mixture sticking.
2 Blend in the flour and then gradually add the stock, stirring constantly, season then cover and simmer for 10 minutes.
3 Purée in a liquidiser, cool a little and then stir in the yogurt and mint. Chill until cold before serving.

Top tip Do not put the yogurt in while the soup is very hot or it may split.
Variation For a Scandinavian flavour, make with dill rather than mint.

Italian bean and rosemary soup

2 Points per serving	Points per recipe 10½

Ⓥ if using vegetable stock ● Serves 6 ● Preparation time 15 minutes + overnight soaking ● Cooking time 1¼ hours ● Calories per serving 140 ● Freezing recommended *A little planning is needed for this recipe if you are using dried beans as they need to be soaked overnight. For a quick canned bean alternative see Top tip below.*

>   low-fat cooking spray
>   2 garlic cloves, crushed
>   1 large onion, diced
>   1 large carrot, diced
>   250 g (9 oz) cannellini beans, soaked overnight then rinsed and drained
>   8 sprigs of rosemary, chopped finely
>   2 litres (3½ pints) chicken or vegetable stock
>   salt and freshly ground black pepper

1 Heat a large saucepan and spray with the low-fat cooking spray then gently fry the garlic, onion and carrot for about 4 minutes until beginning to soften, adding a little water if necessary to stop the mixture sticking.
2 Add the beans, rosemary and stock and bring to the boil. Boil for 10 minutes, skimming the top occasionally, then keep at a low simmer for 40–50 minutes or until the beans are tender.
3 Carefully remove half the soup to a liquidiser and whizz until smooth. Return to the pan and stir it in. Check the seasoning and then serve.

Top tip Use canned beans for a much faster recipe. Add 3 × 300 g cans of cannellini beans, rinsed and drained, to the sautéed vegetables. Reduce the stock to 1.2 litres (2 pints) and reduce the cooking time to 10 minutes. The points per serving will be 1½.
Variations Use any small beans such as flageolet, pinto, black-eyed, haricot blanc.

Vichyssoise

1½	Points per serving	Points per recipe	7½

 if using vegetable stock ● Serves 6 ● Preparation time 10 minutes ● Cooking time 1 hour ● Calories per serving 135 ● Freezing recommended *A classic cold summer soup, although you could serve it hot and then call it Leek and Potato Soup.*

    low-fat cooking spray
    6 large leeks, halved, sliced thinly then rinsed and drained
    1 large onion, chopped coarsely
    6 medium potatoes, peeled and chopped coarsely
    1 litre (1¾ pints) stock
    300 ml (½ pint) skimmed milk
    a pinch of freshly grated nutmeg
    a pinch of cayenne
    salt and freshly ground black pepper
    1 bunch of chives, snipped, to garnish

1 Heat a large, heavy-based saucepan and spray with the low-fat cooking spray. Add the leeks, and onion, cover with a piece of baking paper tucked down the sides of the pan then cover with a lid and sweat over the lowest possible heat for 25 minutes. Occasionally remove the lid and paper and give the mixture a stir. They should soften without browning.

2 Add the potatoes and stock to the pan and gently simmer for 30 minutes until the potatoes are well cooked.

3 Purée the soup in a liquidiser then return to the pan and add the milk, nutmeg, cayenne and season to taste. Leave to cool and then chill until cold. Serve garnished with snipped chives.

Top tip Put peeled potatoes in a bowl and cover with water until ready to use to prevent them discolouring. Drain before use.

Middle Eastern lentil soup

2½	Points per serving	Points per recipe	15

 if using vegetable stock ● Serves 6 ● Preparation time 5 minutes ● Cooking time 40 minutes ● Calories per serving 195 ● Freezing not recommended *This soup makes an ideal meal on a blustery day, which in this country means there are lots of opportunities to enjoy it! Hearty, quick and easy to prepare, it is full of warming flavours.*

    low-fat cooking spray
    1 large onion, chopped
    1 stalk celery, with leaves, chopped
    1 large carrot, chopped
    350 g (12 oz) dried lentils
    2 litres (3½ pints) stock
    juice of ½ lemon
    1 teaspoon ground cumin
    salt and freshly ground black pepper

1 Heat a large non-stick saucepan and spray with the low-fat cooking spray. Stir-fry the onion, celery and carrot for 5 minutes until softened, adding a little water if necessary to stop the mixture sticking.

2 Add the lentils and stock and bring to the boil. Skim off any froth that rises to the surface, cover and simmer gently for about 30 minutes until the lentils are soft – the cooking time depends on the type and age of the lentils used.

3 When the lentils are cooked, season the soup and add the lemon juice and cumin. Liquidise, return to the pan and reheat gently then serve.

Top tip Any type of lentil is good in this recipe but I like the orange ones for their colour and fluffy texture.

Eat a variety of foods –

   this will help to ensure you get all the vitamins and minerals you need

In this chapter you will find ideas for light meals, snacks and starters. Most of the recipes are for 1 or 2 people and can easily be doubled or tripled if you are feeding a family or friends. The recipes are simple and most are under 5 points per serving.

light lunches

Club sandwich

Serves 1 ● Preparation and cooking time 20 minutes ●
Calories per serving 385 ● Freezing not recommended
*A huge, double-decker of a sandwich made with
succulent turkey breast and crispy turkey
rashers with low-fat mayonnaise and whole-
grain mustard.*

2 medium slices low-fat turkey rashers
3 medium slices bread, toasted
1 tablespoon low-fat mayonnaise
approximately 4 lettuce leaves, shredded
1 teaspoon whole-grain mustard
2 or 3 slices of ripe tomato
40 g (1½ oz) wafer-thin roast turkey slices
salt and freshly ground black pepper

1 Grill the turkey rashers for a minute on each side
until crispy.
2 Spread one slice of toast with mayonnaise, top with
the lettuce. Spread another with mustard and top with
the tomato slices then season them both.
3 Place the wafer-thin turkey slices on the lettuce
and the turkey rashers on the tomato then build the
sandwich: lettuce and turkey slices on the bottom,
followed by toast, then the turkey rashers and tomato,
followed by the last slice of toast.
4 Spear the sandwich with four cocktail sticks 1 cm
(½-inch) in from each corner then cut into quarters
diagonally. Each triangle should be held together by a
cocktail stick.

Variations Use a tablespoon of reduced-fat
hummous instead of the turkey rasher
(for the same points) or a medium
sliced hard-boiled egg instead of the
turkey slices. The points per serving
with egg will be 6½.

Tuna mayo pitta

5 Points per serving	Points per recipe **10½**

Serves 2 ● Preparation time 5 minutes ● Calories per serving 470 ● Freezing not recommended *A delicious, classic lunch-time sandwich – tuna with mayonnaise, sweetcorn and salad in pitta bread.*

> 150 g can tuna in brine, drained
> 2 tablespoons low-fat mayonnaise
> 2 spring onions, sliced
> 200 g can sweetcorn, drained
> 2 tablespoons capers or chopped gherkins (optional)
> 2 medium pitta breads
> a large handful of salad leaves
> salt and freshly ground black pepper

1 Mix all the ingredients except the pitta breads and salad leaves together and season.

2 Meanwhile, warm the pitta breads under the grill or in the toaster, then split them and divide the salad between them, add the tuna mixture and serve.

Variations You could use ½ small red or Spanish onion instead of the spring onions.

This recipe is also good on toast; the points per serving will be 3½.

Chunky tomato and avocado salsa

3 Points per serving	Points per recipe **6**

Ⓥ Serves 2 ● Preparation time 5 minutes ● Calories per serving 155 ● Freezing ● not recommended *This is a variation on traditional guacamole which packs a punch and really wakes up those taste buds! Serve with the flatbreads on page 187 or a medium pitta bread (2½ points).*

> 2 medium, ripe tomatoes, quartered, de-seeded and diced finely
> 1 medium avocado, peeled, stoned and diced
> juice of 2 limes
> 1 small red onion, diced finely
> 1 small red chilli, de-seeded and diced finely
> a small bunch of fresh coriander, chopped finely

1 Place all the ingredients in a bowl. Toss together to mix thoroughly and serve.

Top tip Remember to wash your hands well after handling chillies or wear gloves.

Variations You can use lemon instead of the lime juice or you could try a crushed garlic clove instead of the chilli.

Roasted pepper pockets

4 Points per serving	Points per recipe 4

 if using vegetarian cheese ● Serves 1 ● Preparation and cooking time 15 minutes ● Calories per serving 265 ● Freezing not recommended *Pitta bread is delicious with creamy soft cheese and sweet roasted peppers.*

> 1 medium red pepper, halved and de-seeded
> 1 medium pitta bread
> 1 tablespoon Quark soft cheese
> a large handful of watercress, rinsed, drained and chopped roughly
> 2 teaspoons balsamic vinegar
> 1 teaspoon olive oil
> salt and freshly ground black pepper

1 Preheat the grill to high and put the pepper skin-side-up on the grill pan. Grill for 5 minutes until the skin is blackened and blistered.

2 Remove the pepper, wrap it in a plastic bag and set aside. Put the pitta in the toaster or heat under the grill for 30 seconds to 1 minute until warmed through, then slice in half across the middle and push the sides to open them up. Spread the inside of each half with some Quark. Season lightly.

3 When the pepper is cool enough to handle, peel away the skin and cut the flesh into strips. Put in a bowl together with the watercress and sprinkle over the balsamic vinegar and olive oil then season.

4 Toss together well then fill both halves of the pitta with the roasted pepper mixture. Serve immediately.

Top tip Recycle clean old shopping bags by using them to wrap the hot peppers in.

Simple summer salad

2 Points per serving	Points per recipe 4

 Serves 2 ● Preparation time 5 minutes ● Calories per serving 185 ● Freezing not recommended *This recipe would taste even better made with fresh artichoke hearts, but these can be difficult to find and prepare so I have used canned ones. Serve with a medium warm roll adding 2 points per serving.*

> 400 g can artichoke hearts in brine, rinsed, drained and quartered
> 1 small garlic clove, finely chopped
> 2 medium tomatoes, skinned (see Top tip on page 67), de-seeded and diced finely
> juice of 1 lemon
> 2 teaspoons balsamic vinegar
> 2 teaspoons hazelnut oil
> 25 g (1 oz) hazelnuts, chopped and toasted

1 Place all the ingredients except the hazelnuts in a bowl and toss together. Spoon on to serving plates and sprinkle the toasted nuts over.

Variation Substitute walnut oil and chopped walnuts for the hazelnuts and hazelnut oil. The points will remain the same.

Aim for five portions of fruit and vegetables every day

Sweetcorn fritters

3 Points per serving   Points per recipe **6½**

V if using free-range eggs ● Serves 2 ● Preparation time 15 minutes + 30 minutes standing ● Cooking time 15 minutes ● Calories per serving 260 ● Freezing not recommended *These little sweetcorn fritters can be prepared in minutes for a snack that's loved by all the family. Serve with a crunchy point-free salad.*

3 tablespoons seasoned flour
1 medium egg, separated
3 tablespoons skimmed milk
200 g can sweetcorn, drained
low-fat cooking spray

For the salsa
250 g (9 oz) cherry tomatoes, quartered
½ medium cucumber, diced
1 small red chilli, de-seeded and chopped finely
juice of 1 lemon
a small bunch of coriander, chopped
salt and freshly ground black pepper

1 Place the seasoned flour in a bowl. Add the yolk to the flour and place the egg white in a separate bowl.
2 Stir the milk into the flour and mix thoroughly, add the sweetcorn and, if you have time, set aside for 30 minutes.
3 Meanwhile, make the salsa by mixing all the ingredients together in a bowl.
4 Beat the egg white until stiff and gently fold into the batter mix with a large metal spoon. Heat a large frying-pan and spray with the low-fat cooking spray, then drop in 5–6 tablespoonfuls of the batter at a time.
5 Cook for 3–4 minutes, then flip over with a palette knife and cook the other sides for 3–4 minutes until golden brown. Put on a plate and keep warm while you cook the remaining batter in the same way (making about 10 fritters altogether), then serve with the salsa.

Top tip Always make sure the bowl and whisks for the egg whites are scrupulously clean and dry or else they will not fluff up.
Variation Look for cans of sweetcorn with red pepper for a change.

Broad bean 'guacamole'

1½ Points per serving	Points per recipe 3½

V Serves 2 ● Preparation time 5 minutes ● Calories per serving 75 ● Freezing not recommended This dish is derived from an ancient Arab recipe for 'bessara', a purée of broad beans and herbs. Serve with lightly toasted medium pitta bread, adding 2½ points per serving.

    300 g can broad beans, rinsed and drained
    a small bunch of fresh coriander or parsley,
        chopped roughly
    1 small green chilli, de-seeded and chopped
        finely (optional)
    1 garlic clove, crushed
    ½ teaspoon ground cumin
    1 small red onion, chopped roughly
    juice of 1 lemon
    salt and freshly ground black pepper

1 Place all the ingredients in a food processor and purée to a rough paste. Alternatively crush the ingredients together with a pestle and mortar to achieve the same result. Check the seasoning and serve.

Variation Stir two thin slices of chopped ham into the purée. The points per serving will be 2.

Sticky corn-on-the-cob

1 Point per serving	Points per recipe 5

V Serves 4 ● Preparation time 5 minutes ● Cooking time 15 minutes ● Calories per serving 145 ● Freezing not recommended These corn-on-the-cobs are ideal for the BBQ and make a great starter.

    4 medium corn cobs, stripped of husks
    1 tablespoon clear honey
    2 tablespoons soy sauce
    juice and zest of 1 lime

1 Cook the corn cobs in plenty of boiling salted water for 10–15 minutes until tender. Meanwhile, in a small pan gently heat together the honey and soy, then squeeze in the lime juice and zest and stir to mix.
2 Preheat the grill. Brush the cooked corn cobs with the honey mixture and grill for 1 minute, turn the corn cobs over, brush again and grill another minute and so on until slightly caramelised, then serve.

Variation Substitute lemon for the lime.

Tuna melt

4 Points per serving   Points per recipe **8½**

Serves 2 ● Preparation and cooking time 10 minutes ●
Calories per serving 335 ● Freezing not recommended
A substantial lunch for two, these tuna melts go
down a treat with the kids, but you may wish to
omit the capers.

> 4 medium slices bread
> 150 g can tuna in brine, drained
> 1 tablespoon Worcestershire sauce
> 125 g tub low-fat soft cheese
> 2 tablespoons capers
> salt and freshly ground black pepper

1 Preheat the grill and toast the bread on one side.
Meanwhile, in a bowl mix together all the other
ingredients.
2 Divide the mixture into four and spread over the
untoasted side of each slice of bread. Return to the
grill for a couple of minutes until the topping turns
golden brown.

Variations Substitute Quark for the low-fat soft cheese;
the points per serving will be 3½.

Instead of capers, or in addition to the capers, you
can add two sun-dried tomatoes, soaked in boiling water
for 5 minutes and then finely chopped. The points per
serving will be 4½.

Garlic bread with pickled vegetable salsa

5 Points per serving   Points per recipe **10½**

Ⓥ if using vegetarian cheese ● Serves 2 ● Preparation
time 10 minutes ● Cooking time 15 minutes ● Calories
per serving 260 ● Freezing not recommended This
recipe is for hot garlic bread served with a pickled
vegetable salsa; we used to make a variation of this
to serve with baked fish at Villandry Dining Room
in London.

> ½ granary baguette, halved lengthways and then halved
>   crossways to make four pieces
> 100 g (3½ oz) low-fat garlic roulé cheese
> **For the pickled vegetable salsa**
> 2 medium carrots, chopped finely
> 1 small red onion, chopped finely
> 2 tablespoons capers, rinsed and drained
> 2 medium pickled gherkins, chopped finely
> 1 garlic clove, crushed
> 2 tablespoons white wine vinegar
> 2 teaspoons caster sugar
> 1 teaspoon olive oil
> salt and freshly ground black pepper

1 Preheat the oven to Gas Mark 4/180°C/350°F. Spread
the bread with the roulé then reassemble as a loaf and
wrap in foil. Bake for 15 minutes until hot.
2 Meanwhile, make the pickle by mixing together all the
ingredients in a bowl. Serve the garlic bread with the
pickle to the side.

Top tip The pickled vegetable salsa is good made a few
hours in advance and left to marinate.
Variations You could substitute 25 g (1 oz) sun-dried
tomatoes, soaked and chopped, for the capers or
gherkins (5½ points per serving) and/or add some
stoned olives but remember to add a ½ point for every
ten used.

Garlic is good for you! It cleanses your bloodstream, boosts your immunity,
helps digestion and lowers cholesterol levels; it is also a natural antibiotic

Summer vegetable omelette

 if using free-range eggs ● Serves 2 ● Preparation time 5 minutes ● Cooking time 20 minutes ● Calories per serving 240 ● Freezing not recommended *A large, Spanish-style, thick omelette that you can slice into wedges and eat hot or cold. Delicious served with a crispy no-point cucumber and mint salad.*

100 g (3½ oz) asparagus spears, sliced into rounds
200 g (7 oz) green beans, sliced into small rounds
4 medium eggs, beaten
a small bunch coriander or thyme, chopped
a small bunch of parsley, chopped
a medium bunch of spring onions, chopped
4 tablespoons skimmed milk
low-fat cooking spray
salt and freshly ground black pepper

1 Blanch the asparagus and green beans in boiling, salted water for 2 minutes, drain, then place in a large bowl.
2 Add the eggs, herbs, spring onions, milk and seasoning to the bowl and mix together. Heat a large heavy-based non-stick frying-pan and spray with the low-fat cooking spray.
3 Pour the egg mixture in and reduce the heat to very low. Cook, without stirring, for 15–20 minutes or until the eggs have set and the base is golden brown (check by gently lifting the edge with a palette knife).
4 Heat the grill to high and place the pan under it to quickly grill the top of the omelette, 2 minutes should be long enough, then slide it out of the pan on to a plate and serve cut in slices.

Top tip The secret to cooking the omelette through without burning it is to have a very low heat and leave it for a long time. Use your smallest ring with the heat on the lowest setting and be patient.
Variations Any quick-cooking summer vegetables would be great in this recipe. Try mange-tout peas, sugar snap peas or tiny baby carrots with their tops merely trimmed.

Mushroom pâté

 if using vegetarian cheese ● Serves 4 ● Preparation time 5 minutes ● Calories per serving 215 ● Freezing not recommended *A fresh-tasting, smooth pâté that goes well with toast, garnished with slices of tomato.*

200 g (7 oz) mushrooms, wiped
100 g (3½ oz) low-fat soft cheese
3 spring onions, chopped
a small bunch of fresh parsley, chopped
juice of 1 small lemon
salt and freshly ground black pepper
To serve
8 medium slices toast
2 medium tomatoes, sliced

1 Place all the ingredients except the toast and tomatoes in a food processor and blend until smooth.
2 Spoon into four ramekin dishes and either serve immediately with the toast and tomatoes or cover and chill until needed.

Top tip This pâté is best eaten immediately as it discolours when left.
Variation Add a dash or two of Tabasco to spice up the pâté.

Turkey frittata

Serves 4 ● Preparation and cooking time 25 minutes ●
Calories per serving 405 ● Freezing not recommended
This is a flexible recipe that is a great way to use
up any left-over food you have – turkey, chicken,
ham or vegetables like Brussels sprouts or cabbage.
Served here with a home-made cranberry sauce.

> low-fat cooking spray
> 1 large onion, chopped
> 1 medium green pepper, de-seeded and diced
> approximately 400 g (14 oz) left-over cooked turkey,
>   brown and white meat, diced
> 10 stoned black olives, chopped
> 4 medium eggs, beaten
> 4 tablespoons skimmed milk
> 1 tablespoon grated Parmesan cheese
> salt and freshly ground black pepper
> **For the cranberry sauce**
> 250 g (9 oz) cranberries
> 100 g (3½ oz) caster sugar
> zest and juice of 1 small orange

1 First make the cranberry sauce as it needs to cool
and thicken before use. Put the cranberries, sugar,
orange juice and zest in a pan, add 50 ml (2 fl oz) water
and bring to the boil. Boil vigorously for 2 minutes then
simmer for 5 minutes. Set aside until ready to use.
2 Heat a large non-stick frying-pan and spray with the
low-fat cooking spray. Stir-fry the onion and green
pepper together for 5 minutes until softened. Add the
diced turkey, season and stir-fry for a further 5 minutes.
3 Stir in the olives and then pour the eggs and milk
over. Leave to cook for 5 minutes on the lowest
possible heat.
4 Preheat the grill. Sprinkle the Parmesan over the
frittata then grill until golden brown and set. Loosen the
edges with a palette knife, place a plate over the pan
and invert giving the pan a little shake so that the frittata
falls on to the plate. Serve with the cranberry sauce.

Variation If you prefer, you can also use ready-made
cranberry sauce; points per serving with 2 tablespoons
will be 3½.

Spinach and poached egg muffins

V if using free-range eggs and vegetarian crème fraîche
● Serves 2 ● Preparation and cooking time 15 minutes ●
Calories per serving 220 ● Freezing not recommended
This delicious recipe is very healthy and makes a
satisfying light lunch.

> 2 tablespoons vinegar
> 1 medium muffin, halved
> 200 g (7 oz) frozen cooked spinach (or 400 g/14 oz fresh,
>   washed spinach, large stems removed)
> freshly grated nutmeg
> 2 tablespoons half-fat crème fraîche
> 2 medium eggs
> salt and freshly ground black pepper
> a few chives, to garnish (optional)

1 Put a pan of water with the vinegar on to boil.
2 Toast the muffin halves in a toaster or under the grill
until lightly browned. Meanwhile, warm the spinach
through in a small saucepan, season and add a pinch or
two of fresh nutmeg with the crème fraîche.
3 When the water is at a boil, break the eggs into a
small cup and then carefully slide out of the cup and into
the water. Simmer for 3 minutes. When the white is
firm but the yolk still soft, remove with a slotted spoon.
4 Spoon the spinach on top of the toasted muffin halves
then put the eggs on top of the spinach. Garnish with
chives, if using, and serve.

Top tip The water for poaching the eggs should be boiling
rapidly when you add the egg to prevent them from
sticking to the bottom. After adding, turn the heat down
so that the water is gently simmering. Skim any scum
that rises to the top with a spoon.
Variation Use 2 medium slices of toast instead of
muffins. The points per serving will be 3.

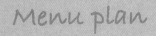

Menu plan

The Big Brunch

~

100 ml (3½ fl oz) freshly squeezed orange juice
1 serving . . . ½ point

~

Spinach and Poached Egg Muffins, page 30
(pictured here)
1 serving . . . 4½ points

~

Fluffy Breakfast Pancakes, page 175
1 serving . . . 5 points

Total points per meal 10 points

Tandoori chicken

4½ Points per serving   Points per recipe **18½**

Serves 4 ● Preparation time 10 minutes + ½ hour–12 hours marinating ● Cooking time 20 minutes ● Calories per serving 220 ● Freezing not recommended This popular Indian starter is quick and easy to make. Serve on a bed of shredded lettuce with the raita.

4 boneless, skinless chicken breasts, weighing 175 g (6 oz) each
4 teaspoons tandoori paste

To garnish (optional)
2 medium red onions, sliced finely
a small bunch of coriander
lemon wedges

For the raita
4 tablespoons low-fat plain yogurt
½ medium cucumber, grated
½ small garlic clove, crushed
salt and freshly ground black pepper

1 Make three slashes in each of the chicken breasts, then rub with the tandoori paste and leave to marinate for up to 12 hours, but for at least 30 minutes.

2 Meanwhile, make the raita by mixing together all the ingredients in a serving bowl, cover and refrigerate until required.

3 Heat the grill to high and grill the chicken breasts for 8–10 minutes on each side, allowing them to char slightly.

4 Place the cooked chicken on a board, slice into pieces then transfer to serving plates and, if using, serve scattered with the onion and coriander, and accompanied by the lemon wedges. Serve with the raita to the side.

Variations Add some chopped spring onions and chopped fresh mint to the raita for a fresh-tasting variation, or, if you prefer it hot, add a little coriander and some fresh, chopped chilles.

Scandinavian trout sandwich

6 Points per serving	Points per recipe **12**

Serves 2 ● Preparation time 10 minutes + 4–24 hours cooling time for the onion pickle ● Cooking time 5 minutes ● Calories per serving 435 ● Freezing not recommended
This appetisingly pretty, open sandwich makes a refreshing lunch or light supper.

For the onion pickle
2 medium red onions, sliced finely, skins reserved
2 tablespoons white wine vinegar
1 tablespoon mustard seeds
2 teaspoons caster sugar
salt and freshly ground black pepper
For the trout
1 bay leaf
6 peppercorns
onion skins, reserved from making the onion pickle
2 trout fillets, weighing approximately 150 g (5½ oz) each
2 small pickled gherkins, sliced
2 tablespoons low-fat mayonnaise
2 teaspoons whole-grain mustard
a small bunch of fresh dill, chopped, plus a few whole sprigs to garnish
2 slices (50 g/1¾ oz each) German rye bread

1 To make the onion pickle place the sliced onion in an old jam jar with the vinegar, mustard seeds, sugar and seasoning. Pour in boiling water to cover and leave to cool before putting the lid on. Leave until completely cool, preferably overnight.
2 Bring a frying-pan of water with the bay leaf, peppercorns and onion skin to the boil then add the trout fillets and poach for 3–5 minutes until just cooked through. Drain and set aside to cool.
3 Flake the trout fillets into a bowl and then add all the other ingredients except the bread and fold gently together. To serve spoon on to pieces of rye bread and top with some of the onion pickle and the reserved dill sprigs.

Top tip The onion pickle really needs to be made a day in advance but it will keep for up to 5 days in the refrigerator.
Variation For a vegetarian alternative, use 100 g (3½ oz) half-fat Cheddar cheese slices instead of the trout. The points per serving will be 5½.

Thai fish cakes with sweet chilli dip

2 Points per serving	Points per recipe **8**

Serves 4 ● Preparation time 15 minutes + 10 minutes–1 hour chilling ● Cooking time 20 minutes ● Calories per serving 115 ● Freezing not recommended Eat these with your fingers, dipping the fish cakes first into a bowl of sweet and hot sauce accompanied by a point-free salad.

300 g (10½ oz) cod fillets
100 g (3½ oz) frozen cooked prawns, thawed
1 tablespoon red or green curry paste
2 dried Kaffir lime leaves soaked in 2 tablespoons boiling water for 10 minutes, then chopped finely or zest of a small lemon
a small bunch of fresh coriander
100 g (3½ oz) green beans, thawed if frozen, chopped into fine rings
1 teaspoon salt
low-fat cooking spray
For the sweet chilli dip sauce
1 small cucumber, quartered lengthways
1 small chilli, de-seeded and sliced finely
2 teaspoons caster sugar
3 tablespoons rice vinegar (or white wine vinegar)
coriander leaves, to garnish

1 Put the fish, curry paste, lime leaves and coriander in a food processor and chop to a fine paste then add the beans and salt and pulse to mix in. Transfer to a clean bowl, cover with clingfilm and refrigerate for up to an hour, though 10 minutes will do.
2 Meanwhile, to make the dip finely slice the cucumber and put in a bowl with the chilli. Combine the sugar, vinegar and 1 tablespoon water in a saucepan and heat until the sugar has dissolved. Leave to cool, then pour over the cucumber. Spoon into little dipping bowls and garnish with the coriander leaves.
3 Lightly oil your hands to stop the fishcake mixture sticking to them then take a tablespoon of the fish mixture at a time and shape into a small patty. Heat a frying-pan and spray with the low-fat cooking spray then fry the fishcakes, a few at a time, for 5 minutes on each side until golden and cooked through. Lift out with a fish slice, keep warm while you cook those remaining. Serve with the dipping sauce.

Satay chicken

7 Points per serving   Points per recipe **28**

Serves 4 ● Preparation and cooking time 35 minutes +
½ hour–12 hours marinating ● Freezing not recommended
Satays are always popular served as finger-food
at parties, but also make a tasty lunch with a
crisp no-point salad.

4 skinless chicken breasts weighing 175 g (6 oz) each,
    sliced into long strips
For the marinade
2 garlic cloves, crushed
2.5 cm (1-inch) piece of fresh root ginger, peeled and grated
2 tablespoons soy sauce
1 tablespoon honey
lime wedges to serve, optional
For the satay sauce
6 teaspoons crunchy peanut butter
1 small red chilli, de-seeded and chopped finely
juice of 2 medium limes
4 tablespoons stock
2 tablespoons reduced-fat coconut milk
salt and freshly ground black pepper

1 Mix together the marinade ingredients in a bowl and
add the chicken pieces. Mix together well to ensure that
the chicken is well coated and leave to marinate in the
fridge for at least 30 minutes but preferably overnight.
2 Make the sauce by blending all the ingredients
together either in a food processor or just mix together in
a bowl. Cover with clingfilm and keep in the refrigerator
until ready to use.
3 Soak twenty wooden skewers in cold water for 10
minutes. Preheat the grill to high. Thread the chicken on
to the skewers and grill for 3 minutes on each side until
golden brown and cooked through. Keep brushing with
the left-over marinade.
4 Serve the chicken satay skewers with the peanut sauce
as a dip and lime wedges to squeeze over, if using.

Top tip Pre-soak the satay sticks so that they do not
burn under the grill or on the BBQ.
Variations You could use 700 g (1 lb 9 oz) extra-lean pork,
turkey, lamb or braising steak instead of the chicken. The
points per serving for extra-lean pork will be 5, 6½ for
turkey, 8 for extra-lean lamb and 7½ for beef.

Smoked turkey and spinach wrap

3 Points per serving   Points per recipe **6½**

Serves 2 ● Preparation and cooking time 20 minutes ●
Calories per serving 280 ● Freezing not recommended
This tortilla sandwich makes a great lunch-on-
the-run or it can be sliced into rounds and served
as canapé or starter.

100 g (3½ oz) baby spinach, rinsed and drained
100 g (3½ oz) smoked turkey breast slices
2 medium flour tortillas
For the red onion relish
low-fat cooking spray
2 large onions, sliced thinly
125 ml (4 fl oz) red wine
a few thyme sprigs, chopped
salt and freshly ground black pepper

1 First make the relish. Heat a frying-pan and spray with
the low-fat cooking spray. Stir-fry the onions for 5 minutes
until softened, add the wine, thyme and seasoning and
bring to the boil. Simmer gently for 10 minutes until most
of the wine has evaporated and the onions are soft.
2 To assemble the wraps, place half the spinach and
turkey on each tortilla, spoon 2 teaspoons of the relish
over and roll up to serve.

Top tip Smoked turkey breast slices are available in the
pre-packed cooked meat section of supermarkets.
Variations Alternatives to smoked turkey are roast
turkey or cooked chicken slices. The points per serving
remain the same with both options.

Smoked haddock on potato pancakes

3½ Points per serving   Points per recipe **7½**

Serves 2 ● Preparation time 15 minutes ● Cooking time 30 minutes ● Calories per serving 300 ● Freezing not recommended *These fluffy pancakes make a satisfying brunch or supper dish.*

> 2 smoked haddock fillets, weighing approximately 125 g (4½ oz) each
> fresh parsley, to garnish (optional)
> salt and freshly ground black pepper
> **For the pancakes**
> 250 g (9 oz) peeled potatoes, cut into chunks
> 25 g (1 oz) plain flour
> 50 ml (2 fl oz) hot skimmed milk
> freshly grated nutmeg
> 2 medium egg whites
> low-fat cooking spray
> **For the mustard sauce**
> 2 tablespoons half-fat crème fraîche
> 1 teaspoon Dijon mustard

1 Boil the potatoes in plenty of salted water for about 15 minutes until tender. Then mash in a large bowl and leave to cool slightly.

2 Mix in the flour, milk, seasoning and a little grated nutmeg. Whisk the egg whites until stiff then fold gently into the mixture.

3 Heat a large frying-pan and spray with the low-fat cooking spray. Drop tablespoonfuls of the mixture into the pan and cook for 2–3 minutes, flip over with a palette knife and cook for another 2–3 minutes until golden. Set aside on a plate and keep warm while you cook the remaining mixture (making 10 pancakes altogether).

4 Meanwhile, preheat the grill. Lay the haddock fillets on a piece of foil on the grill pan. Season and spray with the low-fat cooking spray. Grill for 2–3 minutes each on side until cooked through.

5 Make the sauce by stirring together all the ingredients.

6 Divide the potato pancakes between two serving plates. Add a smoked haddock fillet and some of the sauce to each plate. Serve garnished with parsley sprigs, if using.

Sardines on pesto toasts

3½ Points per serving   Points per recipe **7½**

Serves 2 ● Preparation and cooking time 10 minutes ● Calories per serving 215 ● Freezing not recommended *A very quick and simple recipe using canned sardines in tomato sauce. Combined with a good wholemeal bread, pesto and fresh basil you have an aromatic, light lunch.*

> 120 g can sardines in tomato sauce
> 2 medium slices wholemeal bread
> 1 tablespoon pesto sauce
> 1 medium tomato, sliced
> a bunch of fresh basil, chopped roughly
> freshly ground black pepper

1 Preheat the grill to hot. Place the sardines on a piece of foil on the grill pan and grill for 3–4 minutes. Meanwhile, toast the bread, spread with the pesto sauce and arrange the tomato slices on top. Spoon the warmed sardines and tomato on top of the bread and scatter with basil and lots of freshly ground black pepper.

Salads can be very satisfying dishes; gone are the days of a few lettuce leaves on a plate! And for Weight Watchers Members, they have the extra advantage of filling you up without spending too many points.

salad days

Sweet potato and sausage salad

4½	Points per serving	Points per recipe	**18½**

Serves 4 ● Preparation time 15 minutes + cooling ●
Cooking time 30 minutes ● Calories per serving 190 ●
Freezing not recommended *Roast sweet potatoes*
are delicious eaten hot or cold and make a great
salad ingredient, especially when combined with
sausage and a creamy mustard dressing.

> 4 medium sweet potatoes
> low-fat cooking spray
> 8 thin low-fat sausages
> 4 shallots, chopped finely
> a small bunch of fresh chives, chopped
> salt and freshly ground black pepper
> **For the dressing**
> 4 tablespoons half-fat crème fraîche
> 1 tablespoon Dijon mustard

1 Preheat the oven to Gas Mark 7/220°C/425°F. Scrub
the potatoes and cut into wedges. Place in a roasting tin,
spray with the low-fat cooking spray, season then roast
for 30 minutes until tender.

2 Meanwhile, preheat the grill and grill the sausages for
about 5 minutes on each side until browned and cooked
through. Leave to cool, then chop into pieces.

3 Heat a non-stick frying-pan and spray with low-fat
cooking spray, then stir-fry the shallots for 5 minutes
until softened, adding a little water if necessary to stop
them from sticking.

4 Place the sweet potato, sausages, shallots and chives
in a bowl. In a separate bowl stir together the dressing
ingredients then spoon over the potatoes. Toss the salad
together and serve.

Variation Use ordinary potatoes instead of sweet potatoes.
The points per serving will be 4.

vitality rice salad

3½ Points per serving   Points per recipe **15**

Ⓥ Serves 4 ● Preparation time 10 minutes ● Cooking time 30 minutes ● Calories per serving 310 ● Freezing not recommended *A good pick-me-up meal, full of complex carbohydrates for slow-releasing energy and essential vitamins and minerals. The recipe is for four servings but if you only need one or two servings you can keep it in the refrigerator and have it again the next day. Great for the lunchbox.*

125 g (4½ oz) brown basmati rice, rinsed and drained
125 g (4½ oz) wild rice, rinsed and drained
2 medium courgettes, grated
a small bunch of fresh parsley, chopped
a small bunch of fresh coriander, chopped
4 spring onions, chopped
1 medium red pepper, de-seeded and chopped finely
100 g (3½ oz) mange-tout peas or snow peas,
    blanched for 30 seconds in boiling water
1 tablespoon sunflower seeds, toasted
1 tablespoon sesame seeds, toasted
For the dressing
2 tablespoons soy sauce
juice of 1 lemon
1 teaspoon Tabasco sauce

1 Put the rice in a large saucepan and cover with boiling water. Bring back to the boil and simmer for 25–30 minutes until the grains are tender then drain and leave to cool.
2 Put all the salad ingredients, including the cooked rice, in a bowl. Put all the dressing ingredients together in an empty jam jar with a screw-top lid, shake well then pour over the salad. Toss everything together and serve or keep, covered, in the refrigerator for up to 2 days.

Variation For a quicker alternative, use white basmati rice which cooks in 10 minutes.

Greek salad

4½ Points per serving   Points per recipe **17½**

Ⓥ if using vegetarian cheese ● Serves 4 ● Preparation time 10 minutes ● Calories per serving 175 ● Freezing not recommended *An everyday salad in Greece that is made with crumbly, salty feta cheese. This one has the addition of a tangy yogurt and lemon dressing.*

200 g (7oz) feta cheese, diced
1 small cucumber, quartered and sliced into small wedges
8 medium ripe tomatoes, cut into wedges
2 small red onions, cut into wedges
12 stoned black olives
1 teaspoon dried oregano
juice and zest of 1 lemon
a small bunch of fresh basil, chopped
For the yogurt dressing
1 garlic clove, chopped finely
2 tablespoons low-fat plain yogurt
salt and freshly ground black pepper

1 Put all the salad ingredients except the basil in a large bowl.
2 Put all the dressing ingredients plus 2 tablespoons of water in a clean jam jar with a screw-top lid, shake vigorously then pour over the salad and gently toss together. Serve scattered with the basil.

Cycle your way to fitness:

   it's fun, cheap and environmentally friendly

Roasted tomato bruschetta

2½ Points per serving	Points per recipe 10

Ⓥ Serves 4 ● Preparation time 2 minutes ● Cooking time 15 minutes ● Calories per serving 160 ● Freezing not recommended *A simple recipe for garlic toast, that could be served with a variety of toppings. Serve with a crisp, green salad for lunch, Italian-style.*

200 g (7 oz) ripe cherry tomatoes, quartered
low-fat cooking spray
2 tablespoons balsamic vinegar
4 × 1 cm (½-inch thick) slices of bread, but not pre-sliced and preferably a rustic loaf
1 garlic clove, peeled
4 teaspoons extra-virgin olive oil
a small bunch of fresh basil, chopped
salt and freshly ground pepper

1 Preheat the oven to Gas Mark 7/220°C/425°F. Place the tomatoes in a baking tray sprayed with the low-fat cooking spray, season and sprinkle with the vinegar. Spray again with the low-fat cooking spray and roast for 10–15 minutes until softened and charring at the edges.
2 Toast the bread under a pre-heated grill until golden on both sides. Cut the garlic clove in half and rub the cut side over the toast.
3 Drizzle the olive oil over, pile with the roasted tomatoes, scatter the basil over, season to taste and serve while still hot.

Variations This can also be served plain: without the tomato and/or with some crispy, blanched mange-tout peas with a tiny amount of whole-grain mustard or with dry-fried mushrooms with black pepper and a squeeze of lemon.

Carrot and apple salad

2 Points per serving	Points per recipe 4

Ⓥ Serves 2 ● Preparation time 10 minutes ● Calories per serving 165 ● Freezing not recommended *This salad is dressed in honey and sesame seeds and served in attractive rounds on individual serving plates. It makes an ideal starter or light lunch.*

2 large carrots, peeled and grated coarsely
2 medium dessert apples, grated coarsely
1 tablespoon clear honey
1 tablespoon white wine vinegar
1 teaspoon sesame oil
2 teaspoons sesame seeds, toasted
salt and freshly ground black pepper
a handful of salad leaves and/or chervil, to garnish

1 Place all the ingredients in a bowl and mix together with your hand. Place a 10 cm (4-inch) pastry cutter or something similar on a small serving plate.
2 Stuff half the salad ingredients down into the ring on one plate then carefully lift the ring upwards to leave the salad in a short, round pile on the plate. Repeat with the remaining mixture on another plate then arrange the salad leaves and /or chervil on top of both and serve.

Top tip If possible, use lollo rosso or lollo blonda lettuce so you can achieve more height on the plate by first making a nest with the lollo and then piling the carrot and apple salad on top.

Lentil and red pepper salad

| 4½ | Points per serving | Points per recipe | 18 |

v if using vegetarian cheese ● Serves 4 ● Preparation time 10 minutes + cooling ● Cooking time 20–30 minutes ● Calories per serving 230 ● Freezing not recommended

This is a modern lentil salad – no longer a mushy, dry, brown affair but made using the tasty little green Puy lentils, which have the added advantage of cooking in only about 20 minutes. They are tossed with fresh herbs, roasted peppers and yogurt for an aromatic, flavoursome feast.

150 g (5½ oz) green lentils
4 medium red peppers, halved and de-seeded
150 ml (5 fl oz) low-fat plain yogurt
100 g (3½ oz) soft goats' cheese, chopped
1 garlic clove, crushed
a small bunch of fresh mint, chopped finely
a small bunch of fresh parsley, chopped finely
juice of ½ lemon (optional)
salt and freshly ground black pepper

1 Cook the lentils in plenty of boiling water for 20–30 minutes until tender, then drain and set aside to cool. Meanwhile, preheat the grill and place the red peppers beneath it skin-side-up. Grill for about 10 minutes until blistered and charred then take out, wrap in a plastic bag and leave to cool.

2 Place all the other salad ingredients in a bowl, add the warm lentils and toss together. When the peppers are cool enough to handle, peel them and dice the flesh. Add to the salad and toss together again.

3 Check the flavour as the lentils may have absorbed a lot of the flavour and need additional seasoning and/or lemon juice. Serve warm or cool.

Top tip This is one salad that definitely improves with age. Cover and keep in the refrigerator for up to 3 days to allow the flavours to mature.

Oriental noodle salad

| 4 | Points per serving | Points per recipe | 15½ |

Serves 4 ● Preparation and cooking time 15 minutes ● Calories per serving 255 ● Freezing not recommended

Try this with Malaysian BBQ Pork (see page 142).

200 g (7 oz) dried glass noodles, soaked according to
    packet instructions and drained
low-fat cooking spray
2 garlic cloves, sliced thinly
2.5 cm (1-inch) piece of fresh root ginger,
    peeled and grated
200 g (7 oz) lean pork tenderloin, sliced thinly
2 tablespoons light soy sauce
1 medium tomato, quartered, de-seeded and sliced
2 celery stalks, sliced thinly
4 spring onions, sliced thinly
1 medium green pepper, de-seeded and chopped finely
juice of 2 limes
2 small green chillies, de-seeded and chopped finely
2 teaspoons caster sugar
salt and freshly ground black pepper
a small bunch of fresh coriander, chopped

1 Put the noodles in a large bowl and snip them with scissors into shorter lengths.

2 Heat a non-stick frying-pan and spray with the low-fat cooking spray, then stir-fry the garlic and ginger for a few seconds. Add the pork and stir-fry for 5 minutes until the pork is cooked through and golden.

3 Add the soy and stir-fry a further 30 seconds then pour everything from the pan over the noodles. Add all the other ingredients, toss together then serve.

Top tip Glass noodles are very thin rice noodles which need soaking in cold water for 30 minutes rather than cooking. They can be found in some supermarkets or in Asian food stores.

Variations Any kind of noodle could be used for this salad – just cook according to the packet instructions and then follow the recipe instructions from step 2.

Substitute a 200 g (7 oz) skinless, sliced chicken breast for the pork. The points per serving will be the same.

Oriental noodle salad: A very pretty salad that makes a satisfying lunch; it's also ideal as an accompaniment to an Oriental meal

Warm vegetable salad

1 Point per serving	Points per recipe **4½**

ⓥ Serves 4 ● Preparation and cooking time 10 minutes ●
Calories per serving 165 ● Freezing not recommended
*The warmth of the vegetables brings out the best
in this aromatic dressing since it enhances their
fresh flavours. Perfect on its own or serve with a
grilled 120 g (4 oz) cod fillet, (1½ points per
serving) or a medium skinless chicken breast
(2½ points per serving).*

1 large head of broccoli, chopped into florets
1 large head of cauliflower, chopped into florets
200 g (7 oz) mange-tout peas or green beans
100 g (3½ oz) frozen peas
100 g (3½ oz) baby corn
100 g (3½ oz) asparagus, trimmed and cut into 2.5 cm
   (1-inch) lengths
100 g (3½ oz) baby carrots or 2 medium carrots cut into
   2.5 cm (1-inch) batons
salt and freshly ground black pepper
For the dressing
juice and zest of 2 lemons
1 small red onion, chopped finely
a small bunch of parsley, chopped finely
a small bunch of dill chopped finely
a small bunch of mint, chopped finely
4 teaspoons olive oil

1 Bring a large pan of salted, boiling water to the boil.
Blanch all the vegetables for 2 minutes then place in a
large bowl.
2 While the vegetables are still hot add all the dressing
ingredients, toss together, season then serve.

Top tip Blanching the vegetables for just a few minutes
retains their crunch and also most of their nutrients.
Variations Vary the herbs according to what you have
available – basil, thyme, chervil and/or tarragon would
be delicious.

Tomato, mozzarella and basil salad

2 Points per serving	Points per recipe **4**

ⓥ if using vegetarian cheese ● Serves 2 ● Preparation
time 5 minutes ● Calories per serving 160 ● Freezing not
recommended *A Mediterranean salad that needs
good, ripe, flavoursome Italian plum tomatoes to
really come into its own.*

4 medium, ripe plum tomatoes, sliced
75 g (2¾ oz) light mozzarella cheese, sliced
1 tablespoon balsamic vinegar
2 teaspoons olive oil
a small bunch of fresh basil, chopped
salt and freshly ground black pepper

1 Interleave the tomatoes and cheese around two
serving plates. Sprinkle the seasoning over, drizzle
with the vinegar and oil then scatter with basil leaves
and serve.

Top tip This salad benefits from being made 30 minutes
before you eat it so that the flavours can mingle.
Variation Try with goats' cheese instead of the mozzarella.
The points per serving will be 4½.

Green bean and shallot salad

1 Point per serving　　　Points per recipe **2**

Ⓥ Serves 2 ● Preparation and cooking time 15 minutes ●
Calories per serving 105 ● Freezing not recommended
*A simple, classic salad that can be enjoyed hot
or cold, on its own or as an accompaniment to
poached eggs or cold meats, adding the extra
points as necessary.*

300 g (10½ oz) French beans
low-fat cooking spray
4 small shallots, chopped finely
2 tablespoons balsamic vinegar
2 teaspoons Dijon mustard
2 teaspoons olive oil
salt and freshly ground black pepper

1 Bring a pan of salted water to the boil and blanch the
beans for 2–4 minutes until just tender.
2 Meanwhile, heat a non-stick frying-pan and spray with
the low-fat cooking spray then stir-fry the shallots for 4
minutes until they have softened, adding a little water if
necessary to stop the mixture sticking.
3 Add the blanched beans to the pan along with all the
other ingredients. Toss together and serve hot or chill
and serve cold.

Top tip Trim the tops of the beans but leave the tails
intact as they look attractive.

Chicken Caesar salad

5 Points per serving　　　Points per recipe **9½**

Serves 2 ● Preparation time 10 minutes + 30 minutes
marinating ● Cooking time 10 minutes ● Calories per
serving 295 ● Freezing not recommended *A slight
variation on a well-known salad. Here the chicken
is first marinated in yogurt, then grilled before
being placed on top of Cos lettuce, sprinkled
with croûtons and Parmesan and served with
a hummous dressing.*

1 medium skinless, boneless chicken breast,
　sliced into strips
1 tablespoon low-fat plain yogurt
2 teaspoons whole-grain mustard
2 medium slices of bread, cubed
1 Cos lettuce, chopped, rinsed and dried
25 g (1 oz) Parmesan cheese, grated finely
salt and freshly ground black pepper
For the dressing
2 tablespoons reduced-fat hummous
juice of ½ lemon

1 Place the chicken in a non-metallic bowl with the
yogurt, seasoning, and mustard. Toss to coat and
leave to marinate for at least 30 minutes.
2 Meanwhile, toast the bread cubes under the grill until
golden and divide the Cos lettuce between two serving
bowls. Scatter the croûtons over.
3 Shake the dressing ingredients plus 2 tablespoons of
water together in a jar with a screw-top lid then pour
over the lettuce. Toss together.
4 Preheat the grill then grill the chicken for 10 minutes,
turning once, until cooked through. Place on top of the
salad, sprinkle over the Parmesan and serve
immediately.

Variations For a vegetarian version, leave out the chicken
to reduce the points to 3½ per serving or replace it with
2 tablespoons of toasted seeds such as sesame or
pumpkin. This will make the points 4½ per serving.

**As a goal, keep in mind a picture
of something you want to be able to wear**

New potato, pea and ham salad

5 Points per serving	Points per recipe **20½**

(v) if not using the ham ● Serves 4 ● Preparation time 10 minutes ● Cooking time 25 minutes ● Calories per serving 325 ● Freezing not recommended This fresh summer salad is perfect for eating 'al fresco'.

> 1 kg (2 lb 4 oz) new potatoes, large ones halved
> 200 g (7 oz) frozen petit pois
> 200 g (7 oz) ham, diced finely
> 250 ml (9 fl oz) low-fat plain yogurt
> a small bunch of mint, chopped
> ½ teaspoon caster sugar
> salt and freshly ground black pepper

1 Boil the potatoes in plenty of salted water for 15–20 minutes until just tender, then add the peas and cook for 2 minutes more. Drain, rinse under cold water to refresh and drain again then put in a bowl.
2 Add the ham, seasoning, yogurt, mint and sugar, toss together then serve.

Leeks and crispy ham salad

1 Point per serving	Points per recipe **2**

(v) if not using the ham ● Serves 2 ● Preparation time 10 minutes ● Cooking time 15 minutes ● Calories per serving 85 ● Freezing not recommended A light and healthy starter, lunch or accompaniment to grilled fish, adding the extra points as necessary.

> 8 baby leeks or 2 medium leeks, halved and halved again lengthways, rinsed and drained
> 100 g (3½ oz) tomatoes, quartered
> low-fat cooking spray
> 1 tablespoon balsamic vinegar
> 1 teaspoon caster sugar
> 2 thin slices Parma ham
> salt and freshly ground black pepper

1 Bring a large pan of salted water to the boil then blanch the leeks for 4–8 minutes depending on their size and tenderness. Check with the point of a sharp knife to see if they are tender.
2 Meanwhile, preheat the oven to Gas Mark 7/220°C/425°F. Place the tomato quarters on a baking tray. Season and spray with the low-fat cooking spray then roast for 10 minutes, until softened and slightly charred.
3 Put the tomatoes in a liquidiser with the vinegar and sugar and blend to a vinaigrette, then push through a sieve to remove all the seeds.
4 Preheat the grill and grill the Parma ham for 2 minutes until curled and crispy. Arrange the leeks on two serving plates, pour the tomato vinaigrette over and top with a piece of crispy ham and serve.

Top tip If they are available baby leeks make this salad especially good, as they are so tender and sweet.
Variation Use 2 medium slices of lean back bacon, grilled and then chopped and sprinkled over, instead of the Parma ham. The points per serving will be 2.

Warm spinach and turkey rasher salad

3 Points per serving	Points per recipe **6½**

Serves 2 ● Preparation and cooking time 10 minutes ●
Calories per serving 215 ● Freezing not recommended

This quick-fix salad makes a satisfying brunch.

1 tablespoon white wine (or malt) vinegar
225 g (8 oz) baby spinach, rinsed and drained
1 tablespoon balsamic vinegar
2 teaspoons olive oil
2 medium eggs
4 medium turkey rashers
salt and freshly ground black pepper

1 Put a saucepan of water on to boil with the tablespoon of white wine vinegar in it. Put the spinach in a bowl with the balsamic vinegar, olive oil and seasoning and toss together. Divide the dressed spinach between two serving bowls.

2 When the water is at a rolling boil, crack the eggs into a cup and then slide gently into the water. Cook for 3 minutes then lift out with a slotted spoon.

3 Meanwhile, preheat the grill. Grill the turkey rashers for 1 minute on each side until starting to turn crispy. Chop them into pieces and scatter over the spinach, top with a poached egg and lots of ground pepper.

Malaysian chicken salad

| 1½ | Points per serving | Points per recipe | 6½ |

Serves 4 ● Preparation time 15 minutes ● Calories per serving 200 ● Freezing not recommended It speeds things up to shred all the vegetables in a food processor or vegetable mandolin if you have one; otherwise chop them by hand with a very sharp knife.

2 medium skinless, boneless cooked chicken breasts, shredded
2 large carrots, sliced into thin matchsticks
½ large cucumber, sliced into thin matchsticks
6 spring onions, shredded
1 medium red pepper, de-seeded and sliced into thin matchsticks
200 g (7 oz) beansprouts, rinsed and drained
85 g (3 oz) watercress, rinsed, drained and chopped roughly
a small bunch of mint or coriander, chopped roughly
For the dressing
juice of 2 limes
1 tablespoon light soy sauce
2 teaspoons sesame oil

1 Combine all the salad ingredients in a bowl and either shake the dressing ingredients together in a screw-top jar or whisk them together in a bowl. Pour over the salad, toss together then serve.

Top tip Shred the chicken breast by hand, just pull it apart along the grain of the meat.

Broad bean and Parma ham salad

| 3 | Points per serving | Points per recipe | 13 |

Serves 4 ● Preparation and cooking time 15 minutes ● Calories per serving 140 ● Freezing not recommended A satisfying, bright green salad that is best made with small, tender broad beans which can be bought fresh or frozen.

450 g (1 lb) shelled fresh or frozen broad beans
8 thin slices Parma ham, sliced into little strips
juice of ½ lemon
a small bunch of parsley, chopped finely
2 teaspoons olive oil
salt and freshly ground black pepper

1 Bring a large pan of salted water to the boil and blanch the beans for 2 minutes then drain and refresh under cold water.
2 Put the beans in a serving bowl, add all the other ingredients, toss together and serve.

Variation Use wafer-thin honey roast ham instead of Parma ham. The points per serving will remain the same.

Treat yourself to at least one pleasurable experience every day. It could be as simple as a walk in the park, listening to a favourite piece of music, manicuring your nails – whatever makes you feel good!

Blue cheese and croûton salad

4½   Points per serving   Points per recipe   **9**

V if using vegetarian cheese ● Serves 2 ● Preparation and cooking time 10 minutes ● Calories per serving 270 ● Freezing not recommended *It is important to try to use bitter salad leaves like frisée, raddichio or chicory for this salad as their flavour really sets off the rich creaminess of the blue cheese.*

2 medium bread slices, cubed
low-fat cooking spray
1 head frisée lettuce or 2 heads chicory or raddichio,
    washed and sliced
50 g (1¾ oz) Danish blue cheese
salt and freshly ground black pepper
For the dressing
1 tablespoon white wine vinegar
2 teaspoons olive oil
1 small garlic clove, crushed
1 teaspoon French mustard
salt and freshly ground black pepper

1 Preheat the grill and place the bread on the grill pan. Season and spray with low-fat cooking spray. Toast for 1–2 minutes, then turn over with a fish slice, spray again and toast the other sides. Cut into cubes to make the croûtons.

2 Place all the dressing ingredients and 2 tablespoons water in an empty jam jar with a screw-top lid and shake vigorously. Place the lettuce in a bowl and pour the dressing over. Toss together and then divide the dressed salad between two serving plates.

3 Scatter the toasted croûtons over, then crumble the blue cheese on top and serve.

Spicy sausage and bean salad

4½   Points per serving   Points per recipe   **18**

Serves 4 ● Preparation and cooking time 20 minutes + 30 minutes marinating (optional) ● Calories per serving 220 ● Freezing not recommended *A satisfying and colourful salad full of robust flavours.*

8 thin low-fat sausages
1 small red onion, chopped finely
1 small red chilli, de-seeded and chopped finely
    (or 1 teaspoon dried chilli flakes)
4 medium ripe tomatoes, sliced
2 × 400 g cans cannelllini beans, rinsed and drained
a small bunch of parsley, basil or coriander, chopped
salt and freshly ground black pepper
For the dressing
2 tablespoons balsamic vinegar
4 teaspoons olive oil
1 teaspoon Tabasco sauce
1 tablespoon light soy or Worcestershire sauce

1 Preheat the grill then grill the sausages for about 5 minutes on each side until browned and cooked through. Set aside to cool.

2 Meanwhile, place all the other salad ingredients in a bowl. Shake all the dressing ingredients together in an empty screw-top jam jar and pour over the salad.

3 Chop the sausages into small pieces, add to the salad and toss everything together. Leave to marinate for as long as possible before serving.

Variations Try a tablespoon of whole-grain mustard in the dressing instead of the Tabasco and soy sauce, and possibly omit the chilli too.

You could also use flageolet beans for the same amount of points per serving.

In the pink fish salad

2   Points per serving   Points per recipe   **4**

Serves 2 ● Preparation time 10 minutes ● Calories per serving 200 ● Freezing not recommended *The vibrant shocking pink and purple of this coleslaw is in complete contrast to the delicate pink fish placed on top, however the flavours complement each other beautifully.*

125 g (4½ oz) smoked trout
½ small red cabbage, shredded thinly
1 small red onion, sliced thinly
2 small, uncooked beetroots, peeled and grated
25 g (1 oz) sultanas
a small bunch of dill, chopped

For the dressing
1 teaspoon Dijon mustard
1 teaspoon clear honey
1 teaspoon red wine vinegar
2 tablespoons virtually fat-free fromage frais

1 Put all the salad ingredients together in a large bowl. Shake all the dressing ingredients together in a jam jar with a screw-top lid then pour over. Toss together and divide between two serving plates. Top with the smoked fish and serve.

Top tip Grated raw beetroot is delicious and well worth a try. It is not nearly as messy to handle as cooked beetroot, but wear kitchen rubber gloves if you are worried about staining your hands.

Variation Using the same amount of smoked salmon in place of the trout adds 2½ points per serving.

Chilli crab and mango salad

3   Points per serving   Points per recipe   **12½**

Serves 4 ● Preparation time 5 minutes ● Calories per serving 205 ● Freezing not recommended *This recipe is based on a South East Asian salad and is delicious.*

240 g (8½ oz) fresh crab meat or 2 × 120 g cans white crabmeat, drained
1 medium cucumber, grated
8 small pink radishes, halved and sliced thinly
2 medium ripe mangos or papayas, peeled and sliced
2 teaspoons caster sugar
1½ teaspoons fish or soy sauce
1 teaspoon crushed dried chilli
juice of 2 limes
1 small red chilli, de-seeded and chopped
50 g (1¾ oz) roasted peanuts, chopped
a small bunch of chives or coriander, chopped
salt

1 Put all the ingredients except the chilli, peanuts and chives or coriander in a bowl and toss together gently. Pile on to serving plates, then sprinkle with the chilli, nuts and chives or coriander and serve.

Menu plan

Go Tropical

~

Chilli Crab and Mango Salad, page 48
(pictured here)
1 serving . . . 3 points

~

Thai Fishcakes with Sweet Chilli Dip, page 33
1 serving . . . 2 points

~

Coconut and Raspberry Cup Cakes, page 200
1 serving . . . 4½ points

Total points per meal 9½ points

Potato salad with bacon

4 Points per serving	Points per recipe **16**

 if not using the bacon bits ● Serves 4 ● Preparation time 5 minutes ● Cooking time 30 minutes ● Calories per serving 205; with bacon 255 ● Freezing not recommended

A classic potato salad to accompany a BBQ meal or to take on a picnic.

    800 g (1 lb 11 oz) medium potatoes
    a small bunch of chives, chopped
    1 tablespoon Dijon mustard
    4 tablespoons low-fat mayonnaise
    2 medium rashers lean back bacon,
        cut into small strips
    salt and freshly ground black pepper

1 Boil the potatoes in plenty of salted water for 20–30 minutes until tender then drain and set aside to cool. Chop into large dice.

2 Add all the other ingredients except the bacon to the potato and toss together. Dry-fry the bacon in a non-stick frying-pan for 5 minutes until really crispy, then scatter over the top of the salad and serve.

Top tip The potato skins can be left on but you may wish to peel them after they are cooked before dicing.
Variation Vegetarians can omit the bacon. The points per serving will be 3.

Smoked mackerel and beetroot salad

| 4 | Points per serving | Points per recipe | 16 |

Serves 4 ● Preparation time 10 minutes + 30 minutes soaking ● Calories per serving 270 ● Freezing not recommended *In this recipe salty, smoked mackerel is complemented by sweet beetroot and nutty bulgar wheat to make a salad full of interesting flavours and textures, served with a creamy mustard dressing.*

100 g (3½ oz) bulgar wheat
8 small beetroot, cooked, peeled and diced finely
1 peppered smoked mackerel fillet, approximately
    150 g (5½ oz), skinned and flaked
a small bunch of chives, chopped, plus extra to garnish
juice of ½ lemon
2 tablespoons half-fat crème fraîche
2 teaspoons whole-grain mustard
225 g (8 oz) rocket or mixed baby salad leaves, rinsed
    and drained

1 Soak the bulgar wheat for 30 minutes in 300 ml (½ pint) boiling water. Meanwhile, place the beetroot, mackerel flakes and chopped chives together in a large bowl. Squeeze the lemon juice over and add the crème fraîche and mustard.

2 Arrange the salad leaves in nests on four serving plates. When the bulgar wheat is swollen, drain and rinse in cold water. Add to the beetroot mixture in the bowl and very gently mix together.

3 Pile spoonfuls of the salad on top of the lettuce, sprinkle with chives and serve.

Warm floret salad

| 2½ | Points per serving | Points per recipe | 10 |

Serves 4 ● Preparation and cooking time 15 minutes ● Calories per serving 175 ● Freezing not recommended *A warm salad of broccoli and cauliflower served with a tangy anchovy mayonnaise. The mayonnaise does not taste fishy and it heightens the flavours in the salad.*

1 medium head of cauliflower, chopped into florets
1 medium head of broccoli, chopped into florets
6 anchovy fillets, rinsed and patted dry on kitchen paper
100 ml (3½ fl oz) low-fat mayonnaise
1 garlic clove, crushed
juice of 1 lemon
freshly ground black pepper
To serve
1 tablespoon sesame seeds, toasted
1 tablespoon sunflower seeds, toasted

1 Bring a large pan of salted water to the boil and blanch the cauliflower and broccoli florets for about 4 minutes until only just tender. Drain and put in a large bowl.

2 Meanwhile, mash the anchovy fillets in a pestle and mortar then stir with the mayonnaise, garlic, lemon juice and season well with pepper. Add to the warm florets and toss together. Serve scattered with the seeds.

Variation Meat lovers can try replacing the seeds with 4 medium lean back rashers of smoked bacon, grilled until crispy then chopped finely and scattered over. The points per serving will be 3½.

This chapter will show you how interesting, tasty and satisfying it is to prepare vegetarian meals. And for more meat-free meals, have a look in the chapter called Oodles of Noodles, Rice and Beans on page 70.

vibrant veggies

Lasagne verde

7 Points per serving	Points per recipe **27½**

V if using vegetarian cheese ● Serves 4 ● Preparation time 20 minutes ● Cooking time 50 minutes ● Calories per serving 580 ● Freezing recommended *A lovely twist on traditional lasagne.*

250 g (9 oz) no-precook lasagne sheets, preferably spinach
For the filling
1 medium round lettuce, shredded
450 g (1 lb) frozen peas
125 ml (4 fl oz) vegetable stock
low-fat cooking spray
2 garlic cloves, chopped finely
225 g (8 oz) courgettes, diced finely
125 ml (4 fl oz) white wine
a small bunch of fresh mint, chopped
500 g (1 lb 2 oz) frozen spinach, cooked
200 g (7 oz) Quark cheese
a pinch of freshly grated nutmeg
salt and freshly ground black pepper
For the topping
2 medium eggs
4 tablespoons skimmed milk
300 g (10½ oz) low-fat plain yogurt
100 g (3½ oz) low-fat soft cheese
50 g (1¾ oz) reduced-fat strong-flavoured Cheddar
   cheese, grated

1 Cook the lettuce with the peas and the stock in a covered saucepan for 20 minutes over a low heat.
2 Meanwhile, heat a large frying-pan. Spray with the cooking spray. Sauté the garlic for 2 minutes. Add the courgettes. Stir-fry for 4 minutes over a high heat until the courgettes brown slightly. Add the wine. Boil rapidly until all but a few tablespoons evaporate. Add the mint, toss and remove from the heat.
3 In another pan, gently heat the spinach and Quark. Add the nutmeg and seasoning.
4 Preheat the oven to Gas Mark 6/200°C/400°F. Spray a 30 cm (12-inch) ovenproof dish with the cooking spray then line the bottom with lasagne. Mix the cooked lettuce and peas together with the courgette mixture.
5 Cover the bottom of the dish with a layer of vegetables in their juices, then top with lasagne and repeat twice more. Finish with a layer of lasagne.
6 Beat together the topping ingredients, except the Cheddar cheese. Pour over the lasagne. Sprinkle with cheese and bake for 30 minutes until golden.

Mushroom stroganoff with a rice pilaff

3½ Points per serving	Points per recipe **14½**

ⓥ Serves 4 ● Preparation time 10 minutes ● Cooking time 40 minutes ● Calories per serving 285 ● Freezing not recommended *This is two recipes in one. The recipes for the pilaff and the stroganoff can be used separately from one another but together they make a very satisfying vegetarian meal.*

For the pilaff
1 medium onion, chopped roughly
1 teaspoon ground cumin
2 teaspoons ground coriander
200 g (7 oz) brown lentils
100 g (3½ oz) brown basmati rice
1 litre (1¾ pints) vegetable stock
a small bunch of parsley or coriander, to garnish
For the mushrooms
low-fat cooking spray
2 garlic cloves, crushed
400 g (14 oz) mushrooms
1 small red chilli, de-seeded and chopped finely
juice of 1 lemon
100 ml (3½ fl oz) low-fat plain yogurt
a small bunch of fresh parsley or thyme, chopped
salt and freshly ground black pepper

1 Put all the ingredients for the pilaff except the garnish, into a large saucepan. Bring to the boil, cover then simmer gently for 35–40 minutes or until the rice is tender and the liquid absorbed.
2 Meanwhile heat a large frying-pan and spray with the low-fat cooking spray then fry the garlic for 1 minute. Add the mushrooms and stir-fry over a high heat for 5 minutes, then add the chilli, seasoning and lemon juice.
3 Cook for a further 2 minutes, turn off the heat and stir the yogurt through then add the parsley or thyme. Serve with the pilaff, garnished with parsley or coriander.

Top tip Use large, flat field mushrooms as they are easy to clean and chop and full of flavour. Chestnut mushrooms are also very good.
Variation For a special occasion, wild mushrooms are unrivalled for flavour but they can be expensive.

Potato pizza

4½ Points per serving	Points per recipe **8½**

ⓥ Serves 2 ● Preparation time 5 minutes ● Cooking time 15–20 minutes ● Calories per serving 395 ● Freezing not recommended *This pizza is always a hot favourite at dinner parties. Serve in thin wedges as a starter.*

250 g (9 oz) waxy potatoes, peeled, sliced thinly, rinsed and patted dry on kitchen paper
2 garlic cloves, crushed
leaves from 1 sprig of rosemary
low-fat cooking spray
1 large, thin, (30 cm/12-inch) fresh pizza base
1 teaspoon olive oil
plain flour, for dusting
salt and freshly ground black pepper

1 Preheat the oven to Gas Mark 7/220°C/425°F. Put the potatoes, garlic, rosemary and seasoning in a bowl, spray with the low-fat cooking spray, toss together then spray again.
2 Place the pizza base on an oven tray sprayed with the low-fat cooking spray and dusted with a little flour.
3 Spread the potato mixture evenly over the pizza base, drizzle with olive oil and bake for 15–20 minutes until the potatoes are tender and the pizza lightly golden and crisp.

Top tip This is best made with waxy potato varieties which include Desirée (the red-skinned potato) and new and early potatoes such as Pentland Javelin and Maris Peer.

Spring vegetable stew

2½ Points per serving   Points per recipe **9½**

ⓥ Serves 4 ● Preparation time 2 minutes ● Cooking time 20 minutes ● Calories per serving 190 ● Freezing not recommended *A fresh-tasting spring stew full of cheerful colours and goodness which is simplicity itself to make.*

400 g (14 oz) new potatoes
600 ml (1 pint) boiling vegetable stock
40 g (1½ oz) pesto sauce from a jar
1 bunch spring onions, chopped roughly
2 garlic cloves, sliced into slivers
200 g (7 oz) sugar snap peas
200 g (7 oz) runner beans, cut diagonally
200 g (7 oz) baby carrots, halved or quartered lengthways
100 g (3½ oz) frozen petit pois
100 g (3½ oz) frozen, shelled broad beans
1 bunch fresh basil or mint, chopped

1 Put the potatoes in a saucepan, pour the boiling stock over and boil for 15–20 minutes until just tender.
2 Add the pesto sauce and the rest of the vegetables. Cook for 5 minutes more then serve sprinkled with the basil or mint.

Top tips Pesto sauce is available in jars from the pasta sauce section of supermarkets or it can be bought from the chilled sauces or delicatessan.

Pesto is also good on baked potatoes instead of butter or cheese; spread it sparingly over fish and then grill, or swirl into soup instead of fresh herbs.
Variations Use red pepper purée, hot harissa paste (1 tablespoon is 1 point) or tapenade instead of the pesto.

Potato and spinach curry (Saag aloo)

2½ Points per serving   Points per recipe **10**

ⓥ Serves 4 ● Preparation time 5 minutes ● Cooking time 50 minutes ● Calories per serving 220 ● Freezing recommended *This is a classic Indian dish that is satisfying on its own or as an accompaniment to meat or fish.*

1 kg (2 lb 4 oz) fresh spinach, rinsed, drained and large stalks removed, or 500 g (1 lb 2 oz) frozen spinach
low-fat cooking spray
2 teaspoons whole black mustard seeds
1 medium onion, sliced thinly
2 garlic cloves, chopped finely
900 g (2 lb) potatoes, peeled and cut into 2.5 cm (1-inch) cubes
½ teaspoon cayenne or dried chilli flakes
1 teaspoon ground cumin
1 teaspoon ground coriander
salt and freshly ground black pepper

1 If using fresh spinach, cook in a large pan with very little water, covered, for 5 minutes until wilted. Season, drain and chop.
2 Spray the same saucepan with the low-fat cooking spray, cook the mustard seeds for a couple of seconds, until they pop then add the onion and garlic and stir-fry for 2 minutes.
3 Add the potatoes and cayenne or chilli flakes and fry another 2 minutes. Add the spinach, cumin, coriander and seasoning and 300 ml (½ pint) water. Bring to the boil then simmer over the lowest possible heat with a lid on for 30–40 minutes until the potatoes are tender.
4 Stir occasionally, adding a little more water if the mixture looks like it might become too dry and stick.

Keep track – knowing what you've eaten and how much exercise you've done can go a long way towards helping you to feel in control

vegetable moussaka

2	Points per serving	Points per recipe	9

Ⓥ if using vegetarian cheese ● Serves 4 ● Preparation time 50 minutes ● Cooking time 20 minutes ● Calories per serving 250 ● Freezing recommended *This classic Greek dish is a family favourite, full of satisfying textures and soothing flavours.*

600 g (1lb 5 oz) aubergines, sliced into 2.5 cm (1-inch) thick rounds
a small bunch of fresh basil, leaves only, to garnish (optional)
½ teaspoon paprika
For the tomato sauce
low-fat cooking spray
2 large onions, chopped roughly
2 garlic cloves, crushed
2 large carrots, chopped finely
4 medium courgettes, sliced into 1 cm (½-inch) thick rounds
200 g (7 oz) mushrooms, sliced
2 × 400 g cans chopped tomatoes
2 tablespoons balsamic vinegar
1 teaspoon Tabasco sauce
1 tablespoon honey
salt and freshly ground black pepper
For the yogurt topping
2 teaspoons cornflour, mixed to a paste with 1 tablespoon water
450 ml (16 fl oz) low-fat plain yogurt
100 g (3½ oz) low-fat soft cheese

1 First, make the sauce. Heat a large frying-pan and spray with the low-fat cooking spray. Stir-fry the onions, garlic and carrots for 5 minutes until softened and lightly browned, then add all the other ingredients. Bring to the boil and simmer for 20 minutes.
2 Meanwhile, preheat the grill to high and place some of the aubergine slices in one layer on the grill rack. Grill for 2 minutes on each side until lightly browned, set aside and continue to grill the rest.
3 Meanwhile, make the topping by beating all the ingredients together in a bowl.
4 Preheat the oven to Gas Mark 4/180°C/350°F. Place the aubergine slices in the bottom of an ovenproof dish, cover with the tomato sauce, then spoon over the topping.
5 Bake for 20 minutes until the top is set and browned then sprinkle with fresh basil leaves, if using, and a little paprika and serve.

Jerk sweet potatoes

2½	Points per serving	Points per recipe	10½

Ⓥ Serves 4 ● Preparation time 15 minutes ● Cooking time 50 minutes ● Calories per serving 175 ● Freezing not recommended *'Jerking' is a Jamaican marinate - and-grill method of cooking,*

4 medium sweet potatoes, halved lengthways
low-fat cooking spray
salt and freshly ground black pepper
1 lime, quartered, to serve
For the jerk
juice of 1 lime
1 tablespoon honey
1 teaspoon olive oil
1 tablespoon Jamaican jerk seasoning
For the dip
4 tablespoons low-fat plain yogurt
1 garlic clove, crushed
a small bunch of fresh mint, chopped finely

1 Preheat the oven to Gas Mark 6/200°C/400°F. Using a sharp knife, slash the flesh of each sweet potato half in a criss-cross fashion. Place on an oven tray, flesh-side up, and spray with the low-fat cooking spray. Season and bake for about 40 minutes until tender.
2 Meanwhile, put all the jerk ingredients in a small pan and stir together over a gentle heat. Brush this mixture over the nearly cooked sweet potatoes then return them to the oven for at least another 10 minutes until they turn golden.
3 Make the dip by mixing together all the ingredients in a bowl. Serve the potatoes with lime wedges and the dip.

Top tip Jerk seasoning is available in the spice section of supermarkets.

Roast Mediterranean vegetables

0 Points per serving	Points per recipe 0

(V) Serves 6 ● Preparation time 15 minutes ● Cooking time 25 minutes ● Calories per serving 65 ● Freezing not recommended *Since this recipe is point-free, you can 'afford' to serve it with lovely crusty bread as a filling meal for only 1 point per medium slice. You could also use it as an accompaniment to grilled meat or fish, counting the points as necessary.*

2 large aubergines, cubed
450 g (1 lb) courgettes, sliced fairly thickly
2 medium red peppers, de-seeded and cut into
   8 lengthways
2 medium yellow peppers, de-seeded and cut into
   8 lengthways
low-fat cooking spray
a small bunch of basil, chopped roughly
salt and freshly ground black pepper
For the sauce
400 g can chopped tomatoes
1 tablespoon balsamic vinegar
1 garlic clove, crushed
1 small red chilli, de-seeded and chopped finely

1 Preheat the oven to Gas Mark 8/230°C/450°F. Place the aubergines, courgettes and peppers in a roasting tin, season well and spray with the low-fat cooking spray. Bake for about 25 minutes until they are tender and slightly charred.

2 Place all the roasted vegetables together with the basil and any cooking juices from the trays into a bowl.

3 Meanwhile, make the sauce. Put all the ingredients in a small saucepan, season, bring to the boil and simmer gently for 15 minutes.

4 Pour the sauce over the vegetables, toss gently together then serve.

Variation This is also good as a pasta sauce.

Chicory gratin

5 Points per serving	Points per recipe 20

(V) if using vegetarian cheese ● Serves 4 ● Preparation time 10 minutes ● Cooking time 50 minutes ● Calories per serving 295 ● Freezing not recommended *This recipe for chicory baked in a cheese sauce is simple to prepare and the usually bitter heads of chicory become sweet and caramelised.*

50 g (1¾ oz) polyunsaturated margarine
8 slim heads of chicory
50 g (1¾ oz) plain flour
600 ml (1 pint) skimmed milk
100 g (3½ oz) low-fat soft cheese
1 tablespoon French mustard
50 g (1¾ oz) mature Cheddar cheese, grated
salt and freshly ground black pepper

1 Melt the margarine in a large frying-pan then add the chicory, turning to coat. Season then cover with a piece of baking paper tucked down the sides of the pan and cover with a lid. Sweat over the lowest possible heat for 35 minutes until tender and caramelised.

2 Remove from the pan with a slotted spoon and place in an ovenproof dish, packing them tightly together. Preheat the oven to Gas Mark 5/190°C/375°F. Put the flour in the pan used for the chicory and cook for 30 seconds, then add the milk a little at a time, whisking between additions to make a smooth sauce.

3 Add the cheese, mustard and seasoning and stir until smooth over a gentle heat. Pour over the chicory, sprinkle the cheese on top and bake for 15 minutes until bubbling and golden.

Roasted autumn roots

2½	Points per serving	Points per recipe	9½

Ⓥ Serves 4 ● Preparation time 10 minutes ● Cooking time 1 hour ● Calories per serving 235 ● Freezing not recommended *In this recipe, the ingredients can be changed to suit your mood or the season. Just make sure that all the vegetables are chopped into pieces roughly the same size so they need the same cooking time as each other. Keep the size quite small so you do not have to cook them for too long.*

4 medium carrots, sliced diagonally into thick slices
4 medium parsnips, quartered lengthways
4 medium potatoes, peeled and sliced into wedges
4 small turnips, peeled quartered
1 medium swede, halved and sliced into wedges
1 garlic bulb, broken into cloves
4 small red onions, quartered
leaves from 4 sprigs of rosemary
low-fat cooking spray
juice of ½ lemon
2 teaspoons olive oil
salt and freshly ground black pepper

1 Preheat the oven to Gas Mark 7/220°C/425°F. Place all the vegetables and the rosemary in a large, deep baking tray, spreading out as much as possible.
2 Season and spray with the low-fat cooking spray. Toss to mix together and then spray again. Roast for 45 minutes – 1 hour until the vegetables are tender and beginning to brown at the edges. Toss them once half-way through the cooking to turn them.
3 Remove the garlic and squash the cloves using a wooden spoon, discard the skins and return the flesh to the other vegetables. Pour the lemon juice and oil over and toss again to mix in the garlic then serve.

Aubergine Madras

2	Points per serving	Points per recipe	4

Ⓥ Serves 2 ● Preparation time 10 minutes ● Cooking time 40 minutes ● Calories per serving 140 ● Freezing not recommended *Aubergines are like sponges, absorbing the flavours around them making this an intensely-flavoured but silky-textured curry.*

2 medium aubergines, halved lengthways
4 teaspoons Madras curry paste
low-fat cooking spray
1 small onion, sliced thinly
2 garlic cloves, sliced thinly
150 ml (5 fl oz) stock or water
150 ml (5 fl oz) low-fat plain yogurt
a small bunch of fresh coriander, chopped

1 Preheat the oven to Gas Mark 4/180°C/350°F. Score the cut side of the aubergine halves with a sharp knife in a deep criss-cross fashion, then spread a teaspoon of the curry paste over each scored face and place them curry-side-up on a baking tray.
2 Bake for 30 minutes until softened.
3 Meanwhile, spray a large frying-pan with the low-fat cooking spray and stir-fry the onion for 5 minutes until softened. Add the garlic and stir-fry another couple of minutes then turn off the heat.
4 When the aubergines are baked, transfer them to a board and chop them into cubes as marked by the score lines. Add them to the onion with the stock or water and bring to the boil. Boil rapidly, uncovered, for 10 minutes until nearly all the liquid has evaporated.
5 Remove from the heat, stir in the yogurt and coriander and serve.

Sweet onion tart

4 Points per serving   Points per recipe **15½**

Ⓥ if using free-range eggs ● Serves 4 ● Preparation time 15 minutes + 30 minutes cooling ● Cooking time 1 hour 10 minutes ● Calories per serving 305 ● Freezing not recommended *Serve with 200 g (7 oz) new potatoes and a crisp green salad, adding on 2 points per serving.*

For the pastry
50 g (1¾ oz) polyunsaturated margarine
50 g (1¾ oz) plain flour
50 g (1¾ oz) wholemeal flour
a pinch of salt

For the sweet onion filling
low-fat cooking spray
1 kg (2 lb 4 oz) onions, sliced very thinly
a small bunch of thyme, chopped
2 medium eggs
150 ml (5 fl oz) skimmed milk
2 teaspoons French mustard
salt and freshly ground black pepper

1 Make the pastry by rubbing the margarine into the flours and salt until the mixture resembles fresh breadcrumbs then add about 1 tablespoon of water and mix the dough quickly into a ball with your hand. Wrap in clingfilm and chill in the refrigerator for 30 minutes.

2 Meanwhile, heat a large frying-pan and spray with the low-fat cooking spray then add the onions, thyme and seasoning and stir-fry for 2 minutes over a high heat.

3 Cover the pan with a piece of baking paper tucked down the sides to seal the onion mixture in, then cover with a lid and sweat over the lowest possible heat for 20 minutes. Pull the paper to one side occasionally and stir to make sure the mixture is not sticking to the pan, adding a little water to prevent this if necessary.

4 Preheat the oven to Gas Mark 5/190°C/375°F. Roll the pastry out to a circle about 5 mm (½-inch) thick and use to line a 19 cm (7½-inch) loose-bottomed flan tin. Line with foil then fill with baking beans.

5 Bake for 15 minutes then remove the beans and foil lining and bake for a further 10 minutes or until evenly golden brown.

6 Meanwhile, beat the eggs with the milk, mustard and seasoning in a jug.

7 Spoon the cooked onions into the pastry case, pour the egg mixture over and bake for 20 minutes until the filling is set and lightly golden.

Variation Try filling the tart with roasted vegetables instead of the onions.

Vegetarian chilli

2 Points per serving	Points per recipe **9**

Ⓥ if using vegetable stock ● Serves 4 ● Preparation time 10 minutes ● Cooking time 30 minutes ● Calories per serving 345 ● Freezing not recommended *You won't miss meat with this chunky vegetable stew flavoured with a tiny amount of chocolate for an authentic Aztec sweetness. Serve with 4 tablespoons cooked rice per person, adding 3 points per serving.*

low-fat cooking spray
2 large onions, chopped
2 garlic cloves, crushed
2 medium carrots, peeled, quartered lengthways then
    chopped
1 medium butternut squash or ½ pumpkin, peeled and
    cut into 1 cm (½-inch) cubes
2 medium sweet potatoes, peeled and cubed
4 sun-dried tomatoes, soaked in 150 ml (5 fl oz)
    boiling water
1 tablespoon low-fat drinking chocolate
2 teaspoons ground cinnamon
1 teaspoon chilli powder (or more to taste)
400 g can chopped tomatoes
300 ml (½ pint) stock
400 g can kidney beans, rinsed and drained
salt and freshly ground black pepper

1 Heat a large saucepan and spray with the low-fat cooking spray then fry the onions and garlic for 5 minutes until softened, adding a little water if necessary to prevent them from sticking. Add the carrots, squash and sweet potatoes and stir-fry for 2 minutes.
2 Chop the sun-dried tomatoes, and add together with their soaking liquid to the vegetable mixture along with the chocolate, cinnamon and chilli. Stir everything together well. Add the chopped tomatoes, stock and season liberally.
3 Bring to the boil, cover and simmer gently for 20 minutes or until all the vegetables are tender. Finally add the kidney beans and boil rapidly, uncovered, for another 5 minutes until the sauce is rich and thick.

Mexican beanburgers

5 Points per serving	Points per recipe **20½**

Ⓥ if using a free-range egg but not using Worcestershire sauce ● Serves 4 ● Preparation and cooking time 20 minutes + 30 minutes chilling ● Calories per serving 370 ● Freezing recommended *These spicy Mexican-style beanburgers have a really satisfying texture and give a gentle kick! Serve with relish and a big green salad for no extra points.*

2 × 400 g cans mixed beans, rinsed and drained
1 small onion, chopped roughly
1 garlic clove, chopped
400 g can mixed peppers in brine, rinsed, drained
    and chopped roughly
1 medium red chilli, de-seeded and chopped finely
1 teaspoon ground cumin seeds
2 tablespoons Worcestershire sauce
1 tablespoon tomato purée, diluted with 1 tablespoon water
a small bunch of fresh parsley, coriander or chives
1 medium egg, beaten
2 tablespoons plain white flour
low-fat cooking spray
4 medium burger buns
salt and freshly ground black pepper
salad leaves of your choice, to serve

1 Put all the ingredients except the flour and cooking spray in a food processor and whizz to a rough paste. Shape the mixture into 4 burgers, put the flour on a plate and coat the burgers in it. Refrigerate for 30 minutes to allow them to firm up.
2 Heat a large frying-pan and spray with the low-fat cooking spray then fry the burgers for about 4 minutes on each side until browned and heated through.
3 Split the buns and fill with the burgers and salad leaves, then serve.

See yourself slimmer;

visualisation can be a powerful weight loss tool

Menu plan

Spice Up Your Life

~

Spiced Cauliflower Soup, page 17
1 serving . . . 0 points

~

Mexican Beanburgers, page 60
(pictured here)
1 serving . . . 5 points

~

Tropical Mango Creams, page 166
1 serving . . . 2 points

Total points per meal 7 points

Mixed vegetable sushi

3½	Points per serving	Points per recipe	15

ⓥ if using free-range eggs ● Serves 4 ● Preparation time 30 minutes ● Cooking time 20 minutes ● Calories per serving 280 ● Freezing not recommended Now that the ingredients are widely available in the Oriental sections of supermarkets as well as Oriental food stores, it is surprisingly easy to make your own sushi... and it doesn't have to include raw fish!

225 g (8 oz) sushi rice
3 tablespoons seasoned rice vinegar or sherry
low-fat cooking spray
2 medium eggs, lightly beaten
8 sheets nori seaweed
140 g (5 oz) mixed vegetables, cut into matchsticks
    e.g. blanched carrot, cucumber, blanched baby corn,
    cooked beetroot

To serve
½ teaspoon wasabi paste
½ teaspoon pickled ginger
1 tablespoon soy sauce

1 Cook the rice according to the packet instructions then stir in the vinegar or sherry and set aside.
2 Heat a small omelette pan and spray with the low-fat cooking spray then pour in the beaten eggs and swirl around so that they cover the pan base. Cook until just set and then tip out and allow to cool. Cut into strips the same size as the vegetables.
3 Lay one sheet of seaweed on a bamboo mat or a board and trim off the top third. Spread about 50 g (1¾ oz) of the rice along the front end, flatten slightly then place a strip of omelette and strips of vegetables on top.
4 Roll up tightly to form a log and stick the seaweed to itself by dampening with a brush dipped in water. Cut into 5–6 thick slices.
5 Repeat with the remaining rice, omelette and vegetable strips to make a selection of different fillings. Arrange on individual serving plates and serve each with a little pile of wasabi, pickled ginger and a dish of soy for dipping.

Irish leek and potato bake

4½	Points per serving	Points per recipe	19

ⓥ if using vegetarian cheese ● Serves 4 ● Preparation time 15 minutes ● Cooking time 50 minutes ● Calories per serving 315 ● Freezing recommended A lovely, soothing bake full of comforting flavours and textures to take the chill out of any wintery day.

450 g (1 lb) small, floury potatoes, unpeeled
low-fat cooking spray
450 g (1 lb) leeks, sliced thickly, rinsed and drained
1 garlic clove, crushed
50 g (1¾ oz) low-fat Cheddar cheese, grated
salt and freshly ground black pepper
For the sauce
2 tablespoons polyunsaturated margarine
2 tablespoons plain flour
600 ml (1 pint) skimmed milk
100 g (3½ oz) low-fat soft cheese
1 tablespoon French mustard

1 Put the potatoes in a large pan of boiling, salted water and cook for 30 minutes until tender.
2 Meanwhile, heat a large casserole and spray with the low-fat cooking spray then add the leeks and season. Cover and leave to sweat for 20 minutes over the lowest possible heat.
3 To make the cheese sauce, melt the margarine in a small saucepan then add the flour. Cook for 2 minutes then gradually add the milk a little at a time, stirring between additions to make a smooth sauce. Add the soft cheese and heat gently, stirring, until melted in. Add mustard then season and set aside.
4 Preheat the oven to Gas Mark 4/180°C/350°F. Drain the potatoes, peel and chop into cubes and add to the leeks along with the garlic and cheese sauce, stirring gently to combine. Sprinkle the grated cheese over and bake for 20 minutes until bubbling and golden on top.

vegetarian shepherd's pie

6½	Points per serving	Points per recipe	26

Ⓥ if using vegetarian cheese ● Serves 4 ● Preparation time 10 minutes ● Cooking time 20 minutes ● Calories per serving 460 ● Freezing not recommended *A delicious low-Point vegetarian alternative to the original shepherd's pie.*

> 1 kg (2¼ lb) potatoes, peeled and diced
> low-fat cooking spray
> 2 medium carrots, diced finely
> 2 medium onions, chopped finely
> 2 garlic cloves, crushed
> 200 g (7 oz) red lentils, rinsed and drained
> 600 ml (1 pint) vegetable stock
> 400 g can chopped tomatoes
> a dash of Tabasco sauce
> 4 tablespoons skimmed milk
> 50 g (1¾ oz) frozen peas
> 50 g (1¾ oz) mature Cheddar cheese
> salt and freshly ground black pepper

1 Cook the potatoes in a large pan of boiling salted water for 10–15 minutes until tender.

2 Meanwhile heat a large frying-pan and spray with the low-fat cooking spray then stir-fry the carrots, onions and garlic for 5 minutes until softened, adding a little water if necessary to prevent them from sticking.

3 Add the lentils and stock, bring to the boil and simmer rapidly for 10 minutes. Add the tomatoes and Tabasco and simmer for a further 10 minutes until the mixture is thick and the lentils tender.

4 Preheat the grill to high. Drain the potatoes and mash with the milk and seasoning.

5 Stir the peas into the lentil mixture, season and cook for 1 minute more then spoon into an ovenproof dish. Top with the mash, sprinkle over the cheese and grill for 2 minutes until the top is bubbling and golden.

Variations For a meat alternative, add 200 g (7 oz) of lamb (8½ points per serving) or beef mince (8 points per serving) with the carrot and onion at Step 2.

For a vegetarian 'meaty' version, add vegetarian mince (7 points per serving with Quorn and 7½ points per serving with soya) at Step 2.

Pepperonata (Italian red pepper stew)

½	Point per serving	Points per recipe	1

Ⓥ Serves 2 ● Preparation and cooking time 20 minutes ● Calories per serving 155 ● Freezing not recommended *This is a bright, tangy stew which goes well with cold meats, fish or as part of a vegetarian meal adding the points as necessary, and can be served hot or cold. It is quick to prepare as it uses canned products and keeps well in the refrigerator for a couple of days.*

> low-fat cooking spray
> 1 medium onion, chopped
> 2 large garlic cloves, sliced thinly
> 400 g can red peppers, chopped
> 400 g can chopped tomatoes
> 1 tablespoon white wine vinegar
> 1 tablespoon clear honey
> salt and freshly ground black pepper

1 Heat a large frying-pan and spray with the low-fat cooking spray then stir-fry the onion and garlic for 5 minutes until softened, adding a couple of tablespoons of water if necessary to prevent the mixture from sticking.

2 Add the peppers, tomatoes, vinegar, honey and seasoning. Bring to the boil then simmer gently for 10 minutes until slightly thickened. Check the seasoning and serve.

Variation Serves 4 as an accompaniment and the points will be 0 per serving.

Red cabbage and apple

2½	Points per serving	Points per recipe	10

V Serves 4 ● Preparation time 15 minutes ● Cooking time 2–2¼ hours ● Calories per serving 190 ● Freezing not recommended *It does take a long time to cook this cabbage but the results are meltingly smooth and the flavours a delicious combination of sweet and sour. Serve with grilled or roasted meats, especially pork, adding the points as necessary.*

30 ml (1 fl oz) sunflower oil
450 g (1 lb) red cabbage
150 ml (5 fl oz) red wine
2 medium eating apples, peeled and diced finely
2 tablespoons dark brown sugar
2 tablespoons white wine vinegar
2 tablespoons redcurrant jelly

1 Heat the oil in a large saucepan then add the cabbage and toss to coat. Cover the pan with baking paper tucked down the sides then cover with a lid and sweat over a low heat for 10 minutes.
2 Remove the paper, add the wine, increase the heat and cook, uncovered, until the liquid has reduced by half. Add the rest of the ingredients, cover and simmer over the lowest possible heat for 2 hours. Then remove the lid, increase the heat and boil fiercely until the liquid has reduced to a sticky sauce at the bottom of the pan. Then serve.

Cauliflower cheese soufflé

5	Points per serving	Points per recipe	20

V if using vegetarian cheese and free-range eggs ● Serves 4 ● Preparation time 15 minutes ● Cooking time 50 minutes ● Calories per serving 305 ● Freezing not recommended *This recipe is a little more involved than the traditional family favourite Cauliflower cheese, but it is really quite easy and the results are sensational!*

1 small cauliflower, cut into florets
low-fat cooking spray
1 tablespoon fresh breadcrumbs
40 g (1½ oz) polyunsaturated margarine
40 g (1½ oz) plain flour
425 ml (¾ pint) skimmed milk
3 medium egg yolks
a pinch of freshly ground nutmeg
1 teaspoon French mustard
50 g (1¾ oz) mature Cheddar cheese, grated
4 medium egg whites
salt and freshly ground black pepper

1 Cook the cauliflower in salted, boiling water for 10 minutes until quite soft, then mash.
2 Meanwhile, preheat the oven to Gas Mark 6/200°C/ 400°F and prepare an 18 cm (8-inch) soufflé dish by spraying with low-fat cooking spray and dusting the sides with breadcrumbs.
3 Melt the margarine in a small saucepan and stir in the flour. Add the milk a little at a time stirring well between each addition to make a smooth sauce.
4 Remove the sauce from the heat and stir in the egg yolks, nutmeg, mustard, cauliflower and all but a little of the grated cheese and season to taste.
5 Whisk the egg whites until stiff and then gently fold into the sauce. Sprinkle the remaining cheese over the top and bake for 35–40 minutes, until well risen. Serve immediately.

Mustard mash

3 Points per serving	Points per recipe **11½**

V Serves 4 as a side dish ● Preparation time 15 minutes ● Cooking time 30–45 minutes ● Calories per serving 225 ● Freezing not recommended *Simple mashed potato is one of the best comfort foods.*

1 kg (2 lb 4 oz) potatoes
150 ml (5 fl oz) skimmed milk
50 g (1¾ oz) hot English mustard
salt and freshly ground black pepper

1 Put the potatoes into a large pan of boiling salted water and boil for at least 30 minutes until tender when you insert the point of a knife into the largest one.
2 Drain and, holding each hot potato in a tea towel, peel them using the back of a knife. Return to the pan and mash them with a hand masher. Do not be tempted to use a food processor as you will end up with a sticky mess!

3 Add the milk, mustard and seasoning. Stir together then serve.

Variations For horseradish mash, replace the mustard with the same amount of a good horseradish sauce. The points per serving will be 3½.

For spring onion mash (known as 'champ' in Ireland), omit the mustard, add 100 g (3½ oz) finely chopped spring onions to the milk in a small pan and heat gently for 10 minutes then add to the mash. The points per serving will be 3.

For cabbage mash (or colcannon), use the mustard mash recipe but stir 450 g (1 lb) cooked, chopped Savoy cabbage into the mash. You could leave out the mustard. The points per serving will be 3.

Sicilian stuffed peppers: Bold, brightly-coloured peppers make the perfect baking pots for this delicious filling and you can eat them too for only 4 points per serving

Sicilian stuffed peppers

4	Points per serving	Points per recipe	16

Ⓥ if not using the anchovies ● Serves 4 ● Preparation time 15 minutes ● Cooking time 20 minutes ● Calories per serving 365 ● Freezing not recommended *Delicious served with 4 tablespoons cooked rice (3 points) and a crunchy salad.*

4 medium red or yellow peppers, halved lengthways
and de-seeded
For the filling
6 canned anchovy fillets, washed, drained and chopped finely
a small bunch of parsley, chopped finely
a small bunch of fresh oregano, chopped finely
2 tablespoons capers, washed, drained, patted dry on
kitchen paper then chopped
1 garlic clove, crushed
200 g (7 oz) fresh breadcrumbs
4 ripe tomatoes, skinned, de-seeded and diced finely
(see Top tip)
2 tablespoons currants
20 stoned black olives in brine, drained and chopped
50 g (1¾ oz) pine kernels, toasted until golden
juice and zest of 1 lemon
salt and freshly ground black pepper

1 Preheat the oven to Gas Mark 6/200°C/400°F. Place the peppers cut-side-up on a baking tray.
2 Mix all the filling ingredients together in a bowl and use to fill the pepper halves. Bake for 20 minutes until tender and golden on top then serve.

Top tip To skin tomatoes easily, put the tomatoes in a bowl and cover with boiling water. Leave for about 10 seconds, then remove with a slotted spoon. Cool under cold water and the skin should peel off easily. If it doesn't, then return the tomatoes to the hot water for about 5 seconds then try to peel them again and use according to the recipe. This method of preparation is also perfect for preparing tomatoes for including in salsas.
Variations Large beef or plum tomatoes or courgettes can be stuffed with the same mixture.

Grilled Oriental aubergine

1½	Points per serving	Points per recipe	6½

Ⓥ Serves 4 ● Preparation and cooking time 40 minutes ● Calories per serving 90 ● Freezing not recommended *Aubergine slices toasted in a ginger and sesame coating then served with soy and coriander create an Oriental-style starter or accompanying vegetable dish.*

2 tablespoons soy sauce
1 tablespoon honey
low-fat cooking spray
1 medium onion, chopped finely
50 g (1¾ oz) sesame seeds
2.5 cm (1-inch) piece of fresh root ginger,
peeled and grated
½ teaspoon dry chilli flakes (optional)
2 medium aubergines, sliced lengthways into thick slices
a small bunch of fresh coriander, chopped, to serve

1 Heat the soy and honey together gently in a small pan or microwave.
2 Preheat the grill to medium. Heat a small frying-pan and spray with low-fat cooking spray then stir-fry the onion for 4 minutes until softened. Blend the onion, sesame seeds, ginger and chilli flakes, if using, in a pestle and mortar or spice grinder, to make a paste.
3 Lay the aubergine slices on the grill pan and spray with low-fat cooking spray then brush with a little of the soy and honey mixture. Grill for 5 minutes until browned.
4 Turn the slices over and spray again with low-fat cooking spray then brush with the remaining soy and honey mixture and grill for another 5 minutes.
5 Spread the sesame mixture over the aubergine slices and grill for another 2–5 minutes until hot and golden.
6 To serve, lay two pieces of aubergine on each serving plate, drizzle a little soy sauce over and scatter with fresh coriander.

Thai red curry

| **2** Points per serving | Points per recipe **8** |

Ⓥ Serves 4 ● Preparation time 20 minutes ● Cooking time 20 minutes ● Calories per serving 130 ● Freezing not recommended *A fresh-tasting vegetarian Thai curry with a hot kick. Serve with cooked Thai fragrant rice, adding 3 points per 4 tablespoon serving.*

2 tablespoons red curry paste
6 medium shallots, chopped finely
2 medium red peppers, de-seeded and diced finely
2 medium carrots, peeled and cut into matchsticks
300 ml (½ pint) vegetable stock
2 dried or fresh kaffir lime leaves or zest of 1
   lemon or 2 limes
100 g (3½ oz) mushrooms
150 g can sliced bamboo shoots, rinsed and drained
100 ml (3½ fl oz) reduced-fat coconut milk
300 ml (½ pint) soya milk
200 g (7 oz) beansprouts
2 heads bok choy, sliced
a small bunch of fresh coriander, chopped

1 Heat a large frying-pan or wok and add the curry paste; dry-fry for 30 seconds. Add the shallots, red peppers and carrots and stir-fry over a high heat for 2 minutes until just browning on the edges, then add the stock and lime leaves.

2 Bring to the boil and simmer for 5 minutes then add the mushrooms, bamboo shoots, coconut milk and soya milk. Cook for a further 15 minutes on a low heat but do not allow to boil.

3 Add the beansprouts and bok choy and cook for 2 minutes, then stir in the coriander and serve.

Top tips Bok choy is a Chinese green leafy vegetable now available in most large supermarkets in the fresh vegetable section.

Soya milk can also be bought in supermarkets. It comes in cartons and is usually found with the long-life milk/powdered milk. Buy the unsweetened version.

Spring vegetables with crusty polenta

| **2½** Points per serving | Points per recipe **10½** |

Ⓥ Serves 4 ● Preparation time 10 minutes + 1 hour cooling for polenta ● Cooking time 20 minutes ● Calories per serving 205 ● Freezing not recommended *The quick-cook, 'instant' polenta is very easy to prepare and makes a welcome change from potatoes, rice and pasta in your diet.*

For the polenta
200 g pack of polenta
3–4 fresh sage leaves, chopped
low-fat cooking spray
fresh thyme leaves
salt and freshly ground black pepper
For the vegetables
low-fat cooking spray
8 baby leeks or spring onions, halved lengthways
200 g (7 oz) small, young asparagus spears
200 g (7 oz) mushrooms, preferably wild
2 tablespoons balsamic vinegar
150 ml (5 fl oz) vegetable stock
salt and freshly ground black pepper

1 Make the polenta according to the packet instructions. Season and stir in the chopped sage. Line a shallow dish or baking tray with clingfilm, pour in the polenta and leave to cool and set for at least 1 hour.

2 Preheat the grill or a griddle pan to high and spray with low-fat cooking spray to prevent sticking. Turn out the set polenta and cut into 4 or 8 thin slices. Grill for 4 minutes on each side until crusty.

3 Meanwhile, heat a large frying-pan or wok over a high heat and spray with the low-fat cooking spray. Stir-fry all the vegetables for 4–5 minutes until turning brown at the edges. Season then pour in the vinegar and stir-fry another minute. Add the stock and boil vigorously for 2 minutes.

4 Place the grilled polenta on four serving plates, spoon the vegetables over, scatter with fresh thyme leaves and serve.

Top tip Wild mushrooms can be found in the fresh vegetable section of most supermarkets and in delicatessans.

Perfect roast potatoes

4½ Points per serving	Points per recipe 18½

Ⓥ Serves 4 ● Preparation time 20 minutes ● Cooking time 1 hour ● Calories per serving 290 ● Freezing not recommended *Always popular, but these have fewer points than the traditional roast potatoes – and they taste just as good.*

    1 kg (2 1b 4 oz) peeled potatoes, each cut into 3
        even-sized pieces
    8 teaspoons olive oil
    1 tablespoon plain flour
    low-fat cooking spray
    salt and freshly ground black pepper

1 Boil the potatoes in plenty of boiling salted water for 10 minutes.

2 Preheat the oven to Gas Mark 7/220°C/425°F and heat a large baking tray with the olive oil in it.

3 Drain the potatoes and return them to the saucepan. Cover with a lid and shake them about to soften their edges a bit, then sprinkle over the flour, replace the lid and shake again to part-coat.

4 Carefully remove the hot baking tray from oven and transfer the potatoes on to it. Season well and turn the potatoes to coat them in oil. Spray with low-fat cooking spray and roast for 30 minutes.

5 Remove from the oven, turn the potatoes, spray again and return to the oven for another 30 minutes after which they should be golden brown and crispy on the outside, but soft in the middle.

Brussels sprouts with chestnuts

1 Point per serving	Points per recipe 5½

Ⓥ if using vegetarian crème fraîche ● Serves 6 ● Preparation and cooking time 20 minutes ● Calories per serving 75 ● Freezing not recommended *Delicious at any time of the year but the perfect seasonal accompaniment to the Christmas roast turkey; see page 103.*

    700 g (1 lb 9 oz) Brussels sprouts, washed and trimmed
    100 g pack vacuum-sealed chestnuts
    4 tablespoons half-fat crème fraîche
    a pinch of freshly grated nutmeg
    salt and freshly ground black pepper

1 Bring a large pan of salted water to the boil. Make a cross in the bottom of the Brussels sprouts with a sharp knife, add to the water and cook for 10 minutes until just tender.

2 Drain and return to the hot pan. Add the chestnuts, crème fraîche, a pinch of nutmeg and season. Toss together and serve.

Notice how your clothes feel, instead of relying on the scales to tell you about a weight gain or loss

We are all eating more and more noodles, pasta, rice and bean dishes and this chapter is devoted to illustrating their versatility and the wide array of flavours that can be created with them.

oodles of noodles, rice and

beans

Spaghetti meatballs

8 Points per serving	Points per recipe **31½**

Serves 4 ● Preparation time 20 minutes ● Cooking time 25 minutes ● Calories per serving 465 ● Freezing recommended for the meatballs and sauce only *Ideal for a cold wintery evening!*

low-fat cooking spray
300 g (10½ oz) spaghetti
For the meatballs
2 medium courgettes, grated
400 g (14 oz) extra-lean minced beef
2 garlic cloves, crushed
1 medium onion, chopped finely
1 egg white
2 tablespoons Worcestershire sauce
a small bunch of basil, chopped, plus extra to garnish
salt and freshly ground black pepper
For the sauce
400 g can chopped tomatoes
150 ml (5 fl oz) stock
4 sun-dried tomatoes, soaked for 10 minutes in boiling
    water then chopped, soaking liquid reserved
1 tablespoon clear honey

1 Place all the meatball ingredients in a bowl and mix together well. Roll small amounts into meatballs about the size of golf balls and place on a tray sprayed with the low-fat cooking spray.

2 Heat a large frying-pan and spray with the cooking spray. Gently fry a few meatballs at a time for about 10 minutes, turning them until browned all over.

3 Remove with a slotted spoon to a clean tray. Set aside.

4 To make the sauce, drain any oil left in the frying-pan but do not wash it. Add the sauce ingredients, stir well, scraping up any meat juices. Bring to the boil.

5 Simmer for 10 minutes. Add the meatballs and seasoning and simmer for a further 15 minutes, stirring occasionally to ensure that the meatballs don't stick.

6 Meanwhile, cook the spaghetti according to the packet instructions. Drain, reserving 4 tablespoons of the cooking liquid. Add the reserved liquid to the tomato sauce.

7 To serve, pile the spaghetti on plates and top with the meatballs in sauce, then scatter with basil.

Nasi goreng

7 Points per serving	Points per recipe **28½**

Serves 4 ● Preparation and cooking time 15 minutes ●
Calories per serving 430 ● Freezing not recommended
*Nasi goreng means 'fried rice' in Indonesia where
it is enjoyed as a quick family meal.*

4 teaspoons Indonesian or Thai red curry paste
250 g (9 oz) pork fillet, cut into thin strips
200 g (7 oz) frozen cooked, peeled prawns, thawed
600 g (1 lb 5 oz) rice, cooked (240 g/8½ oz uncooked weight)
1 tablespoon soy sauce
200 g (7 oz) frozen petit pois, defrosted
2 medium eggs, beaten
a small bunch of fresh coriander, chopped, to garnish

1 Heat the curry paste in a wok or large frying-pan then
add the pork and stir fry for 4–5 minutes, until cooked
through.
2 Add all the other ingredients, except the eggs and
stir-fry for 5 minutes then push everything to one side of
the wok or pan and pour in the eggs. Stir until lightly set
like scrambled egg, then stir in the other ingredients.
3 Scatter with chopped coriander and serve.

Chicken biryani

6 Points per serving	Points per recipe **24½**

Serves 4 ● Preparation time 40 minutes ● Cooking time
50 minutes ● Calories per serving 430 ● Freezing not
recommended *A delicious and satisfying supper.*

For the rice
low-fat cooking spray
4 cloves
4 cm (1½-inch) cinnamon stick
2 garlic cloves
4 cm (1½-inch) root ginger, peeled
300 g (10½ oz) basmati rice, rinsed and drained
For the chicken
2 boneless, skinless chicken breasts weighing 175 g (6 oz)
   each, cut into bite-size pieces
150 ml (5 fl oz) low-fat plain yogurt
1 teaspoon cumin powder
1 teaspoon chilli powder
1 teaspoon turmeric powder
2 medium onions, chopped
400 g can chopped tomatoes
2 teaspoons garam masala powder
salt and freshly ground black pepper
To serve (optional)
a small bunch of fresh coriander or mint
1 teaspoon rose water

1 Heat a saucepan and spray with the cooking spray,
then fry the cloves, cinnamon, garlic and ginger for 1
minute. Add the rice and 600 ml (1 pint) of water. Bring
to the boil and simmer for 25 minutes until most of the
water has been absorbed. Cover and cook for a further
5 minutes then turn off the heat and leave.
2 Meanwhile, mix the chicken with the yogurt, seasoning,
cumin, chilli and turmeric and set aside.
3 Heat a large frying-pan. Spray with cooking spray.
Stir-fry the onions until softened. Add the tomatoes and
garam masala. Cook for 10 minutes. Add the chicken
mixture and 300 ml (½ pint) of hot water.
4 Bring to the boil and simmer for 20 minutes until the
sauce is thick and the chicken cooked through.
5 Preheat the oven to Gas Mark 6/200°C/400°F. Layer
the chicken and rice in a deep oven-proof dish, finishing
with a rice layer, then bake for 10 minutes.
6 To serve, sprinkle with fresh coriander or mint and the
rose water, if using.

Turkey pilaff

5½ Points per serving	Points per recipe 21½

Serves 4 ● Preparation and cooking time 35 minutes ●
Calories per serving 340 ● Freezing not recommended
*A 'pilaff' or 'pilau' is a Central Asian or Middle
Eastern rice dish with many variations.*

> 250 g (9 oz) long-grain rice, rinsed and drained
> 1.2 litres (2 pints) chicken stock
> low-fat cooking spray
> 200 g (7 oz) turkey mince
> 1 tablespoon Worcestershire sauce
> 2 bay leaves
> 1 onion, chopped
> 50 g (1¾ oz) raisins
> 25 g (1 oz) flaked almonds, toasted
> ½ teaspoon ground cinnamon
> salt and freshly ground black pepper
> a small bunch of fresh coriander or mint,
>   chopped, to serve (optional)

1 Place the rice in a saucepan with the stock, bring to
the boil and then simmer for 20 minutes, until all the
stock has been absorbed and the rice is tender.
2 Meanwhile, heat a large frying-pan and spray with the
low-fat cooking spray then add the mince, seasoning,
Worcestershire sauce and bay leaves and stir-fry for
5 minutes until golden brown and cooked through.
Remove from the pan and set aside. Discard the bay
leaves.
3 Spray the frying-pan again with the low-fat cooking
spray and stir-fry the onion for 4 minutes until softened,
then add the raisins, almonds and cinnamon. Return
the turkey mixture and cooked rice to the pan, stir well
together and cook for 1 minute until warmed through.
4 Serve sprinkled with chopped coriander or mint, if
using.

Variation Try using vegetarian mince, available frozen
from supermarkets, for a meat-free version that meat-
eaters would be hard-pushed to notice. With Quorn the
points per serving will be 3.

Spicy tomato rice

3 Points per serving	Points per recipe 13

Ⓥ Serves 4 ● Preparation time 5 minutes ● Cooking
time 25 minutes ● Calories per serving 290 ● Freezing
not recommended *This rice dish can either be served
as a light, vegetarian meal accompanied by some
steamed vegetables or as an accompaniment to
meat or fish. Don't forget to add on the extra points.*

> low-fat cooking spray
> 2 large onions, chopped
> 2 garlic cloves, chopped
> 2 × 400 g cans chopped tomatoes
> 1 teaspoon cumin seeds, dry-fried until they pop
> 1 teaspoon caster sugar
> 250 g (9 oz) long-grain rice, rinsed and drained
> salt and freshly ground black pepper

1 Heat a large saucepan and spray with the low-fat
cooking spray then fry the onions and garlic for about
4 minutes until softened. Add all the other ingredients
and 850 ml (1½ pints) water.
2 Bring to the boil and then simmer for 20 minutes or
until most of the liquid has been absorbed and the rice
is tender, then serve.

Variation Add 50 g (1¾ oz) sun-dried tomatoes for a
more intense tomato flavour. The points per serving
will be 3½.

Relax, visualise and set goals...

Menu plan

Sunshine Food

~

Cold Cucumber and Mint Soup, page 20
1 serving . . . 1½ points

~

Paella, page 75
(pictured here)
1 serving . . . 5½ points

~

Summer Berry Mousse Cake, page 163
1 serving . . . 2 points

Total points per meal 9 points

Paella

5½ Points per serving	Points per recipe **23**

Serves 4 ● Preparation time 25 minutes ● Cooking time 25 minutes ● Calories per serving 550 ● Freezing not recommended *Paella is the national dish of Spain and is traditionally cooked in a large, open, shallow pan called a paellera. Rice and saffron are the only essential ingredients as it can be made with just vegetables, meat, fish or a mixture of all three.*

low fat cooking spray
2 medium skinless chicken breasts, cut into bite-size pieces
1 medium onion, chopped
1 medium red pepper, de-seeded and chopped
3 garlic cloves, crushed
3 medium ripe tomatoes, chopped
a generous pinch of saffron
2 teaspoons paprika
a small bunch of thyme, woody stems removed, chopped
250 g (9 oz) rice, preferably brown or long-grain and wild mixed
1.2 litres (2 pints) chicken stock
400 g (14 oz) frozen seafood, defrosted
125 g (4½ oz) frozen peas
salt and freshly ground black pepper
lemon wedges, to serve

1 Spray a large pan with the low-fat cooking spray then sauté the chicken pieces for 5 minutes, stirring frequently. Season, then remove from the pan and set aside.

2 Spray the pan again with the low-fat cooking spray then stir-fry the onion, red pepper and garlic for 5 minutes or until softened. Then add the tomatoes, saffron, paprika and thyme and cook for a further 2 minutes.

3 Add the rice and stir until well mixed in then add half the stock. Bring to the boil then simmer for 10 minutes. Add the rest of the stock and the chicken and cook for a further 10 minutes, without stirring. Lastly add the seafood and the peas, stir once, gently, and cook for 5 minutes or until the rice is tender.

4 Taste to check the seasoning and serve with lemon wedges.

Bacon and mushroom risotto

8 Points per serving	Points per recipe **16½**

Serves 2 ● Preparation time 20 minutes ● Cooking time 25 minutes ● Calories per serving 450 ● Freezing not recommended *An easy supper dish made from rice cooked in stock with mushrooms and crispy bacon.*

4 medium rashers of lean back bacon
100 g (3½ oz) mushrooms, sliced
juice of 1 lemon
2 dried mushrooms (porcini), soaked in 150 ml (5 fl oz) boiling water for 10 minutes
low-fat cooking spray
1 medium onion, chopped finely
175 g (6 oz) risotto rice
150 ml (5 fl oz) white wine
300 ml (½ pint) hot stock
a small bunch of parsley, chopped
salt and freshly ground black pepper

1 Preheat the grill to high, grill the bacon until crispy then chop into little pieces. Set to one side. Meanwhile, heat a frying-pan and add the sliced mushrooms. Season and stir-fry for 5 minutes then add the lemon juice and cook for 1 minute until absorbed. Set aside.

2 Drain the porcini, reserving the soaking liquid. Chop finely and add to the cooked mushrooms.

3 Heat a saucepan and spray with the low-fat cooking spray then fry the onion for 4 minutes, until softened. Add the rice, stir, then pour in the wine and porcini soaking liquid and stir vigorously. Add the warmed stock a ladleful at a time after the stock is absorbed which should take about 5 minutes. Stir between each addition. It will take around 20 minutes before all the stock is absorbed.

4 Stir in the cooked mushrooms, bacon and chopped parsley, check the seasoning and then serve.

Variation Serve with a few shavings of fresh Parmesan (10 g per person) and add 1 point per serving.

Pad Thai noodles

7 Points per serving	Points per recipe **14**

Serves 2 ● Preparation and cooking time 20 minutes + 30 minutes soaking ● Calories per serving 505 ● Freezing not recommended *Versions of this Thai noodle dish vary widely in terms of ingredients. An authentic version should combine sweet and tart flavours using prawns, spring onions and beansprouts against a backdrop of tender noodles.*

175 g (6 oz) flat rice noodles
low-fat cooking spray
2 garlic cloves, chopped finely
½ teaspoon chilli flakes
100 g (3½ oz) raw prawns, without shells
2 medium eggs, beaten
2 tablespoons fish sauce
1 tablespoon light brown sugar
4 spring onions, cut into 5 cm (2-inch) lengths then shredded finely
50 g (1¾ oz) beansprouts
a small bunch of fresh coriander, chopped

1 Soak the noodles in cold water for 30 minutes, then drain and set aside. Heat a wok or large frying-pan and spray with the low-fat cooking spray. Add the garlic, chilli and prawns and stir-fry for 2–3 minutes, until the prawns are pink.
2 Pour in the eggs and stir-fry for a few seconds until they just begin to look scrambled, then add the noodles, fish sauce and sugar and toss together.
3 Add the spring onions, beansprouts and coriander and toss together again, then serve.

Variations You could use cooked prawns but add them with the noodles at Step 2.

You could use egg noodles rather than the rice noodles, cooked according to the packet instructions. The points per serving will be 6½.

Quick peanut noodles

6 Points per serving	Points per recipe **24**

Ⓥ Serves 4 ● Preparation and cooking time 25 minutes ● Calories per serving 390 ● Freezing not recommended *In this recipe noodles are tossed with raw shredded vegetables and served with a light lime, peanut and soy sauce for a fresh-tasting and quick lunch or supper.*

300 g (10½ oz) medium egg noodles
low-fat cooking spray
2 medium carrots, shredded
½ medium cucumber, shredded
a bunch of spring onions, chopped into 2.5 cm (1-inch) lengths then shredded
a small bunch of fresh coriander, chopped
For the sauce
2 tablespoons crunchy peanut butter
juice of 2 limes
2 tablespoons soy sauce
1 teaspoon dried chilli flakes

1 Cook the noodles according to the packet instructions then drain.
2 Meanwhile, make the sauce. Put all the ingredients in a small saucepan and heat gently, stirring, until the peanut butter melts. Stir in 4 tablespoons water to give a fairly thin consistency.
3 Heat a wok or large frying-pan and spray with the low-fat cooking spray, add the noodles and vegetables and toss together then pour the sauce over and sprinkle in the fresh coriander. Toss together again then serve.

Watch your portion sizes –

part of healthy eating is knowing when to stop

Chinese pork noodles

5 Points per serving	Points per recipe **20**

Serves 4 ● Preparation time 10 minutes + overnight marinating ● Cooking time 25–30 minutes ● Calories per serving 380 ● Freezing not recommended *This marinated pork makes a fragrant and rich supper dish. Serve with spinach, cooked until just wilted and/or a little soy sauce or some crunchy blanched broccoli.*

400 g (14 oz) pork tenderloin, cut into 7.5 cm (3-inch) strips
2 tablespoons soy sauce
1 tablespoon tomato ketchup
1 teaspoon brown sugar
1 tablespoon clear honey
3 tablespoons hoisin sauce
2 garlic cloves, crushed
1 tablespoon sweet sherry
1 teaspoon salt
200 g pack egg noodles, cooked according to packet instructions
1 teaspoon sesame seeds, toasted
a small bunch of fresh coriander, chopped, to garnish (optional)

1 Place the pork in a bowl with the soy, ketchup, sugar, honey, 1 tablespoon of the hoisin, garlic, sherry and salt. Toss around to mix well and then refrigerate overnight, turning the pork a couple of times so the liquid can really soak in.

2 Preheat the oven to Gas Mark 7/220°C/425°F. Place the pork strips in the oven on a grill rack with a foil-lined tray underneath to catch the drips.

3 Roast for 15 minutes, then turn the heat down to Gas Mark 4/180°C/350°F and cook a further 10–15 minutes, until just cooked through. Brush the meat frequently with the marinade to get a baked-on coating of the sauce.

4 Meanwhile toss the noodles in the remaining 2 tablespoons hoisin sauce. Slice the cooked pork strips diagonally and arrange on top of the noodles. Sprinkle with a few toasted sesame seeds and the fresh coriander and serve.

Chicken chow mein

5 Points per serving   Points per recipe **20½**

Serves 4 ● Preparation and cooking time 30 minutes ●
Calories per serving 420 ● Freezing not recommended
Forget the Chinese take-away!

    300 g (10½ oz) egg noodles
    1 teaspoon sesame oil
    low-fat cooking spray
    4 spring onions, sliced finely
    1 tablespoon oyster sauce
    200 g (7 oz) chicken mince
    400 g (14 oz) Savoy cabbage, shredded thinly
    150 g (5½ oz) oyster, shiitake or button mushrooms,
      sliced thinly
    2 medium carrots, cut into matchsticks
    125 ml (4 fl oz) hot chicken stock
    2 tablespoons soy sauce

1 Cook the noodles according to the packet instructions,
drain and toss with the sesame oil.
2 Heat a wok or large frying-pan and spray with the
low-fat cooking spray, stir-fry the spring onions, oyster
sauce and mince for 3–4 minutes.
3 Add the cabbage, mushrooms, carrots and stock,
cover and simmer for 3–4 minutes, or until the carrots
are just tender. Uncover and cook for 3 minutes more,
or until the liquid has evaporated.
4 Stir in the soy, add the noodles and stir-fry until
heated through. Serve immediately.

Variations Try using spinach, peas, bamboo shoots or
beansprouts.
    Any fish or meat can be used, for example pork
(5½ points per serving) or turkey mince (5 points per
serving) or raw, shelled prawns (5 points per serving).

Honeyed pork stir-fry

5 Points per serving   Points per recipe **20½**

Serves 4 ● Preparation and cooking time 20 minutes ●
Calories per serving 385 ● Freezing not recommended
*A very versatile recipe to which you can add your
favourite point-free vegetables.*

    low-fat cooking spray
    1 teaspoon sesame oil
    2 garlic cloves, sliced
    400 g (14 oz) pork tenderloin, sliced thinly
    1 tablespoon honey
    4 tablespoons soy sauce
    2.5 cm (1-inch) fresh root ginger, sliced into matchsticks
    100 g (3½ oz) mange-tout peas, sliced into thin strips
    2 medium carrots, sliced into matchsticks
    100 g (3½ oz) baby spinach, rinsed and drained
    a bunch of spring onions, shredded
    200 g pack noodles, cooked according to pack instructions
    2 tablespoons seasoned rice vinegar or lemon juice

1 Heat a wok or large frying-pan and spray with the
low-fat cooking spray then add the sesame oil. Add the
garlic and pork and stir-fry over a high heat for 4 minutes,
then add the honey, soy and ginger and cook for a further
2 minutes.
2 Add the vegetables and toss together. Roughly cut up
the cooked noodles with a pair of scissors and add them
with the rice vinegar or lemon juice then toss together
and serve immediately.

Top tip Fresh root ginger keeps for up to 3 months in
the freezer. Whenever you need some, just take it out,
slice the required amount off and put the remaining root
back in the freezer.
Variations You could use turkey or a skinless chicken
breast instead of the pork and any shredded vegetables
that you fancy, e.g. cabbage, green beans, fennel,
asparagus, spinach etc. The points remain the same.

Crab and ginger noodles

5½ Points per serving	Points per recipe 11

Serves 2 ● Preparation and cooking time 20 minutes ● Calories per serving 460 ● Freezing not recommended *The combination of crab meat, fresh ginger, crunchy beansprouts, hot chilli and noodles is both luxurious, tantalising and surprisingly low in points.*

175 g (6 oz) egg noodles
low-fat cooking spray
1 garlic clove, sliced
200 g (7 oz) bok choy or spring greens or spinach, rinsed, drained and sliced
120 g can white crab meat, drained
2.5 cm (1-inch) piece of fresh root ginger, peeled and grated coarsely
3 tablespoons oyster sauce
½ teaspoon dried chilli flakes
100 g (3½ oz) beansprouts

1 Cook the noodles according to the packet instructions.
2 Meanwhile, heat a wok or large frying-pan and spray with the low-fat cooking spray. Fry the garlic for 1 minute until turning golden, then add the bok choy, crab, ginger, oyster sauce, chilli and beansprouts.
3 Stir-fry together for a couple of minutes then serve with the drained noodles.

Spaghetti bolognese

5½ Points per serving	Points per recipe 22½

Serves 4 ● Preparation time 15 minutes ● Cooking time 30 minutes ● Calories per serving 435 ● Freezing recommended *This low-Point version of spaghetti bolognese will save you plenty of points compared with the full-fat version and is equally delicious.*

low-fat cooking spray
2 medium onions, chopped finely
2 garlic cloves, chopped finely
400 g (14 oz) turkey mince
3 medium carrots, chopped finely
2 celery sticks, chopped finely
400 g can chopped tomatoes
2 tablespoons tomato purée
leaves from 2 sprigs fresh thyme (or 1 teaspoon dried)
150 ml (5 fl oz) red wine
2 tablespoons Worcestershire sauce
250 g (9 oz) spaghetti
a small bunch of fresh parsley
salt and freshly ground black pepper

1 Heat a large frying-pan and spray with low-fat cooking spray. Fry the onions and garlic for 5 minutes until softened. Add the turkey mince and fry until it is browned all over, breaking it up with the back of a wooden spoon
2 Add the carrots, celery, tomatoes, tomato purée, thyme, seasoning, red wine and Worcestershire sauce. Stir together and leave to simmer for 30 minutes.
3 While the sauce is simmering, cook the spaghetti according to the packet instructions, then drain.
4 Check the sauce for seasoning, stir in the fresh parsley and serve with the spaghetti.

Variations Use lean beef (6½ points per serving) or lamb mince (8 points per serving).

Pasta primavera

| **5** Points per serving | Points per recipe **19½** |

v if using vegetarian cheese ● Serves 4 ● Preparation and cooking time 15 minutes ● Calories per serving 430 ● Freezing not recommended *Primavera means 'spring' in Italian and this pasta recipe will fill you with the joys of spring as you crunch on all the fresh, young vegetables.*

> 350 g (12 oz) pasta shapes
> low-fat cooking spray
> 200 g (7 oz) asparagus, cut into 2.5 cm (1-inch) lengths
> 300 g (10½ oz) sugar snap peas
> 300 g (10½ oz) baby carrots, trimmed
> 2 tablespoons white wine
> 100 g (3½ oz) low-fat soft cheese
> a small bunch of fresh dill, chopped
> salt and freshly ground black pepper

1 Cook the pasta in plenty of boiling salted water according to the packet instructions, then drain.
2 Spray a wok or large frying-pan with the low-fat cooking spray and put on a medium heat. Stir-fry all the vegetables for a few minutes then add the white wine and toss.
3 Gently stir in the soft cheese and cook for a further 2 minutes. Season, toss with the pasta and fresh dill then serve.

Variations Any spring vegetables could be used in this recipe as long as they are very quick to cook; green beans, mange-tout peas, baby spinach would work especially well.

Use tarragon instead of dill for a hint of aniseed.

Roasted tomato pasta

| **5** Points per serving | Points per recipe **20** |

v Serves 4 ● Preparation time 15 minutes ● Cooking time 20 minutes ● Calories per serving 405 ● Freezing not recommended *A quick-to-prepare supper dish for the summer, when you can buy really tasty deep red tomatoes.*

> 1 kg (2 lb 4 oz) ripe tomatoes
> low-fat cooking spray
> 4 garlic cloves, sliced into slivers
> 2 teaspoons caster sugar
> 2 teaspoons olive oil
> 2 tablespoons balsamic vinegar
> 350 g (12 oz) pasta ribbons
> a large bunch of fresh basil, chopped roughly
> salt and freshly ground black pepper

1 Preheat the oven to Gas Mark 6/200°C/400°F. Halve the tomatoes around their circumference and place in a deep baking tray sprayed with low-fat cooking spray.
2 Push slivers of garlic into the tomato flesh, about 2 slivers per half. Season with plenty of salt and pepper and the sugar, then drizzle over the oil and vinegar. Bake for 20 minutes or until the tomatoes have softened and the garlic turned golden brown.
3 Meanwhile, cook the pasta in plenty of boiling salted water, then drain reserving about 4 tablespoons of the cooking water. Toss the pasta and water with the tomatoes in their baking tray, scraping up any stuck-on juices.
4 Add the basil, toss again then serve.

If you're on a tight budget, buy fruits and vegetables when they're in season; look out for special offers in the shops or buy from the market

Creamy mushroom tagliatelle

| **4½** Points per serving | Points per recipe **17½** |

V if using vegetarian fromage frais ● Serves 4 ● Preparation and cooking time 20 minutes ● Calories per serving 350 ● Freezing not recommended *A very quick, easy and satisfying pasta dish with only a few ingredients.*

350 g (12 oz) tagliatelle
low-fat cooking spray
2 garlic cloves, chopped
450 g (1 lb) mushrooms, sliced
juice of ½ lemon
4 tablespoons virtually fat-free fromage frais
salt and freshly ground black pepper
a small bunch of chives, chopped finely, to garnish (optional)

1 Cook the pasta in plenty of boiling salted water according to the packet instructions.
2 Meanwhile, heat a large frying-pan and spray with the low-fat cooking spray and fry the garlic for 1 minute, until turning golden.
3 Add the mushrooms, season and stir-fry on a high heat for 4 minutes until they are soft and have absorbed all their juices. Add the lemon juice and cook for a further minute then turn off the heat and stir in the fromage frais.
4 Drain the pasta, reserving a few tablespoon of the cooking liquid, then toss in the sauce and check the seasoning. Serve garnished with chopped chives, if using.

Top tip When making pasta sauces, always try to reserve a few tablespoon of the pasta cooking liquid to add to the sauce. It improves the sauce's texture and helps it to bind to the pasta.

Spicy pasta and cockles

| **5** Points per serving | Points per recipe **20** |

Serves 4 ● Preparation and cooking time 25 minutes ● Calories per serving 405 ● Freezing not recommended *A scrumptious, quick and spicy recipe, good for lunch or dinner.*

350 g (12 oz) spaghetti (or tagliatelle)
low-fat cooking spray
2 garlic cloves, crushed
4 medium courgettes, diced finely
1 small red chilli, de-seeded and chopped finely
2 × 205 g jars of cockles, rinsed and drained
2 tablespoons soy sauce
juice of 1 lime
salt
a small bunch of fresh coriander or parsley, chopped, to garnish (optional)

1 Cook the spaghetti in plenty of boiling salted water according to the packet instructions, until just tender.
2 Meanwhile, heat a large frying-pan and spray with the low-fat cooking spray, fry the garlic for 1 minute, then add the courgettes and stir-fry for 4 minutes until golden brown round the edges.
3 Add the chilli, cockles and soy and stir-fry a further 2 minutes, then add the lime juice and take off the heat.
4 Drain the pasta, add the cockles and sauce to the pan and toss together. Serve immediately, sprinkled with coriander or parsley, if using.

4 Points per serving	Points per recipe **16½**

ⓥ Serves 4 ● Preparation and cooking time 45 minutes ●
Calories per serving 345 ● Freezing not recommended
A creamy dish with very little fat at all!

500 g (1 lb 2 oz) pumpkin, peeled, de-seeded and cut
    into 2.5 cm (1-inch) cubes
2 medium red peppers, de-seeded and cut into 5 cm
    (2-inch) strips
low-fat cooking spray
1 medium onion, chopped finely
1 garlic clove, chopped finely
300 g (10½ oz) risotto rice
125 ml (4 fl oz) dry white wine
1 litre (1¾ pint) boiling vegetable stock
salt and freshly ground black pepper
a small bunch of parsley, chopped, to garnish (optional)

1 Preheat the oven to Gas Mark 7/220°C/425°F. Put the
pumpkin and peppers on a large baking tray, season and
spray with cooking spray. Roast for 10 minutes then turn
and roast a further 10 minutes until just tender.
2 Heat a large frying-pan and spray with the cooking
spray. Stir-fry the onion and garlic on a low heat for 5
minutes until softened. Add the rice. Mix together.
3 Turn the heat to high, pour in the wine and stir-fry for
a further 2 minutes until all the wine has been absorbed.
4 Reduce the heat to medium. Add a ladleful of hot
stock to just cover the rice. Stir until absorbed. Repeat
until all the stock is used.
5 The rice should now be tender but still firm to the
bite. Gently fold in the roasted vegetables, check the
seasoning and sprinkle with parsley to serve.

Grilled vegetable penne

6 Points per serving	Points per recipe **25**

ⓥ if using vegetarian cheese ● Serves 4 ● Preparation and cooking time 25 minutes ● Calories per serving 460 ● Freezing not recommended *This dish is also very good cold as then the flavours have time to mingle and mellow.*

350 g (12 oz) penne or other pasta shapes
2 medium red onions, cut into wedges
225 g (8 oz) courgettes, cut diagonally into 1 cm (½-inch) slices
2 medium red peppers, de-seeded and cut diagonally into 1 cm (½-inch) strips
1 garlic bulb, split into cloves but not peeled
low-fat cooking spray
50 g (1¾ oz) fresh Parmesan cheese, grated finely
For the dressing
2 tablespoons balsamic vinegar
2 teaspoons olive oil
a small bunch of fresh mint, chopped
salt and freshly ground black pepper

1 Cook the pasta in plenty of boiling salted water according to the packet instructions, then drain.
2 Meanwhile, preheat the grill to high and arrange the vegetables in one layer over the grill pan. You may have to grill the vegetables in two lots as you want to grill them in a single layer.
3 Season well and spray with the low-fat cooking spray then grill for 4–5 minutes until blackened at the edges and tender. Set aside and repeat with the rest of the vegetables until they are all grilled.
4 Add the cooked pasta and dressing ingredients to the bowl, toss together and serve with the Parmesan grated over the top.

Top tips Do not eat the whole, cooked garlic. Squash the cloves with your fork until they split then discard the skins and stir the flesh into the pasta.

Although using the grill is easier, the vegetables in this recipe taste best if they are cooked on a griddle pan or BBQ as they need to dry out and become quite charred.

Cheesy red pepper pasta

5½ Points per serving	Points per recipe **21½**

ⓥ if using vegetarian cheese ● Serves 4 ● Preparation and cooking time 25 minutes ● Calories per serving 395 ● Freezing not recommended *A very speedy pasta sauce that doesn't require any cooking but is creamy and satisfying.*

350 g (12 oz) pasta shapes
4 sun-dried tomatoes, soaked in 4 tablespoons boiling water for 10 minutes, then chopped, soaking liquid reserved
3 medium skinless roasted red peppers from a can or jar (or freshly roasted ones)
2 tablespoons balsamic vinegar
a small bunch of fresh basil, chopped
110 g (4 oz) plain cottage cheese
salt and freshly ground black pepper

1 Cook the pasta according to the packet instructions. (see Top tip before draining).
2 Meanwhile, whizz the sun-dried tomatoes with the roasted peppers, vinegar and seasoning for a few seconds in a food processor, until a smooth purée.
3 Drain the pasta, leaving a few tablespoons of the cooking liquid in the pan, then return the pasta to the pan.
4 Add the sauce, basil and cottage cheese and toss together, then serve with more black pepper ground over the top.

Top tip Adding a little of the pasta cooking liquid to the sauce is an Italian trick to help the sauce to stick to the pasta better when they are tossed together.

Prawn and ginger noodles

4 Points per serving	Points per recipe **17**

Serves 4 ● Preparation and cooking time 15 minutes ●
Calories per serving 355 ● Freezing not recommended
*Prawns with fresh ginger are a wonderful
combination conjuring up images of the East
and sunny climes.*

250 g (9 oz) fine egg noodles
low-fat cooking spray
bunch of spring onions, sliced diagonally
2.5 cm (1-inch) fresh root ginger, peeled and cut into thin
    slivers
2 garlic cloves, sliced
1 medium red chilli, de-seeded and chopped finely (optional)
200 g (7 oz) frozen cooked prawns, defrosted
300 g (10½ oz) sugar snap peas or snow peas, sliced
2 teaspoons sesame oil
juice of 1 lemon
a bunch of fresh coriander, chopped, to garnish

1 Cook the noodles according to pack instructions then
drain, rinse with cold water and drain again.
2 Meanwhile, spray a wok or large frying-pan with the
low-fat cooking spray and put on a high heat. Stir-fry the
spring onions, ginger, garlic and chilli for 2 minutes.
3 Add the prawns, peas, sesame oil and lemon juice
and stir-fry a further 2 minutes then add the noodles
and toss together. Remove from the heat, sprinkle with
coriander and serve.

Quick tomato tuna pasta

5 Points per serving	Points per recipe **21**

Serves 4 ● Preparation time 20 minutes ● Cooking time
15 minutes ● Calories per serving 465 ● Freezing not
recommended *This is one of our staple family meals
as all the ingredients are in the storecupboard and
it can be on the table in less than 30 minutes.*

350 g (12 oz) pasta shapes
low-fat cooking spray
1 large onion, chopped
2 garlic cloves, crushed
2 × 400 g cans chopped tomatoes
2 × 150 g cans tuna steaks in brine, drained
1 teaspoon dried oregano
20 stoned olives in brine, drained and halved (optional)
salt and freshly ground black pepper
a small bunch of fresh parsley or basil, chopped,
    to garnish (optional)

1 Cook the pasta in plenty of boiling salted water
according to the packet instructions.
2 Meanwhile, spray a large frying-pan with the low-fat
cooking spray and fry the onion and garlic for about
5 minutes until softened, adding a few tablespoons of
water if they begin to stick.
3 Add the tomatoes, tuna, oregano, olives and seasoning,
if using. Stir together and break the tuna into chunks.
Bring to the boil then simmer for 15 minutes until thick.
4 Drain the pasta and add to the sauce with 4 tablespoons
of the cooking water. Stir together until well coated with
the sauce and then serve, sprinkled with herbs, if using.

Variation This dish becomes a luxury dinner if you use
2 × 150 g (5½ oz) fresh tuna steaks which should be
grilled first and then flaked into the finished sauce
before tossing with the pasta. The points per serving will
be 5½.

Mushroom and sweet onion pasta

4½ Points per serving   Points per recipe **17½**

V if using vegetarian fromage frais ● Serves 4 ●
Preparation time 20 minutes ● Cooking time 15 minutes
● Calories per serving 375 ● Freezing not recommended
*A lovely, mellow-flavoured pasta, perfect for an
autumnal evening meal.*

350 g (12 oz) pasta shapes
low-fat cooking spray
4 medium onions, sliced
250 g (9 oz) mushrooms, sliced
300 ml (½ pint) vegetable stock
4 tablespoons virtually fat-free fromage frais
leaves from 4 sprigs fresh thyme
salt and freshly ground black pepper

1 Cook the pasta in plenty of boiling salted water
according to the packet instructions.
2 Meanwhile, spray a large frying-pan with the cooking
spray and put on a high heat. Stir-fry the onions and
mushrooms for 5 minutes until they are golden brown,
then add the stock and simmer for 15 minutes.
3 Drain the pasta but add 4 tablespoons of the cooking
liquid to the onion mixture then add the pasta, fromage
frais, thyme and seasoning. Toss and serve.

Variation For a richer flavour use half-fat crème fraîche
instead of the fromage frais. The points per serving
will be 5.

Seafood spaghetti

5½ Points per serving   Points per recipe **22½**

Serves 4 ● Preparation time 20 minutes ● Cooking time
20 minutes ● Calories per serving 480 ● Freezing not
recommended *Take advantage of cooked frozen
seafood in this easy-to-prepare dish.*

350 g (12 oz) spaghetti
low-fat cooking spray
2 medium onions, chopped
2 garlic cloves, crushed
1 medium red chilli, de-seeded and chopped finely
   (optional)
400 g (14 oz) cooked seafood selection, fresh or frozen
   and defrosted
100 ml (3½ fl oz) white wine
2 tablespoons Worcestershire sauce
1 teaspoon caster sugar
2 × 400 g cans chopped tomatoes
4 tablespoons capers, rinsed, drained and patted dry
salt and freshly ground black pepper
a small bunch of fresh basil, to garnish

1 Cook the pasta in plenty of boiling salted water
according to the packet instructions.
2 Meanwhile, spray a large frying-pan with the low-fat
cooking spray and fry the onions, garlic and chilli, if using,
over a medium heat for 5 minutes until the onions are
softened. Add a few tablespoons of water to prevent
them from sticking if necessary.
3 Add the seafood, wine, Worcestershire sauce, sugar,
tomatoes, capers and seasoning and stir together. Bring
to the boil then simmer for 20 minutes or until the sauce
has thickened.
4 Drain the pasta, reserving about 4 tablespoons of
the cooking liquid. Toss the pasta with the sauce and
cooking liquid, sprinkle with basil and serve.

Success is more often the result of hard work than of talent

Tuscan beans

Ⓥ Serves 4 ● Preparation and cooking time 15 minutes ● Calories per serving 170 ● Freezing not recommended *A simple, aromatic garlic and herb bean dish that is great on it's own or as an accompaniment to fish or meat; add the extra points as necessary.*

    low-fat cooking spray
    4 garlic cloves, crushed
    2 × 400 g cans cannellini beans, rinsed and drained,
        or dried beans (see Top tip)
    2 tablespoons olive oil
    3 sage leaves, chopped finely
    juice of ½ lemon
    a small bunch of parsley, chopped
    salt and freshly ground black pepper

1 Heat a large saucepan and spray with the low-fat cooking spray. Fry the garlic for 2 minutes until just softened, then add the beans, olive oil, sage and seasoning and toss together for a few minutes until heated through.
2 Add the lemon juice and parsley, stir and serve.

Top tip This method tells you how to cook dried beans, such as borlotti, cannellini, flack, flageolet, kidney, butter etc.

To serve 4, place 200 g (7 oz) of dried beans in a large bowl, add enough water to cover the beans plus an extra couple of inches. Add a pinch of bicarbonate of soda and leave to soak overnight. Drain and rinse the beans, place in a saucepan, cover with water plus an extra couple of inches. Add half a peeled onion, 2–3 garlic cloves, a handful of mixed herbs (thyme, rosemary, sage, parsley, bay or coriander). Bring to the boil and boil vigorously for 10 minutes. Reduce the heat and simmer for between 50 minutes and 2 hours, topping up the water during cooking time if necessary. Add a teaspoon of salt towards the end of the cooking time (if it is added at the beginning it will cause the beans to remain tough). Cooking time will depend on the type and age of the beans; push the tip of a small knife into a bean to check for tenderness after about 50 minutes. When tender, drain, remove any vegetables and herbs and use the beans as required.

Jamaican potato and beans

Ⓥ Serves 2 ● Preparation time 25 minutes ● Cooking time 30 minutes ● Calories per serving 375 ● Freezing not recommended *This thick, earthy stew is well-loved in Jamaica. It is made with a combination of sweet potato, potato, kidney beans, chilli and coconut. The delicious flavours bring sunny Jamaica a little closer during the winter months.*

    600 ml (1 pint) stock or water
    100 ml (3½ fl oz) reduced-fat coconut milk
    2 medium carrots, cut into 2.5 cm (1-inch) sticks
    1 medium green pepper, de-seeded and sliced
    1 medium onion, chopped finely
    1 medium potato, peeled and diced
    1 bay leaf
    2 sprigs thyme
    2 garlic cloves, chopped
    1 chilli pepper, de-seeded and chopped
    1 medium sweet potato, diced
    1 medium parsnip, cubed
    400 g can kidney beans, drained
    1 tablespoon soy sauce
    salt and freshly ground black pepper

1 Bring the stock or water and coconut milk to the boil in a large saucepan and simmer for 5 minutes. Add the carrots, pepper and onion. Simmer for 10 minutes.
2 Add the potato, bay leaf, thyme, garlic and chilli. Simmer for a further 10 minutes then add the sweet potato and parsnip and simmer for 20 minutes more.
3 When all the vegetables are almost done, add the beans, soy and seasoning and stir well before serving.

Top tip Nearly all the liquid will have evaporated or been absorbed by the end of the cooking time, but add more water if the stew looks too dry before all the vegetables are cooked. If there is too much liquid left after cooking time, then boil the stew rapidly for a few minutes to evaporate the excess.
Variations The beans and vegetables can be varied to include whatever zero point ones you have available.

Boston baked beans and sausages

6 Points per serving	Points per recipe **23½**

Serves 4 ● Preparation time 10 minutes + overnight soaking ● Cooking time 2¼ hours ● Calories per serving 495 ● Freezing not recommended *Don't be put off by the long cooking time, there is very little preparation involved in this simple but satisfying one-pot casserole.*

low-fat cooking spray
1 large onion, chopped
8 reduced-fat sausages
2 garlic cloves, crushed
3 tablespoons molasses
3 tablespoons Dijon or whole-grain mustard
1 tablespoon paprika
2 tablespoons Worcestershire sauce
600 ml (1 pint) tomato juice
300 g (10½ oz) haricot or borlotti beans, soaked overnight
    then rinsed and drained
salt and freshly ground black pepper

1 Preheat the oven to Gas Mark 4/180°C/350°F and heat an ovenproof casserole dish on the hob. Spray the dish with the low-fat cooking spray and fry the onion and sausages for about 10 minutes until the sausages are browned and the onions soft.

2 Add all the other ingredients except the seasoning, stir to combine and bring to the boil. Simmer for 15 minutes then transfer to the oven and cook for a further 2 hours until the beans are tender and the sauce is thick.

3 Taste the sauce and adjust the seasoning if necessary, and serve.

French ham and bean casserole (cassoulet)

2 Points per serving	Points per recipe **9**

Serves 4 ● Preparation time 10 minutes ● Cooking time 15 minutes ● Calories per serving 225 ● Freezing not recommended *Cassoulet is a bean and tomato-based casserole from the Languedoc region in France. This is a very quick cheat's version!*

low-fat cooking spray
2 medium onions, chopped
3 garlic cloves, crushed
400 g can chopped tomatoes
2 tablespoons tomato purée
2 sprigs thyme, woody stems removed, chopped
2 sprigs marjoram, chopped
1 celery stalk, sliced finely
1 bay leaf
200 g (7 oz) thick-sliced lean ham, cubed
2 × 300 g cans haricot beans, rinsed and drained
a small bunch of fresh parsley, chopped
salt and freshly ground black pepper

1 Heat a large frying-pan and spray with the low-fat cooking spray, fry the onions and garlic for 5 minutes until softened, adding a few tablespoons of water to prevent them from sticking, if necessary.
2 Add the tomatoes and tomato purée, thyme, marjoram, celery and bay leaf and bring to the boil, season and simmer for 10 minutes until thick.
3 Add the ham and beans and simmer for a further 5 minutes. Remove the bay leaf, stir in the parsley and serve.

Sardine and bean stew

3½ Points per serving	Points per recipe **14**

Serves 4 ● Preparation time 10 minutes ● Cooking time 25 minutes ● Calories per serving 290 ● Freezing not recommended *A very quick-and-easy, low-point supper dish made from storecupboard ingredients.*

low-fat cooking spray
2 medium onions, chopped
2 garlic cloves, chopped
2 teaspoons ground cumin
2 × 400 g cans chopped tomatoes
1 small red chilli, de-seeded and chopped finely (optional)
2 × 120 g cans sardines in brine, rinsed, drained and patted dry
2 × 400 g cans borlotti beans, drained
salt and freshly ground black pepper
a small bunch of fresh coriander or parsley, to garnish (optional)

1 Heat a large frying-pan with the low-fat cooking spray and fry the onions and garlic for 5 minutes until softened, adding a few tablespoons of water to prevent them from sticking, if necessary.
2 Add the cumin, tomatoes and chilli, bring to the boil then simmer for 20 minutes until thick.
3 Add the sardines and beans and check the seasoning. Simmer for a further 5 minutes, then stir through the coriander or parsley, if using, and serve.

Variation Use cannellini beans instead for 3 points per serving.

Grilled lamb with garlic beans

8 Points per serving	Points per recipe **16½**

Serves 2 ● Preparation and cooking time 25 minutes ●
Calories per serving 530 ● Freezing not recommended
This is a useful way to jazz up a can of flageolet
or other small beans. Here they are served with
grilled lamb chops for a quick supper; just add
the steamed no-point vegetable of your choice.

4 medium lamb loin chops
2 teaspoons pesto sauce
2 teaspoons olive oil
2 garlic cloves, sliced thinly
400 g can haricot blanc or other small beans
salt and freshly ground black pepper
a small bunch of fresh chives, chopped, to garnish (optional)

1 Heat the grill to high and season the lamb chops then
spread with a little pesto and lay on a foil-lined grill pan.
Place under the grill for 3–4 minutes, depending on how
well you like them cooked, then turn over and spread
with a little more pesto and grill for a further 3–4 minutes.
2 Meanwhile, heat the olive oil in a pan and stir-fry the
garlic for a few minutes until lightly golden, then add the
beans and seasoning. Toss together and allow to warm
through for a few minutes. Turn off the heat, cover the
pan and leave to allow the flavours to mingle.
3 Place a large spoonful of the beans on each plate with
two lamb chops and sprinkle with chopped chives, if
using, to serve.

Sweet chilli fish

4½ Points per serving	Points per recipe **19**

Serves 4 ● Preparation and cooking time 35 minutes ●
Calories per serving 380 ● Freezing not recommended
Salmon fillets are perfectly complemented by
the sweet chilli glaze. Delicious on the bed of
creamy beans.

4 medium boneless salmon fillets weighing approximately
    100 g/3½ oz each
a small bunch of coriander or mint, to garnish (optional)
For the sweet chilli glaze
1 teaspoon dried chilli flakes
2 tablespoons brown sugar
2 teaspoons soy sauce
juice of 1 lemon
½ teaspoon ground allspice
For the mixed beans
low-fat cooking spray
2 garlic cloves, chopped
2 teaspoons cumin seeds
1 large red pepper, de-seeded and chopped finely
1 tablespoon paprika
2 × 400 g cans mixed beans, rinsed and drained
4 tablespoons virtually fat-free fromage frais

1 Put all the sweet chilli glaze ingredients in a small pan
and gently bring to the boil. Simmer for 5 minutes until
thickened then remove from the heat.
2 Meanwhile, heat a large frying-pan and spray with the
low-fat cooking spray. Stir-fry the garlic, cumin and red
pepper for 4 minutes until turning golden.
3 Add the paprika, beans and fromage frais and gently
warm through for 2 minutes then turn off the heat,
cover with a lid and leave while you grill the fish.
4 Preheat the grill to hot. Place the salmon fillets, skin-
side-up, on an oiled piece of foil and grill for 2 minutes
on each side. Brush with the chilli glaze and grill for
1 minute more on each side until the glaze begins to
burn. (Watch carefully as this happens very quickly.)
5 Spoon the beans on to separate plates, top with the
salmon and serve garnished with coriander or mint,
if using.

Variation Try canned lentils instead of the mixed beans.
The points per serving will be 5.

Chicken and turkey are both wonderfully versatile ingredients and very low in fat. This chapter is full of great ideas for how to use them and gives you low-point versions of family favourites and more traditional recipes with a slight twist. For more chicken and turkey dishes, turn to Oodles of Noodles, Rice and Beans on page 70.

perfect poultry

Chicken balti

4 Points per serving	Points per recipe **16**

Serves 4 ● Preparation time 20 minutes ● Cooking time 20 minutes ● Calories per serving 260 ● Freezing not recommended A mild, rich curry made with shop-bought balti paste to speed up the preparation. The flavours and textures are far fresher and more interesting than the usual take-away and there's the added advantage of far fewer points too. Serve with 4 tablespoons cooked basmati rice and maybe a tablespoon of low-fat plain yogurt, adding 3 extra points per serving.

low-fat cooking spray
4 medium boneless, skinless chicken breasts, cubed
6 small new potatoes, quartered
1 medium onion, chopped finely
4 garlic cloves, crushed
5 cm (2-inch) piece of fresh root ginger, chopped finely
400 g can chopped tomatoes
300 ml (½ pint) chicken stock
2 tablespoons balti curry paste
1 bunch fresh coriander, chopped
salt and freshly ground black pepper
lemon wedges, to serve

1 Heat a frying-pan and spray with the low-fat cooking spray, then stir-fry the chicken for 4 minutes until golden round the edges and white all over. Add the potatoes, onion, garlic and ginger and fry for a further 4 minutes until turning golden.

2 Add the tomatoes, stock and curry paste and bring to the boil. Simmer gently for 20 minutes until the chicken is tender and cooked through and the sauce thickened.

3 Stir in the coriander, adjust the seasoning if necessary then serve with the lemon wedges.

Jungle curry

| **4** Points per serving | Points per recipe **16** |

Serves 4 ● Preparation time 20 minutes ● Cooking time 15 minutes ● Calories per serving 165 ● Freezing not recommended 'Jungle curry' is the name given to the traditional, very hot curry cooked in the jungles of Thailand. The chicken and aubergine are a modern cook's substitute for wild boar and gathered bamboo shoots. Serve with 4 tablespoons of cooked rice, for 3 extra points per serving.

low-fat cooking spray
500 g (1 lb 2 oz) skinless, boneless chicken thighs,
    fat removed, cut into bite-size pieces
300 ml (½ pint) chicken stock
1 tablespoon Thai fish sauce or Worcestershire sauce
2 dried kaffir lime leaves or the zest of 2 limes
2 medium aubergines, quartered then sliced and placed
    in salted water
a small bunch of fresh coriander, chopped
For the spice paste
2 small birdseye chillis, de-seeded and chopped
    (or 1 teaspoon dried chilli flakes)
1 stalk lemongrass, chopped finely (or 1 teaspoon dried)
2.5 cm (1-inch) piece of fresh root ginger, peeled and
    chopped finely
4 garlic cloves, sliced
3 shallots, sliced

1 First make the spice paste by grinding all the ingredients in a mill on the food processor or in a pestle and mortar.
2 Heat a large frying-pan or wok and spray with the low-fat cooking spray oil. Fry the spice paste for about 30 seconds until aromatic, then add the chicken pieces and stir-fry for 2 minutes until the chicken changes colour. Add the stock, fish or Worcestershire sauce and lime leaves and bring to the boil.
3 Rinse and drain the aubergine and add to the curry. Simmer for 15 minutes until just cooked through. Sprinkle with fresh coriander and serve.

Turkey breast with raspberry sauce

| **6½** Points per serving | Points per recipe **26½** |

Serves 4 ● Preparation and cooking time 25 minutes ● Calories per serving 240 ● Freezing not recommended Raspberries sound unusual for a savoury sauce but game birds are often served with fruity sauces – for example, turkey with cranberry sauce. The tartness of the raspberries complements the escalopes in this very quick and easy recipe. Serve in summer when raspberries are plentiful with 200 g (7 oz) new potatoes per person and beans, adding on 2 extra points per serving.

low-fat cooking spray
4 turkey breast escalopes, weighing approximately
    150 g (5½ oz) each
juice of 1 lemon
1 medium onion, chopped finely
2 medium carrots, chopped finely
150 ml (5 fl oz) stock
1 tablespoon clear honey
100 g (3½ oz) cherry tomatoes, halved
100 g (3½ oz) fresh or frozen raspberries
25 g (1 oz) plain flour
2 tablespoons Worcestershire sauce
salt and freshly ground black pepper

1 Heat a large frying-pan then spray with the low-fat cooking spray, add the turkey escalopes, season and cook for 3 minutes on each side until almost cooked through and golden brown.
2 Add the lemon juice and scrape up any juices stuck to the pan, then add the onion, carrots and stock. Simmer for 4 minutes then add the honey, tomatoes and raspberries. Sprinkle with the flour.
3 Cook for a further 3 minutes, stirring, season and add the Worcestershire sauce. Remove the turkey and put on serving plates. Allow the sauce to continue simmering for a few minutes, then pour over the turkey and serve.

Chinese five-spice chicken

3 Points per serving   Points per recipe **13**

Serves 4 ● Preparation time 10 minutes + 30 minutes – 12 hours marinating ● Cooking time 15 minutes ● Calories per serving 255 ● Freezing not recommended

Chinese five-spice powder contains aniseed, cinnamon, fennel, black pepper and cloves and imparts a very distinctive Chinese smell and warm flavour to chicken. For this recipe the meat is marinated, and then stir-fried with carrots and spring onions. Serve with 4 tablespoons cooked rice or 60 g (2 oz) cooked egg noodles adding 3 points per serving.

4 medium skinless chicken breasts, cut into
  bite-size pieces
450 g (1 lb) carrots, sliced thinly on the diagonal
300 ml (½ pint) chicken stock
1 tablespoon cornflour made into a paste with
  1 tablespoon water
a bunch of spring onions, sliced finely on the diagonal
For the marinade
1 tablespoon Chinese five-spice powder
1 tablespoon honey
2 tablespoons soy sauce
1 tablespoon rice vinegar
1 teaspoon sesame oil
2.5 cm (1-inch) piece of fresh root ginger, peeled
  and grated

1 Place all the marinade ingredients in a small pan and heat gently, stirring. Place the chicken in a shallow bowl or tray and pour the marinade over, cover with clingfilm and leave in the refrigerator for a minimum of 30 minutes, preferably overnight.
2 Heat a large frying-pan or wok and add the chicken, marinade and carrots and stir-fry over a high heat for 5 minutes. Add the stock and bring to the boil. Boil rapidly for 5 minutes then stir in the cornflour and spring onions.
3 Bring the sauce back to the boil, stirring until it becomes thick and glossy, then serve.

Chicken and spring onion burgers

5 Points per serving   Points per recipe **19½**

Serves 4 ● Preparation and cooking time 20 minutes ● Calories per serving 270 ● Freezing not recommended

These little burgers can be made with chicken or turkey mince and go down a treat with adults and children alike. Serve with a crisp salad with crunchy hot radishes and beansprouts or low-fat oven-cooked chips (125 g/ 4½ oz) for 2½ extra points.

500 g (1 lb 2 oz) chicken or turkey mince
6 spring onions, chopped finely
3 garlic cloves, crushed
2 tablespoons chopped fresh parsley
zest and juice of 1 lime
low-fat cooking spray
salt and freshly ground black pepper
To serve
4 medium burger buns
2 tablespoons tomato ketchup
salad leaves, tomato and cucumber

1 Mix together the mince, spring onions, garlic, parsley, lime zest and seasoning.
2 Shape into four patties then heat a frying-pan and spray with the low-fat cooking spray. Fry the patties for 5–10 minutes on each side until cooked through.
3 Meanwhile, split the buns and toast lightly. Spread each half with ½ tablespoon of tomato ketchup then arrange the salad on the base of each bun and place a burger on top. Squeeze a little lime juice over, replace the top half of the bun and serve.

Variation Use low-fat mayonnaise instead of ketchup for 5½ points per serving.

Chicken tikka masala

| **4** Points per serving | Points per recipe **16½** |

Serves 4 ● Preparation time 20 minutes + 1–12 hours marinating ● Cooking time 15 minutes ● Calories per serving 245 ● Freezing not recommended *A great low point version of the traditional favourite.*

150 ml (5 fl oz) low-fat plain yogurt
2 garlic cloves, crushed
2 teaspoons grated fresh ginger
4 medium skinless, boneless chicken breasts, cut into pieces
low-fat cooking spray
a small bunch of fresh coriander or mint
1 small red onion, sliced very finely
For the masala spice
2 teaspoons cumin seeds
2 teaspoons coriander seeds
½ cinnamon stick
½ teaspoon cloves
½ teaspoon chilli powder
1 teaspoon ground ginger
1 teaspoon ground turmeric
½ teaspoon ground mace
1 teaspoon salt
For the yogurt sauce
200 ml (7 fl oz) chicken stock
2 teaspoons masala spice (from mixture above)
150 g (3½ oz) half-fat crème fraîche

1 Dry-fry all the masala ingredients in a frying-pan for 2 minutes until they begin to smoke. Leave to cool, then grind in a spice mill or with a pestle and mortar.

2 In a large bowl, mix 1 tablespoon of the masala powder with the yogurt, garlic and ginger. Add the chicken. Mix well to coat thoroughly. Cover and marinate in the fridge for at least 1 hour, preferably overnight.

3 Preheat the oven to Gas Mark 7/220°C/425°F Spray a baking tray with cooking spray and spread out the chicken and marinade on it. Bake for 15 minutes, until cooked through and slightly charred at the edges.

4 Meanwhile, make the sauce. Put the stock, masala and half the crème fraîche in a small pan. Bring to the boil, then simmer for 15 minutes until slightly thickened. Stir in the rest of the crème fraîche.

5 To serve, place the grilled chicken on serving plates, pour the sauce over and sprinkle with coriander or mint and the sliced onion.

Spicy turkey cakes

| **3** Points per serving | Points per recipe **12** |

Serves 4 ● Preparation and cooking time 40 minutes ● Calories per serving 150 ● Freezing not recommended *These little cakes are good for a light lunch or appetiser with drinks. Serve with a fresh tomato, red onion and red pepper salsa with lots of lime juice and wedges for no extra points.*

350 g (12 oz) minced turkey
2 teaspoons red Thai curry paste
1 medium egg, beaten
2 tablespoons cornflour
zest of 2 limes (use the juice in the salsa)
a small bunch of fresh coriander, chopped
2 spring onions, sliced finely
1 medium red chilli, de-seeded and sliced finely
low-fat cooking spray
To serve
chunky tomato and avocado salsa (page 24)
lime wedges

1 Put the minced turkey, red curry paste and about half the egg in a food processor and process until evenly blended then transfer to a bowl.

2 Add the cornflour, lime zest, coriander, spring onions and chilli and mix well with your fingers. Add more egg if necessary to bind the mixture.

3 Divide the mixture into 12 portions and roll each into a ball then flatten slightly to make a patty.

4 Heat a large frying-pan and spray with the low-fat cooking spray. Fry the cakes in batches for about 5 minutes on each side, until golden and cooked through.

5 Meanwhile, make up the salsa (see page 24) then serve with some lime wedges.

Variation Try serving these turkey cakes with a soy dipping sauce and/or some sweet chilli sauce.

Menu plan

Friends for Dinner

~

Spicy Turkey Cakes, page 94
(pictured here)
1 serving ... 3 points

~

Prawn and Ginger Noodles, page 84
1 serving ... 4 points

~

Panna Cotta, page 161
1 serving ... 1 point

Total points per meal 8 points

Turkey and mushroom pie

| **6** Points per serving | Points per recipe **23½** |

Serves 4 ● Preparation time 45 minutes ● Cooking time 30 minutes ● Calories per serving 430 ● Freezing not recommended *A chunky, satisfying pie, best served with a big, crisp lettuce like Little Gem, Romaine or Cos and cherry tomato salad for no extra points.*

> 900 g (2 lb) potatoes, peeled
> 600 ml (1 pint) skimmed milk
> low-fat cooking spray
> 450 g (1 lb) turkey steaks, cut into bite-size pieces
> 1 onion, sliced
> 200 g (7 oz) mushrooms, sliced
> 2 tablespoons plain flour
> 100 g (3½ oz) low-fat soft cheese
> 2 tablespoons whole-grain mustard
> a small bunch of fresh parsley, chopped
> salt and freshly ground black pepper

1 Boil the potatoes in plenty of salted water for 25 minutes, until tender, then drain, add 4 tablespoons of milk. Season then mash.

2 Meanwhile, preheat the oven to Gas Mark 6/200°C/400°F. Heat a large frying-pan and spray with the low-fat cooking spray, add the turkey, season and stir-fry for 4–5 minutes until golden all over. Remove to a plate.

3 Spray the pan with the low-fat cooking spray again and add the onion, stir-fry for 5 minutes until softened then add the mushrooms, season and cook for a further 4 minutes on a high heat until the mushrooms have re-absorbed all their juices.

4 Put the turkey pieces back in the pan with the mushroom mixture, add the flour and stir together then add the rest of the milk. Stir and scrape up the juices stuck on the bottom of the pan. Keep stirring vigorously until you have a thick sauce.

5 Add the soft cheese and allow to melt then stir in the mustard and parsley. Pour the whole mixture into an oven-proof dish and top with the mashed potato. Bake for 30 minutes, until bubbling hot and crispy on the top.

Variation If you would like an added kick then stir 2 tablespoons horseradish sauce into the mashed potato. The points per serving will be 6½.

Lemon and garlic roast chicken

| **3** Points per serving | Points per recipe **12** |

Serves 4 ● Preparation time 20 minutes ● Cooking time 1 hour ● Calories per serving 255 ● Freezing not recommended *A very easy recipe, with a Mediterranean flavour, to enjoy as a Sunday roast or evening dinner. Serve with crispy roast potatoes (see page 69).*

> 1 medium chicken, weighing approximately 1.5 kg
>   (3 lb 5 oz)
> low-fat cooking spray
> 2 lemons
> 1 garlic bulb
> 300 ml (½ pint) chicken stock
> salt and freshly ground black pepper

1 Preheat the oven to Gas Mark 6/200°C/425°F. Place the chicken in a roasting tray and spray with the low-fat cooking spray. Season well both inside the cavity and all over the skin.

2 Cut each lemon in half and squeeze the juice over the skin of the chicken and then place the squeezed shell inside the cavity.

3 Break off the garlic cloves from the bulb but do not remove the skin. Add about 4 cloves to the lemon inside the cavity of the chicken then scatter the others around the bird in the roasting tray.

4 Roast for about 1 hour until cooked, basting frequently with the juices in the tray. To test if it is cooked, stick a skewer or knife into the meatiest portion of one of the thighs. The juices that come out should be clear rather than bloody.

5 When cooked, remove the chicken from the roasting tray to a carving board, tipping it up to leave behind any juices collected inside in the roasting tray. Cover with foil and allow to rest for a few minutes while you make the gravy.

6 To make the gravy, drain off any excess oil in the roasting tin then place it on the hob. Squash the cooked garlic cloves with a fork until they split, discard the skins and add the flesh to the roasting tin. Heat the tin and add the chicken stock. Use a wooden spoon or spatula to scrape up any juices stuck to the tin, then boil rapidly for a few minutes until reduced a little. Strain into a jug and serve with the carved meat. Divide the meat into four servings.

Coq au vin

Serves 4 ● Preparation time 20 minutes ● Cooking time 30 minutes ● Calories per serving 360 ● Freezing not recommended This rustic French dish of chicken, bacon and mushrooms in a wine-flavoured sauce goes perfectly with boiled, mashed floury potatoes. Add 2 points for two 60 g (2 oz) scoops.

low-fat cooking spray
6 medium boneless, skinless chicken thigh portions, halved
1 tablespoon seasoned plain flour
2 medium onions, chopped
2 medium rashers lean smoked back bacon, cut into strips
200 g (7 oz) button mushrooms, halved
2 garlic cloves, crushed
150 ml (5 fl oz) red wine
425 ml (¾ pint) chicken stock
1 tablespoon tomato purée
2 fresh thyme sprigs
salt and freshly ground black pepper

1 Heat a large non-stick pan and spray with the low-fat cooking spray. Dust the chicken with the seasoned flour and fry in the pan for a few minutes on each side until browned. Remove the chicken to a plate.

2 Add the onions and bacon to the pan and cook for 2–3 minutes, then add the mushrooms and garlic and stir-fry for a further 2 minutes until browned. Replace the chicken.

3 Pour in the red wine and stock and bring to the boil. Add the tomato purée and thyme and simmer gently for 30 minutes until the chicken is cooked. Season and serve.

Variation For added convenience you could use a 300 g can of button mushrooms, drained, instead of the fresh mushrooms.

Thai-style chicken curry

Serves 4 ● Preparation time 20 minutes ● Cooking time 20 minutes ● Calories per serving 265 ● Freezing not recommended Full of the flavours of South East Asia, this quick and easy curry has far fewer points than any you could buy at a take-away. Serve with 4 tablespoons cooked plain rice, adding 3 points per serving.

2 tablespoons finely chopped lemongrass, fresh or dried
4 fresh kaffir lime leaves, shredded
1 medium leek, sliced thinly
2 teaspoons green Thai curry paste
4 medium skinless, boneless chicken breasts, sliced thinly
400 ml (14 fl oz) soya milk
400 ml (14 fl oz) vegetable or chicken stock
2 tablespoons soy sauce
1 medium courgette, thinly sliced
300 g (10½ oz) green beans, halved
400 g (14 oz) pak choy, chopped
1 tablespoon lime juice
To garnish
a small bunch of fresh coriander, chopped
a small bunch of fresh basil, chopped

1 Mix the lemongrass, lime leaves, leek and curry paste, then heat a medium saucepan and stir-fry the mixture for 2–3 minutes. Add the chicken and stir-fry for another 2 minutes.

2 Add the soya milk, stock and soy and simmer uncovered for 10 minutes. Add the remaining vegetables and cook for another 10 minutes.

3 Add the lime juice and then serve in bowls garnished with coriander and basil.

Top tip Kaffir lime leaves can be bought fresh from the fresh herb section of many supermarkets or dried in bottles in the spice section. If using dried leaves, leave them whole and remove them before eating. If you find the fresh leaves, freeze what you don't use in a plastic bag for future use.

Enthusiasm and success go together

Cheesy garlic chicken breasts

5½ Points per serving	Points per recipe **21½**

Serves 4 ● Preparation time 20 minutes + cooling time ●
Cooking time 40 minutes ● Calories per serving 245 ●
Freezing not recommended *A gorgeous, gooey and garlicky-centred baked chicken. Serve with lightly steamed no-point vegetables of your choice.*

- 4 skinless, boneless chicken breasts weighing 175 g (6 oz) each
- 100 g pack 'Light' garlic roulé cheese
- 225 g (8 oz) spinach leaves (not baby), rinsed and drained, thick stems removed
- low-fat cooking spray
- 300 ml (½ pint) chicken stock
- 2 tablespoons balsamic vinegar
- freshly grated nutmeg
- 4 tablespoons virtually fat-free fromage frais
- salt and freshly ground black pepper

1 Preheat the oven to Gas Mark 7/220°C/425°F. Using a small knife, cut a slit lengthways down the side of each chicken breast, opening it out slightly to form a pocket.

2 Divide the roulé into four, push into the pockets then press closed. Season the chicken and then wrap two or three large spinach leaves around each one.

3 Arrange the chicken on a baking dish sprayed with the low-fat cooking spray, season again and pour the stock and vinegar over. Cover with foil and bake for 40 minutes until the chicken is cooked through, basting once or twice during cooking.

4 Meanwhile, put the rest of the spinach in a saucepan with the lid on and a few gratings of nutmeg. Heat and shake the pan until the leaves are just wilted then transfer to a liquidiser. Allow to cool a little. Add the fromage frais and seasoning. Blend to a smooth sauce.

5 Remove the chicken from the oven and allow to rest for 5 minutes before serving. Spoon some sauce on to each plate, carve each breast into thick slices and arrange on the sauce.

Rancher's turkey

7 Points per serving   Points per recipe **14½**

Serves 2 ● Preparation and cooking time 15 minutes ●
Calories per serving 455 ● Freezing not recommended
A tasty, filling supper for all those hungry
ranchers out there.

> 2 turkey breast fillets, weighing 175 g (6 oz) each
> low-fat cooking spray
> 1 large tomato, chopped finely
> 2 tablespoons hickory BBQ sauce
> 2 medium lean, rindless, smoked streaky bacon rashers
> 400 g can baked beans
> 1 tablespoon Worcestershire sauce
> salt and freshly ground black pepper

1 Place the turkey fillets between two sheets of clingfilm
then beat with a rolling pin until flattened to an even
thickness and season on both sides. Heat a large frying-
pan and spray with the low-fat cooking spray, add the
turkey fillets and fry for 2 minutes on each side.
2 Preheat the grill. Mix the tomato with the BBQ sauce.
Place the turkey fillets on the grill pan lined with foil,
and top each with the tomato mixture and then a piece
of bacon.
3 Grill for 3 minutes until the bacon is crispy. Meanwhile,
heat the baked beans and stir in the Worcestershire
sauce. Pile on to serving plates and top with the turkey.

Moroccan chicken

10 Points per serving   Points per recipe **40½**

Serves 4 ● Preparation time 35 minutes ● Cooking time
20 minutes ● Calories per serving 720 ● Freezing not
recommended Couscous is the staple diet of
Morocco; it can refer either to the grain which you
steam then fluff up to eat, or to the dish, a thin,
spice-infused stew served with the grain. Here is
an easy chicken version of the stew with all the
authentic flavours – cinnamon, cumin and chilli
– and a traditional sweetness from dried apricots.

> 250 g (9 oz) couscous
> 1.4 litres (2¼ pints) hot chicken stock
> low-fat cooking spray
> 2 medium onions, sliced thickly
> 8 medium skinless, boneless chicken thighs, cubed
> 150 g can chopped tomatoes
> ½ teaspoon cumin seeds
> 100 g (3½ oz) dried apricots, chopped
> 400 g can chick-peas, rinsed and drained
> ½ teaspoon dried chilli flakes
> 1 teaspoon ground cinnamon
> salt and freshly ground black pepper

1 Place the couscous in a bowl with 700 ml (1¼ pints)
of the hot chicken stock then leave, covered with a
plate, so that the couscous steams and absorbs all
the stock.
2 Meanwhile, heat a large frying-pan and spray with
the low-fat cooking spray. Stir-fry the onions and chicken
for 10 minutes until the chicken is browned and the
onions are soft. Add the tomatoes and cumin seeds
and cook for 5 minutes more.
3 Add the remaining 600 ml (1 pint) stock to the pan
with the apricots, chick-peas, chilli, cinnamon and
seasoning. Bring back to the boil and then simmer,
uncovered, for 20 minutes until the chicken is tender
and the sauce has thickened a little.
4 To serve, divide the couscous between four plates
and top with the chicken stew.

Variations Try stirring a couple of tablespoons of raisins
and/or some fresh chopped herbs such as coriander
or parsley into the couscous grain. Add a ½ point per
serving.

Persian chicken tagine

8 Points per serving	Points per recipe **33**

Serves 4 ● Preparation time 25 minutes ● Cooking time 50 minutes ● Calories per serving 575 ● Freezing not recommended *A warm cinnamon and cumin-flavoured casserole. Serve with 4 tablespoons of cooked rice for an extra 3 points per serving.*

> low-fat cooking spray
> 8 medium skinless chicken thighs
> 1 large onion, chopped
> 4 garlic cloves, crushed
> 1 stick celery, chopped finely
> 2 medium carrots, chopped finely
> 1 tablespoon plain flour
> ½ teaspoon ground cinnamon
> 1 teaspoon ground cumin
> 1 teaspoon ground turmeric
> 150 ml (5 fl oz) white wine
> 600 ml (1 pint) chicken stock
> 2 × 400 g cans chick-peas, rinsed and drained
> a bunch of fresh coriander, chopped
> salt and freshly ground black pepper

1 Heat a casserole or large, heavy-based saucepan on the hob and spray with the low-fat cooking spray. Add the chicken thighs, season and brown on all sides, then remove and set aside. Add the onion, garlic, celery and carrots to the pan and cook for 10 minutes, until softened, stirring occasionally.

2 Mix the flour with the spices and stir in, cooking for 2 minutes. Return the chicken pieces to the pan, pour the wine and stock over, season, cover and cook on a low heat for 45 minutes.

3 Add the chick-peas and cook a further 5 minutes, then sprinkle the coriander over and serve.

Pollo cacciatore

7 Points per serving	Points per recipe **27½**

Serves 4 ● Preparation time 15 minutes ● Cooking time 40 minutes ● Calories per serving 420 ● Freezing not recommended *The title of this recipe means 'hunter's chicken' in Italian. It is a rustic stew full of robust Mediterranean flavours. Serve with a fresh point-free green side salad.*

> low-fat cooking spray
> 4 skinless chicken breasts, weighing 175 g (6 oz) each
> 225 g (8 oz) onions, halved then sliced
> 2 garlic cloves, sliced
> 400 g can chopped tomatoes
> 1 small bunch parsley, chopped, plus extra to garnish
> 150 ml (5 fl oz) red wine
> 200 g pack instant polenta
> salt and freshly ground black pepper

1 Heat a large frying-pan and spray with the low-fat cooking spray, add the chicken pieces, season and brown on both sides then remove from the heat and set aside.

2 Spray the pan with the low-fat cooking spray again and fry the onions and garlic for 4 minutes until softened. Add the tomatoes, parsley and red wine and bring to the boil.

3 Return the chicken to the pan and simmer for 40 minutes until the chicken is cooked through.

4 Meanwhile, cook the polenta by following the instructions on the packet.

5 Spoon the polenta on to serving plates and top with the chicken stew then sprinkle with parsley.

Cut down easily on saturated fats by trimming the visible fat from meat and poultry and choosing leaner cuts of meat

Baked Mediterranean turkey

7 Points per serving   Points per recipe **14½**

Serves 2 ● Preparation time 20 minutes ● Cooking time 20 minutes ● Calories per serving 520 ● Freezing not recommended *A very quick, fresh-tasting dish, best served with a summery point-free salad.*

2 turkey breast steaks, weighing approximately
     125 g (4½ oz) each
juice and zest of 1 lemon
2 teaspoons dried oregano
2 teaspoons olive oil
salt and freshly ground black pepper
For the couscous
175 g (6 oz) couscous
600 ml (1 pint) boiling stock
100 g (3½ oz) cooked beetroot, diced
1 small red onion, diced
a small bunch of fresh parsley, chopped,
     to garnish (optional)

1 Preheat the oven to Gas Mark 6/200°C/400°F and place the turkey steaks on two separate pieces of foil large enough to completely wrap them in.
2 Season, sprinkle half the lemon juice, zest and herbs on each and drizzle each with a teaspoon of oil. Seal in the foil and place on a baking tray and bake for 20 minutes.
3 Meanwhile, place the couscous in a bowl and cover with the boiling stock. Cover with a plate and leave to steam for at least 10 minutes.
4 Fluff up the couscous with a fork and stir in the diced beetroot and red onion.
5 Unwrap the turkey and put on plates with the juices left in the foil poured over. Serve with large spoons of the couscous and sprinkled with parsley, if using.

Variation You could serve a herby pasta with the turkey if you prefer, instead of the beetroot couscous. The points per serving will be the same.

Turkey jambalaya

6 Points per serving   Points per recipe **24**

Serves 4 ● Preparation and cooking time 55 minutes ● Calories per serving 440 ● Freezing not recommended *I once worked in a Creole restaurant in New Zealand, of all places, and became very familiar with jambalaya which is a spicy rice dish made with whatever meat is available.*

low-fat cooking spray
2 large onions, chopped
1 celery stick, chopped
1 medium green pepper, de-seeded and diced
225 g (8 oz) button mushrooms, sliced
500 g (1 lb 2 oz) skinless, boneless turkey, diced in
     approximately 1 cm (½-inch) cubes
100 g (3½ oz) lean ham, diced
400 g can chopped tomatoes
150 ml (5 fl oz) tomato juice
1 teaspoon Tabasco sauce
2 bay leaves
2 garlic cloves, crushed
1 teaspoon cayenne pepper
1 fresh red chilli, de-seeded and chopped finely
225 g (8 oz) long-grain rice
425 ml (¾ pint) chicken stock
salt and freshly ground black pepper

1 Heat a large frying-pan and spray with the low-fat cooking spray. Fry the onions for 4 minutes until softened.
2 Add the celery, green pepper and mushrooms and stir-fry for 5 minutes. Then add the turkey, ham, tomatoes, tomato juice, Tabasco, bay leaves, garlic, cayenne, chilli and seasoning. Stir together and simmer for 15 minutes.
3 Add the rice and stock and cook for 15–20 minutes, stirring every 5 minutes, until the rice is firm but slightly moist and the stock is completely absorbed. Serve immediately.

Chicken Maryland

| 10½ Points per serving | Points per recipe 42 |

Serves 4 ● Preparation and cooking time 35 minutes ●
Calories per serving 660 ● Freezing not recommended
*Chicken Maryland is nearly impossible to find in
restaurants now, so I make it at home for friends.
Delicious served with tomato ketchup, adding a
½ point per 2 tablespoons.*

4 skinless, boneless chicken breasts, weighing
   175 g (6 oz) each
2 level tablespoons plain flour
1 medium egg, beaten
4 medium slices fresh bread, made into breadcrumbs
low-fat cooking spray
2 medium bananas, peeled
2 teaspoons clear honey, warmed
juice of ½ lemon
salt and freshly ground black pepper
For the sweetcorn fitters
100 g (3½ oz) plain flour
1 medium egg
150 ml (5 fl oz) skimmed milk
310 g can sweetcorn, drained

1 Season and then coat each chicken fillet in flour, then
dip in the egg and finally coat in the breadcrumbs.
2 Heat a large frying-pan and spray with the low-fat
cooking spray, then fry the chicken for 5 minutes on
each side until golden brown and cooked through. Keep
warm while you prepare the bananas and make the
sweetcorn fritters.
3 Slice the bananas in half lengthways. Brush with
honey and lemon juice. Grill for 4 minutes until golden.
4 Make the fritters by beating together the flour,
seasoning, egg and milk and then stirring in the
sweetcorn. Spray the frying-pan with the low-fat cooking
spray and fry spoonfuls of the batter for 2–3 minutes on
each side, turning with a fish slice. Put on a plate and
keep warm with the chicken and bananas until all the
fritters are cooked.
5 To serve, each plate should have a piece of the chicken,
a banana half and 2 or 3 corn fritters.

Top tip Keep the different elements warm in oven until
ready to serve.

Oriental chicken parcels

| 3 Points per serving | Points per recipe 12½ |

Serves 4 ● Preparation time 15 minutes ● Cooking time
25 minutes ● Calories per serving 175 ● Freezing not
recommended *Chicken breast fillets are steamed
in baking paper with mushrooms, rice and a
light aromatic sauce of soy, fresh ginger and
spring onions.*

low-fat cooking spray
1 teaspoon sesame oil
4 spring onions, sliced
1 cm (½-inch) piece of fresh root ginger, peeled and grated
2 skinless, boneless chicken breasts, weighing
   175 g (6 oz), cut into 2 cm (¾-inch) cubes
100 g (3½ oz) shiitake mushrooms, sliced
2 tablespoons soy sauce
175 g (6 oz) basmati rice, cooked

1 Heat a large frying-pan and spray with the low-fat
cooking spray. Add the sesame oil, spring onions and
ginger and fry for 1 minute. Add the chicken and
mushrooms and stir-fry for 2 minutes more.
2 Add the soy and cooked rice and cook for a further
minute. Cut four pieces of baking paper approximately
15 cm (6-inch) square and divide the mixture evenly
between them.
3 Fold up the paper to enclose the filling, securing by
folding underneath. Place the parcels in a steamer over
boiling water and steam for 25 minutes.
4 Serve, allowing each guest to open their own parcel.

Top tip Instead of using a steamer, you can use a
colander suspended over a pan of boiling water using
the pan lid to cover the parcels.

Roast turkey with orange and mushroom stuffing

| 7 Points per serving | Points per recipe 42 |

Serves 6 ● Preparation time 40 minutes ● Cooking time 1–1½ hours (depending on size of turkey) + 30 minutes resting ● Calories per serving 630 ● Freezing not recommended These are simple recipes for a succulent roast turkey with stuffing, gravy and a bread sauce. Using a few shortcuts you can enjoy a stress-free Christmas dinner.

Serve with Cranberry sauce (page 30), Perfect roast potatoes (page 69), Brussels sprouts with chestnuts (page 69) and Roasted autumn roots (page 58), adding on the extra points.

1.5–2.25 kg (3½–5 lb) turkey
12 medium rashers streaky bacon
425 ml (¾ pint) chicken or turkey stock
low-fat cooking spray
salt and freshly ground black pepper
For the stuffing
170 g packet parsley and thyme or garlic and herb
   stuffing mix
300 ml (½ pint) boiling water
100 g (3½ oz) mushrooms, chopped
juice and zest of 1 orange
For the bread sauce
425 ml (¾ pint) skimmed milk
1 small onion, peeled and stuck with 3 cloves
1 bay leaf
4 peppercorns
6 medium slices white bread, crusts removed and cubed
freshly grated nutmeg
salt and freshly ground black pepper
For the gravy
1 tablespoon plain flour
300 ml (½ pint) chicken or turkey stock

1 Preheat the oven to Gas Mark 5/190°C/375°F. Rinse the turkey and pat dry with kitchen paper, then season inside and out. Pour 300 ml (½ pint) boiling water over the stuffing mix, add the mushrooms and orange juice and zest and stir well.

2 Stuff the neck cavity of the bird with this mixture, using as much stuffing as necessary to give a good shape, without pressing in too much. Pull the flap of skin over the stuffing to cover and then tuck under the bird.

3 Weigh the turkey then place in a large roasting tin. Stretch the bacon rashers, using the back of a knife, and place in a criss-cross pattern over the top of the bird. Pour the stock into the roasting tin and cover the turkey with a piece of foil that has been sprayed with the low-fat cooking spray.

4 To calculate the cooking time, allow 20 minutes per 500 g (1 lb 2 oz) of the weight of the stuffed bird – for example a 2 kg (4 lb 8 oz) stuffed turkey will take 1 hour and 20 minutes. Place the turkey in the centre of the oven and roast for the appropriate time removing the foil for the last 30 minutes of the cooking time so that the bacon and skin become crisp.

5 Meanwhile, to make the bread sauce put the milk, onion, bay leaf and peppercorns into a pan and heat gently until the mixture comes to the boil. Remove from the heat and leave for the flavours to infuse for at least an hour. Strain the milk and return to the pan. Put on a very low heat and add the bread, seasoning and a couple of gratings of nutmeg and cook for 10 minutes. Set aside. Reheat gently before use.

6 Check that the turkey is cooked by sticking a skewer or thin-bladed knife into the thickest part of the thigh; if the juices run clear then the bird is cooked but if they look bloody then return to the oven for longer. Keep re-testing until they do run clear.

7 Transfer the turkey to a carving board, cover with foil and allow to rest for 30 minutes before carving. Meanwhile cook any accompanying vegetables. Place any left-over stuffing in a baking tray sprayed with the low-fat cooking spray then bake in the hot oven for 20 minutes.

8 To make the gravy, pour or skim any fat off the top of the juices left in the roasting tray, then place the tray on the hob and heat. Stir in the flour then add the stock, bring to the boil, stirring with a wooden spoon and scraping up the juices stuck to the bottom of the pan. If the gravy looks lumpy then whisk and strain into a serving jug. Serve five 25 g (1 oz) slices per person.

Top tips When you eventually finish all the meat from your turkey, boil up the carcass with a little pepper, a bay leaf, a piece of carrot, onion and celery and enough water to cover. This makes a lovely stock to use in soups and risottos.

Sun-drenched turkey towers: You'll love these Mediterranean-inspired stacks of char-grilled turkey and basil-infused vegetables

Sun-drenched turkey towers

2½ Points per serving   Points per recipe **10**

Serves 4 ● Preparation and cooking time 40 minutes ● Calories per serving 205 ● Freezing not recommended *You really need a griddle pan or BBQ to make these.*

4 turkey breast steaks, weighing approximately 100 g (3½ oz) each, sliced into 4 even-sized medallions
juice and zest of 1 lemon
1 garlic clove, crushed
1 teaspoon olive oil
2 medium aubergines, cut into 16 slices, about 5 mm (¼-inch) thick
4 large beef tomatoes, cut into 16 slices, about 5 mm (¼-inch) thick
2 tablespoons pesto sauce, mixed with 2 tablespoons boiling water
2 medium yellow peppers, quartered and de-seeded
salt and freshly ground black pepper
fresh basil, chopped, to garnish

1 Put the turkey steaks on a large plate and season. Mix together the lemon juice, garlic and olive oil and pour over the turkey.
2 Preheat a griddle pan so it's really hot. Brush the aubergine and tomato slices with the pesto sauce. Char the turkey steaks on both sides on the griddle and then turn down the heat and cook them for about 2 minutes more, until cooked through. Remove from the heat and set aside but keep warm.
3 Get the griddle really hot again and then char all the vegetables on both sides, brushing with more pesto sauce as you go. As they are done, remove from the heat and set aside but keep warm.
4 To serve place a slice of aubergine on each plate then top with a piece of turkey, a slice of tomato and a slice of pepper. Repeat the layers to make a tower and serve two towers on each plate, scattered with basil.

BBQ chicken drumsticks

4 Points per serving   Points per recipe **16**

Serves 4 ● Preparation time 5 minutes + 4–12 hours marinating ● Cooking time 15 minutes ● Calories per serving 285 ● Freezing not recommended *These sweet and spicy chicken drumsticks can be cooked on a griddle or under the grill but they are best with that charred flavour you get from a BBQ.*

12 medium skinless chicken drumsticks
For the marinade
2 garlic cloves, crushed
2.5 cm (1-inch) piece of fresh root ginger, peeled and grated
zest and juice of 2 medium oranges
1 small red chilli, de-seeded and chopped finely
2 tablespoons clear honey
2 tablespoons soy sauce
2 tablespoons tomato purée
2 teaspoons sesame oil

1 Mix all the marinade ingredients together into a paste. Put the drumsticks in a shallow dish, add the marinade and turn to coat. Leave to marinate in the fridge for at least 4 hours but preferably overnight.
2 Cook the drumsticks on a griddle, under the grill or on a hot BBQ for 7–8 minutes on each side until thoroughly cooked and golden brown.

Variation For a quicker and more convenient marinade, use 6 tablespoons of ready-made barbecue sauce mixed with 2 tablespoons water. The points per serving will be 3.

At mealtimes, take it slowly.

You'll enjoy your food more and you'll digest it more efficiently

Turkey Bourguignon

4 Points per serving	Points per recipe **15½**

Serves 4 • Preparation time 20 minutes • Cooking time 2 hours • Calories per serving 245 • Freezing not recommended *A thick, rich stew. Good served with a medium jacket potato (adding 2½ points per serving) or 2 scoops of mash (adding 2 points per serving).*

low-fat cooking spray
4 medium rashers lean, back bacon, cut into strips
225 g (8 oz) button mushrooms
2 garlic cloves, crushed
a small bunch of fresh thyme, chopped
450 g (1 lb) turkey steaks, diced
150 ml (5 fl oz) red wine
425 ml (¾ pint) chicken stock
1 tablespoon cornflour
a small bunch of fresh parsley, chopped, to serve (optional)
salt and freshly ground black pepper

1 Preheat the oven to Gas Mark 4/180°C/350°F. Heat a large frying-pan and spray with the low-fat cooking spray. Add the bacon, mushrooms, garlic and thyme and cook gently for 10 minutes.
2 Add the turkey and cook a further 5 minutes. Pour the whole lot into a deep ovenproof casserole dish, season and add the wine and stock. Cover and bake for 2 hours.
3 Blend the cornflour with 2 tablespoons of water to make a paste, and stir into the Bourguignon to thicken the sauce. Serve sprinkled with fresh parsley, if using.

Variation You could also use braising beef for a more traditional Bourguignon. This will be 5 points per serving.

Chicken piri piri

7 Points per serving	Points per recipe **14½**

Serves 2 • Preparation and cooking time 35 minutes • Calories per serving 540 • Freezing not recommended *Piri piri seasoning is a mixture of chillies and citrus peel originating in Portuguese Africa. Serve this dish with 4 tablespoons cooked rice and lemon wedges adding 3 points per serving.*

2 fresh small red chillis, de-seeded and chopped
a small bunch of fresh tarragon, chopped
a small bunch of fresh basil, chopped
1 bay leaf
2 tablespoons raisins
2 tablespoons lemon juice
1 tablespoon olive oil
1 skinless poussin or spring chicken, weighing approximately 1 kg (2 lb 4 oz)
salt and freshly ground black pepper
parsley sprigs, to serve (optional)

1 Make the piri piri marinade by putting all the ingredients except the chicken and parsley sprigs in a bowl and leaving to infuse for 5 minutes.
2 Split the chicken down the back, but don't separate the two halves completely. Press it out flat on a board using a weight if necessary. Fix with crossed skewers to maintain the shape during grilling.
3 Preheat the grill to high and brush the chicken inside and out with the marinade. Place the chicken under the grill skin-side-down and cook for 10 minutes, basting frequently with the marinade. Turn the chicken over and cook the other side for 10 minutes until cooked through, again basting frequently.
4 To serve separate the chicken halves and put on serving plates, garnished with parsley sprigs, if using.

Top tip Spatchcock chicken or poussin gets its name from the way it is flattened out and skewered. It is available from supermarkets or you could ask your butcher to prepare one for you.

Chicken stir-fry

2½ Points per serving   Points per recipe **5½**

Serves 2 ● Preparation and cooking time 35 minutes ●
Calories per serving 180 ● Freezing not recommended
*A quick, autumnal supper. Serve with 4
tablespoons cooked rice (adding 3 points per
serving) or 60 g (2 oz) cooked egg noodles
(adding 3 points per serving).*

225 g (8 oz) pumpkin or butternut squash flesh, cut into
   large chunks
low-fat cooking spray
1 teaspoon sesame oil
1 skinless, boneless chicken breast, weighing 175 g (6 oz),
   cut into thin strips
4 tablespoons oyster or black bean sauce
2 tablespoons soy sauce
150 ml (5 fl oz) stock or water
125 g (4½ oz) spinach, rinsed, drained and large stalks
   removed
a small bunch of fresh coriander, chopped

1 Bring a large pan of water to the boil and cook the
pumpkin or butternut squash for 5–6 minutes until just
tender. Drain well.

2 Meanwhile heat a wok or large frying-pan and spray
with the low-fat cooking spray, add the sesame oil and
the chicken and stir-fry for 2–4 minutes until golden
brown. Add the pumpkin and cook for 3–4 minutes,
tossing frequently.

3 Add the oyster sauce, soy and stock or water and
cook for 2 minutes, then add the spinach and cook for
another minute. Lastly stir in the coriander, then serve.

Variations You could use any meat and vegetables for
this recipe, adjusting the points accordingly.

Chicken chunga

6 Points per serving   Points per recipe **23½**

Serves 4 ● Preparation time 35 minutes ● Cooking time
45 minutes ● Calories per serving 330 ● Freezing not
recommended *'Chunga' is a Caribbean word
for hotpot, into which virtually anything can be
thrown, so think of this recipe as a rough guide
only, and use whatever vegetables you like. Serve
with 4 tablespoons cooked brown rice adding 3
points per serving.*

low-fat cooking spray
4 skinless chicken breasts, weighing 175 g (6 oz) each
2.5 cm (1-inch) piece of fresh root ginger, peeled and
   chopped finely
1 large onion, chopped
1 small red chilli, de-seeded and chopped finely
2 medium carrots, sliced
100 g (3½ oz) button mushrooms
1 medium red pepper, de-seeded and chopped
1 celery stick, chopped
1 tablespoon plain flour
150 ml (5 fl oz) red or white wine
300 ml (½ pint) chicken stock
400 g can black-eyed beans, drained

1 Preheat the oven to Gas Mark 4/180°C/350°F. Heat
a casserole dish on the hob and spray with the low-fat
cooking spray, add the chicken and ginger and fry for
5 minutes until browned all over, then remove from the
heat and set aside.

2 Spray the casserole dish with the low-fat cooking
spray again and fry the onion for 5 minutes until the
onion has softened. Add the chilli and then add the
other vegetables and stir-fry for a few minutes more.
Remove from the heat and set aside.

3 Sprinkle the flour into the casserole dish and mix into
any juices in the bottom then add the wine and stir until
smooth and thick. Add the stock, bring to the boil then
simmer for 5 minutes, stirring.

4 Return the chicken mixture, vegetables and chilli
to the casserole dish, cover and bake in the oven for
45 minutes. Add the beans to the casserole dish 10
minutes before the end of the cooking time.

Chicken hotpot

4 Points per serving	Points per recipe **16**

Serves 4 • Preparation time 35 minutes • Cooking time 45 minutes • Calories per serving 325 • Freezing not recommended *A soothing casserole of chicken pieces with vegetables. It becomes really special if made with the new vegetables of summer – baby carrots, turnips, parsnips, green beans and freshly podded peas, adding extra points for the peas; 2 tablespoons are 1 point per serving. 1 medium parsnip is 1 point per serving.*

low-fat cooking spray
8 chicken joints (4 medium breasts, halved or
    8 medium thighs), skin left on
2 large onions, sliced
4 garlic cloves, sliced
150 ml (5 fl oz) white wine
2 large carrots, sliced
2 large turnips, sliced
½ medium green cabbage, sliced
8 small new potatoes, scrubbed
1 chicken stock cube
salt and freshly ground black pepper
1 bunch fresh parsley, chopped, to garnish

1 Heat a large casserole on the hob and spray with the low-fat cooking spray. Add the chicken pieces and season. Cook until browned all over then remove from the pan and set aside.
2 Spray the pan with the low-fat cooking spray again and fry the onions and garlic for 6 minutes until softened and golden. Add the white wine and scrape up any juices stuck to the bottom.
3 Replace the chicken and add the remaining vegetables and seasoning. Crumble the stock cube over, then cover with water and bring to the boil. Simmer for 45 minutes until the chicken is cooked through and the liquid reduced a little to a thin, flavoursome sauce.
4 To serve, remove the skin from the chicken and skim any fat from the top of the sauce. Ladle into bowls and sprinkle with the parsley.

Variations If using baby summer vegetables then reduce the cooking time to 30 minutes. 5 minutes before the end, add the beans and peas, and any other very quick-cooking point-free vegetables.

Mexican turkey casserole

6 Points per serving	Points per recipe **23½**

Serves 4 • Preparation time 25 minutes • Cooking time 50 minutes–1 hour • Calories per serving 410 • Freezing not recommended *A one-pot meal full of vibrant Mexican flavours. Serve with 4 tablespoons cooked rice (adding 3 points per serving) or medium soft flour tortillas (adding 2 points per tortilla).*

low-fat cooking spray
400 g (14 oz) skinless, boneless turkey, cubed
2 garlic cloves, crushed
1 large onion, sliced
1 large red chilli, de-seeded and chopped finely
1 teaspoon coriander seeds, crushed
1 teaspoon cumin seeds, crushed
200 g (7 oz) brown rice
400 g can chick-peas, rinsed and drained
400 g can chopped tomatoes
1 large aubergine, diced
600 ml (1 pint) stock
a small bunch of fresh coriander, chopped
salt and freshly ground black pepper

1 Heat a heat-proof casserole dish on the hob then spray with the low-fat cooking spray, add the turkey, season, and stir-fry for about 5 minutes until golden all over. Remove the turkey from the dish and set aside.
2 Spray the casserole with the low-fat cooking spray again, add the garlic, onion, chilli and spices and stir-fry for 4–5 minutes until the onions have softened.
3 Return the turkey to the pan together with all the other ingredients except the coriander and only half the stock. Bring to the boil then simmer for 50 minutes – 1 hour, topping up with stock as necessary. Stir in the coriander and serve.

Mexican chicken tortillas

9½ Points per serving   Points per recipe **37½**

Serves 4 ● Preparation and cooking time 40 minutes ●
Calories per serving 690 ● Freezing not recommended
A fun and satisfying dinner.

8 medium flour tortillas
4 medium skinless, boneless, chicken breast fillets,
     cut into thin strips
150 ml (5 fl oz) low-fat plain yogurt
4 medium slices bread, processed to fine breadcrumbs
low-fat cooking spray
salt and freshly ground black pepper
For the salsa
500 g (1lb 2 oz) frozen petit pois, cooked and drained
100 g (3½ oz) cherry tomatoes, quartered
1 small red onion, chopped finely
juice of 1 lime
1 small red chilli, de-seeded and chopped

1 Wrap the tortillas in foil and place in a warm oven to
heat through. Meanwhile, place the chicken strips in a
bowl and season them then toss in the yogurt until well
covered. Place the breadcrumbs on a plate and roll the
chicken strips in them.
2 Heat a large frying-pan and spray with the low-fat
cooking spray then fry the chicken for 4–5 minutes,
turning gently until golden brown all over and cooked
through.
3 Arrange large spoonfuls of the chicken on the centre
of the warmed tortillas and roll up.
4 Place all the ingredients for the salsa in a food
processor with some seasoning and blend very briefly
to a rough textured paste. Alternatively mash the
ingredients together with a fork. Transfer to a bowl
and serve with the tortillas.

Sticky cranberry turkey steaks

3 Points per serving   Points per recipe **12½**

Serves 4 ● Preparation and cooking time 30 minutes ●
Calories per serving 240 ● Freezing not recommended
*These sweet, sticky, tender turkey steaks are
served with a vibrant salsa.*

4 turkey steaks, weighing 175 g (6 oz) each
1 tablespoon honey
100 g (3½ oz) cranberries
250 g (9 oz) cooked beetroot
1 small red onion, sliced finely
salt and freshly ground black pepper
For the salsa
1 tablespoon caster sugar
4 tablespoons white wine vinegar
½ teaspoon chilli flakes
1 teaspoon coriander seeds
a small bunch of fresh coriander, chopped,
     to garnish (optional)

1 Heat the grill to high and lay the turkey steaks on
the grill pan and season. In a small pan heat the honey,
2 tablespoons of the cranberries and 2 tablespoons
of water for about 5 minutes, covered, or until the
cranberries start to pop.
2 Brush the turkey steaks with the cranberry mixture
and grill for 3–4 minutes on each side, brushing
frequently with the honey, cranberry mixture.
3 Meanwhile, make the salsa. In a small pan mix the
sugar, vinegar, chilli, coriander and the rest of the
cranberries. Heat gently, covered, for 5 minutes until
the cranberries begin to break down.
4 Put the beetroot and onion in a bowl and pour the
cranberries over, toss together and serve with the
turkey steaks. Garnish with coriander, if using.

Fish is the ideal food for today. It is quick and easy to prepare and naturally low in points but it contains many of the nutrients we need for good health. Best of all, it lends itself to numerous delicious recipes. For more fish dishes, have a look in the chapter called Oodles of Noodles, Rice and Beans on page 70.

fabulous fish

Pan-fried salmon

4½ Points per serving	Points per recipe **18½**

Serves 4 ● Preparation and cooking time 20 minutes + 30 minutes marinating time ● Calories per serving 320 ● Freezing not recommended *These fillets are delicious served with 200 g (7 oz) cooked egg noodles for 3 extra points.*

4 salmon fillets, weighing approximately 150 g (5½ oz) each, skinned
4 tablespoons soy sauce
2 tablespoons clear honey
4 tablespoons rice vinegar or lemon juice
6 spring onions, chopped finely
For the sauce
zest and juice of 2 limes
3 teaspoons cornflour, mixed to a paste with 1 tablespoon water

1 Place the fillets in a shallow dish large enough to accommodate them all side by side. Gently heat the soy, honey and vinegar or lemon juice together, then pour over the fish and scatter with the spring onions. Leave to marinate for at least 30 minutes.
2 Heat the grill or griddle pan to high and grill the fish pieces for 5 minutes on each side until cooked through.
3 In a small saucepan, heat the remaining marinade with the lime juice and cornflour until boiling. Boil vigorously for 2 minutes, stirring as it thickens, then serve with the salmon.

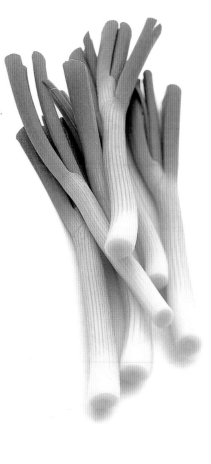

Fish pie

6½ Points per serving   Points per recipe 27

Serves 4 ● Preparation time 45 minutes ● Cooking time 30–40 minutes ● Calories per serving 460 ● Freezing not recommended *A family favourite with a thick, cheesy sauce and a crispy, golden mashed potato top.*

900 g (2 lb) potatoes, peeled
600 ml (1 pint) skimmed milk
400 g (14 oz) undyed smoked haddock, cut into 2.5 cm (1-inch) cubes
200 g (7 oz) broccoli, cut into small florets
150 g (5½ oz) frozen petit pois
30 g (1¼ oz) polyunsaturated margarine
3 tablespoons plain flour
60 g (2 oz) low-fat soft cheese
1 teaspoon French or English mustard
salt and freshly ground black pepper

1 Boil the potatoes in salted water for 20–30 minutes until cooked then drain and mash with a few tablespoons of the milk and season well.

2 Preheat the oven to Gas Mark 3/170°C/325°F. Place the haddock, broccoli and peas in an ovenproof dish, approximately 30 cm (12-inch) long.

3 Melt the margarine in a small saucepan and stir in the flour. Gradually add the milk, stirring well between each addition, to make a smooth sauce. Lastly, add the cheese and mustard. Season and stir until smooth again.

4 Pour the sauce over the fish and vegetables and then top with the mash. Bake for 30–40 minutes or until golden on top and hot and bubbling beneath.

Cod and leek parcels

1½ Points per serving   Points per recipe 5½

Serves 4 ● Preparation time 15 minutes ● Cooking time 20 minutes ● Calories per serving 140 ● Freezing not recommended *Serve with 200 g (7 oz) new potatoes per person for a fresh-tasting quick supper, adding on 2 points per serving.*

4 cod fillets, weighing approximately 125 g (4½ oz) each
2 medium leeks, halved lengthways then sliced and rinsed
zest and juice of 1 lemon
2 teaspoons olive oil
salt and freshly ground black pepper

1 Preheat the oven to Gas Mark 4/180°C/350°F. Cut four pieces of non-stick baking paper about 30 cm (12-inch) square and place a piece of fish in the centre of each.

2 Share the other ingredients between the four fillets so that each is evenly covered with leeks, lemon zest, juice, seasoning and a dribble of oil.

3 Scrunch up the baking paper to make sealed parcels and place on a baking tray. Bake for 20 minutes then serve in the paper for each person to open their own.

Variations Try salmon (4 points per serving), haddock or coley (2 points per serving) instead of the cod.

Horseradish-crusted cod

4 Points per serving	Points per recipe **16½**

Serves 4 ● Preparation time 30 minutes ● Cooking time 20 minutes ● Calories per serving 290 ● Freezing not recommended These cod fillets are roasted with a horseradish crust and served on a bed of creamy green lentils with herbs.

> 200 g (7 oz) green Puy lentils
> a bunch of fresh parsley, chopped finely, plus extra
>   to garnish
> low-fat cooking spray
> 4 cod fillets, weighing approximately 125 g (4½ oz) each
> 1 tablespoon horseradish sauce
> 2 tablespoons fresh breadcrumbs
> 4 tablespoons half-fat crème fraîche
> salt and freshly ground black pepper

1 Place the lentils in a pan, cover with water so it comes about 5 cm (2 inches) above the top of the lentils. Add two sprigs of parsley and bring to the boil. Simmer for 20–30 minutes or until just tender.

2 Meanwhile, preheat the oven to Gas Mark 6/200°C/ 400°F and spray a non-stick baking tray with the low-fat cooking spray. Season both sides of the cod fillets and then spread horseradish sauce thickly over the top of each.

3 Put the breadcrumbs on a plate, press the horseradish side of each fillet down into the breadcrumbs so that they stick. Place on the baking tray and bake for 20 minutes or until the fish is cooked through.

4 When the lentils are cooked, drain and mix with most of the chopped parsley and crème fraîche, seasoning well. Serve as a bed for the fish with the rest of the chopped parsley scattered over the top.

Cod with mustard sauce

2½ Points per serving	Points per recipe **10**

Serves 4 ● Preparation and cooking time 20 minutes ● Calories per serving 205 ● Freezing not recommended This goes well with steamed broccoli or spring greens, which will not add any points.

> low-fat cooking spray
> 4 cod fillets, weighing approximately 125 g (4½ oz) each
> salt and freshly ground black pepper
> a small bunch of chives, chopped, to garnish (optional)
> **For the sauce**
> 2 tablespoons cornflour
> 300 ml (½ pint) skimmed milk
> 1 tablespoon English mustard
> 125 g (4½ oz) low-fat soft cheese

1 Preheat the grill to high and spray a piece of foil on the grill pan with the low-fat cooking spray. Arrange the fish fillets on the foil and season. Grill for 4–5 minutes on each side or until cooked through.

2 Meanwhile, make the sauce by mixing the cornflour with a little of the milk to a paste and bringing the rest of the milk to the boil. Add the other ingredients and the milk paste, season well and cook for 2 minutes, stirring, until thickened.

3 Serve the cod with the mustard sauce poured on top and scattered with a few chopped chives, if using.

Variations Haddock (same points per serving) and salmon (5 points per serving) are also good in this recipe.

Italian fish stew

Serves 4 ● Preparation time 30 minutes ● Cooking time 20 minutes ● Calories per serving 160 ● Freezing not recommended *A colourful fish stew which you'll find versions of all over Italy and the Mediterranean.*

> low-fat cooking spray
> 1 medium onion, chopped finely
> 4 garlic cloves, chopped
> 2 sticks celery, chopped finely
> 2 medium carrots, chopped
> 400 g can chopped tomatoes
> a small bunch of fresh thyme, chopped
> 1 bay leaf
> grated zest and juice of 1 orange
> 700 ml (1¼ pints) fish stock
> 250 g (9 oz) cod or haddock fillet, defrosted if frozen
> 250 g (9 oz) frozen mixed seafood, defrosted
> a small bunch of fresh parsley, chopped, to garnish (optional)
> 2 medium red chillis, de-seeded and chopped finely, to garnish (optional)

1 Heat a large saucepan and spray with the low-fat cooking spray. Add the onion, garlic, celery and carrots. Cook on a low heat for 10 minutes or until all the vegetables are softened.

2 Add the tomatoes, thyme, bay, orange zest and juice and the stock. Bring to the boil then simmer for 20 minutes, uncovered.

3 Meanwhile, cut the fish into large cubes, add to the pan and cook for 3 minutes. Finally, add the seafood and cook for a further 2 minutes.

4 Serve sprinkled with the parsley and chillis, if using, in individual serving bowls.

Spicy cod and sausage kebabs

Serves 4 ● Preparation and cooking time 20 minutes ● Calories per serving 200 ● Freezing not recommended *Ideal for the BBQ but also good grilled, these cod kebabs combine with low-fat sausage and red peppers in a sticky, spicy sauce.*

> 200 g (7 oz) cod fillet, cut into 2.5 cm (1-inch) cubes
> 450 g (1 lb) 95% fat-free fat sausages, quartered lengthways
> 2 medium red peppers, cut into 2.5 cm (1-inch) squares
> **For the sauce**
> 2 tablespoons soy sauce
> 1 tablespoon honey
> 1 red chilli, de-seeded and chopped finely (or 1 teaspoon dried chilli flakes)
> 1 garlic clove, crushed

1 Thread the cod, sausages and red peppers on to eight skewers, alternating them to look attractive.

2 Mix together the sauce ingredients and place in a shallow dish long enough to accommodate the skewers. Lie the skewers in the dish and turn until they are completely covered in the sauce.

3 Preheat the grill or BBQ to high then lay the skewers on a piece of foil on the grill pan or put straight on to the BBQ. Brush with more sauce and grill for 4 minutes, then turn, brush again and grill for a further 4 minutes until cooked through, then serve.

Menu plan

Summer BBQ

~

Spicy Cod and Sausage Kebabs, page 114
(pictured here)
1 serving . . . 3 points

~

Green Bean and Shallot Salad, page 43
1 serving . . . 1 point

~

Jerk Sweet Potatoes, page 56
1 serving . . . 2½ points

~

Instant Raspberry Yogurt Ice Cream, page 166
1 serving . . . 1½ points

Total points per meal 8 points

Baked haddock with tomatoes

3½ Points per serving	Points per recipe **13½**

Serves 4 ● Preparation time 40 minutes ● Cooking time 40 minutes ● Calories per serving 265 ● Freezing not recommended *A quick, no-hassle recipe that, except for the fish, you will probably have all the ingredients for in your storecupboard.*

> 800 g (1 lb 11 oz) potatoes
> low-fat cooking spray
> 2 medium onions, sliced thinly
> 2 garlic cloves, sliced thinly
> 4 haddock fillets, weighing approximately 400 g (14 oz) in total
> 400 g can chopped tomatoes
> 1 tablespoon balsamic vinegar or lemon juice
> salt and freshly ground black pepper
> chopped parsley, to garnish (optional)

1 Boil the potatoes in lots of boiling salted water until soft, approximately 25 minutes, then drain.
2 Preheat the oven to Gas Mark 3/170°C/325°F. Heat a frying-pan and spray with the low-fat cooking spray then fry the onions and garlic for 4 minutes until softened.
3 Spray an ovenproof dish with the low-fat cooking spray and put the fillets in, skin-side-down. Scatter the onions and garlic over the top, pour in the tomatoes, vinegar, 125 ml (4 fl oz) water and season well. Bake for 35–40 minutes.
4 To serve, mash the potatoes, season then spoon on to four plates and top with a piece of fish and some of the sauce. Garnish with chopped parsley, if using.

Variations You could serve the haddock with 225 g (8 oz) cooked pasta or 100 g (3½ oz) couscous per person instead of the potatoes. The points per serving will be 2 with pasta, 2½ with cousous.

Kedgeree

4 Points per serving	Points per recipe **16½**

Serves 4 ● Preparation and cooking time 40 minutes ● Calories per serving 290 ● Freezing not recommended *A quick and easy version of the traditional smoked haddock and rice breakfast, lunch or supper dish.*

> 175 g (6 oz) easy-cook long-grain rice
> a pinch of saffron threads (optional)
> 225 g (8 oz) smoked haddock
> low-fat cooking spray
> 1 medium onion, chopped
> 1 tablespoon curry powder
> 100 ml (3½ fl oz) chicken or vegetable stock
> 2 medium hard-boiled eggs, quartered
> a bunch of fresh parsley, chopped
> 150 ml (5 fl oz) low-fat plain yogurt

1 Cook the rice with the saffron in plenty of boiling water for 10–15 minutes or until tender, then drain, using the boiling water to pour over the haddock. Leave the haddock to stand for 5 minutes. Drain, remove the skin and any bones then flake the fish coarsely.
2 Heat a frying-pan and spray with the low-fat cooking spray then fry the onion for 4 minutes until softened. Add the curry powder and cook a further 2 minutes.
3 Stir the fish, onion, stock, eggs, parsley and yogurt into the cooked saffron rice, heat through and serve.

Variation Use a teaspoon of turmeric to achieve a yellow colour instead of the more expensive saffron.

Poached haddock brunch

8½ Points per serving	Points per recipe **17**

Serves 2 ● Preparation and cooking time 35 minutes ●
Calories per serving 585 ● Freezing not recommended
*The best dish for brunch. It's filling and stodgy
but not so heavy that it will send you back to bed.
The haddock is poached and served on a bed of
wilted spinach with a grating of nutmeg topped
with a lightly poached egg and a cheesy sauce.*

> 600 ml (1 pint) skimmed milk
> 2 × 175 g (6 oz) un-dyed smoked haddock fillets, quartered
> 280 g (10 oz) fresh spinach, rinsed and drained
> grated nutmeg
> 30 g (1¼ oz) polyunsaturated margarine
> 2 tablespoons plain flour
> 60 g (2 oz) low-fat soft cheese
> 1 teaspoon French or English mustard
> 1 tablespoon vinegar
> 2 medium eggs
> salt and freshly ground black pepper

1 Put the milk and fish in a pan large enough to
accommodate the haddock fillets in one layer, skin-side
up. Bring to the boil then turn off the heat and leave the
haddock to poach for 15 minutes.
2 Meanwhile, put the spinach in a large pan over a
gentle heat and cover. Season and add a little grated
nutmeg and cook for about 5 minutes until wilted.
Remove from the heat, still covered and set aside.
3 Drain the milk from the fish and use to make the
cheese sauce. Melt the margarine in a small saucepan
and stir in the flour. Gradually add the milk stirring
well between each addition to make a smooth sauce.
Add the cheese and mustard, season and stir until
smooth again.
4 Boil a pan of water in which to poach the eggs, add
the vinegar. One at a time break the eggs into a cup
then gently slide into the boiling water. Cook for 2–3
minutes then carefully lift out using a slotted spoon.
5 Place a small mound of the spinach on each of two
plates, top with a piece of fish then a poached egg and
lastly spoon over the cheese sauce. Grind black pepper
on top and serve.

Top tip Keep the fish warm once you have drained away
the milk by covering with foil.

Greek fish bake

6½ Points per serving	Points per recipe **26**

Serves 4 ● Preparation time 10 minutes + 30 minutes
marinating ● Cooking time 15 minutes ● Calories per
serving 385 ● Freezing not recommended *Oily fish is
very good for us and, cooked like this, it is lower
in points than you would imagine. Serve with a
Greek salad like the one on page 38.*

> 4 mackerel fillets weighing about 150 g (5½ oz) each,
>   cleaned and trimmed
> low-fat cooking spray
> juice of 2 lemons
> 4 garlic cloves, chopped finely
> a small bunch of fresh thyme, chopped
> 20 stoned olives in brine, rinsed, drained and chopped
>   coarsely
> 400 g can plum tomatoes, chopped roughly
> 100 ml (3½ fl oz) white wine
> salt and freshly ground black pepper

1 Place the fillets in a shallow oven-proof dish that has
been sprayed with the low-fat cooking spray. Season
well and pour the lemon juice over. Leave to marinate
in the fridge for at least 30 minutes.
2 Preheat the oven to Gas Mark 5 /190°C/375°F. Scatter
the garlic, thyme and olives over the top and pour on the
tomatoes and wine. Bake for 15 minutes until the fish is
just cooked through.

Top tip Insist on very fresh mackerel fillets for this
recipe. Check the whole fish at the supermarket for
bright eyes, bright red gills and a fresh sea (rather
than fishy) smell.

Mustard mackerel

| **7** Points per serving | Points per recipe **28** |

Serves 4 ● Preparation and cooking time 15 minutes ●
Calories per serving 390 ● Freezing not recommended

*Quick, grilled fish with a creamy white wine
sauce. Ideal served with a watercress and cherry
tomato salad which will not add any points.*

> 4 medium mackerel fillets, weighing 150 g (5½ oz) each
> 2 tablespoons Dijon mustard
> low-fat cooking spray
> 1 garlic clove, chopped
> 100 ml (3½ fl oz) white wine
> 4 tablespoons half-fat crème fraîche
> salt and freshly ground black pepper

1 Heat the grill to high and place the mackerel fillets,
skin side-down on a piece of foil on the grill pan. Spread
each with a little Dijon mustard and season generously.
Grill for 3–4 minutes until cooked through then place on
serving plates.

2 Meanwhile, heat a frying-pan and spray with the
low-fat cooking spray and fry the garlic for 1 minute
until just beginning to turn golden. Add the wine and
boil until reduced by half then add the crème fraîche,
stir through and boil for 1 minute. Pour over the
mackerel fillets and serve.

Variation You could use English mustard for this recipe
but it has a much harsher, hotter taste than the mild
and smooth Dijon.

Plaice in parsley sauce

| **5** Points per serving | Points per recipe **20½** |

Serves 4 ● Preparation and cooking time 20 minutes ●
Calories per serving 255 ● Freezing not recommended

*A traditional recipe that is wonderful served with
200 g (7 oz) new potatoes per person. Add 2 points
per serving.*

> 600 ml (1 pint) skimmed milk
> a large bunch of fresh parsley
> 2 tablespoons polyunsaturated margarine
> 2 tablespoons plain flour
> 1 tablespoon French mustard
> 12 × 50 g (1¾ oz) skinned plaice fillets
> salt and freshly ground black pepper

1 Heat the milk with the parsley stalks until nearly
boiling, then strain. In another pan cook the margarine
and flour together then pour in the strained milk a little
at a time and stir until smooth.

2 Blanch the parsley leaves in boiling water for 10
seconds then blend with 2 tablespoons of the water
in a food processor to make a green paste. Stir into the
milk sauce with the mustard and season.

3 Preheat the grill to medium. Place the plaice fillets on
a piece of foil on the grill pan which has been sprayed
with the low-fat cooking spray, season and spray them
with the low-fat cooking spray too. Grill for 3–4 minutes
until just cooked through.

4 Put the fillets on to serving plates and coat with the
parsley sauce then serve.

Variations Parsley sauce goes equally well with most
types of fish. Try fillets of trout (points remain the same),
cod (3½ points per serving) or lemon sole (3½ points per
serving).

**Put little encouraging notes on the fridge door, in cupboards, on mirrors –
anywhere you'll see them and they'll help keep you on track**

Monkfish and chick-pea stew

(**4**) Points per serving   Points per recipe **15½**

Serves 4 ● Preparation time 10 minutes ● Cooking time 30 minutes ● Calories per serving 135 ● Freezing not recommended *A simple stew that combines meaty monkfish with the robust, earthy flavours and textures of chick-peas, tomatoes, garlic, chilli and flat-leaf parsley.*

low-fat cooking spray
1 large potato (220 g/7½ oz), peeled and cut into
    small dice and rinsed
4 garlic cloves, crushed
1 teaspoon dried chilli flakes
4 medium plum tomatoes, chopped roughly
300 ml (½ pint) fish or vegetable stock
900 g (2 lb) monkfish fillets, cut into bite-size cubes
200 g can chick-peas, drained
a small bunch of fresh flat-leafed parsley, chopped
salt and freshly ground black pepper

1 Heat a large saucepan and spray with the low-fat cooking spray then fry the potato and garlic for 5 minutes.
2 Add the chilli, tomatoes and the stock and bring to the boil. Simmer for 20 minutes then add the fish and chick-peas.
3 Cook for another 5–10 minutes or until the fish is cooked through. Stir the parsley through, taste and season, then serve.

Variations Monkfish is great for this recipe as it is a meaty fish that holds together well but you could use cubes of swordfish (5 points per serving) or fresh tuna (4½ points per serving) very effectively.

Monkfish curry

(**4**) Points per serving   Points per recipe **15½**

Serves 4 ● Preparation and cooking time 25 minutes ● Calories per serving 215 ● Freezing not recommended *Monkfish is the best fish for this dish as it is so firm and chunky but it can be expensive. Cod and salmon make good alternatives but take care not to overcook them. Serve with 4 tablespoons of cooked basmati rice per person to soak up the soupy, coconut sauce, adding 3 extra points per serving.*

low-fat cooking spray
2 medium onions, diced finely
900 g (2 lb) skinless, boneless monkfish tail, cut into chunks
100 ml (3½ fl oz) 88% fat-free coconut milk
300 ml (½ pint) skimmed milk
225 g (8 oz) fresh leaf spinach, washed and stalks removed
a bunch of fresh coriander, chopped
For the curry paste
6 garlic cloves, peeled
6 cm (2½-inch) piece of fresh root ginger, peeled
1 medium red chilli, de-seeded
2 dried kaffir lime leaves, soaked in 2 tablespoons boiling
    water for 5 minutes then chopped, or zest of 2 limes
1 teaspoon ground star anise
1 teaspoon fennel seeds
salt and freshly ground black pepper

1 Put all the ingredients for the curry paste into a food processor and blend to a fine paste. Alternatively pulverise in a pestle and mortar until a paste.
Heat a frying-pan and spray with the low-fat cooking spray, add the onions and fry for 2 minutes, then add the fish and fry, stirring, for 2 minutes until sealed and white all over.
2 Add the curry paste and stir to cover all the fish. Add the coconut and skimmed milk and bring to a rapid simmer. Add the spinach and cook for 5 minutes, but do not boil, until the fish is just cooked through. Check the seasoning then sprinkle over the chopped coriander and serve.

Variations For a quick alternative, use 2 tablespoons Thai curry paste instead of all the individual curry paste ingredients. Add a ½ point per serving.
    The points per serving would be 4 with cod, 7½ with salmon.

Salmon fishcakes

Serves 4 ● Preparation and cooking time 30 minutes +
20 minutes chilling ● Calories per serving 325 ● Freezing
not recommended *Serve with a fresh tomato and
onion salad for no extra points.*

> 300 g (10½ oz) fresh salmon, cooked or canned salmon,
>   drained
> 300 g (10½ oz) potatoes, boiled in their skins then
>   peeled and mashed
> 2 tablespoons parsley, chopped
> 2 medium eggs, beaten
> 2 tablespoons plain flour
> 75 g (2¾ oz) fresh breadcrumbs
> low-fat cooking spray
> salt and freshly ground
>   black pepper
> chopped chives, to garnish

1 Mix together the salmon, potato, parsley, seasoning
and half the egg. Chill for at least 20 minutes.

2 Place on a floured surface. Shape into a roll. Cut into
8 slices. Shape each one into a flat round, about 6 cm
(2½-inches) in diameter and roll in the flour. Dip into the
remaining egg, then coat in the breadcrumbs.

3 Heat a frying-pan and spray with the low-fat cooking
spray then fry the fish cakes for 2–3 minutes on each
side or until golden brown and heated through. Garnish
sprinkled with chives.

Salmon steaks in foil

4½ Points per serving	Points per recipe 17½

Serves 4 ● Preparation time 10 minutes + 10 minutes–
3 hours marinating ● Cooking time 20 minutes ● Calories
per serving 335 ● Freezing not recommended *Salmon
steaks can be cooked with almost any combination
of your favourite herbs, to create your own version
of this recipe. Serve with green beans and 200 g
(7 oz) new potatoes adding on 2 extra points per
serving.*

4 salmon steaks, weighing approximately 175 g (6 oz) each
low-fat cooking spray
4 teaspoons polyunsaturated margarine
juice of 2 lemons
a small bunch of fresh parsley, chopped
a small bunch of fresh dill, chopped
salt and freshly ground black pepper
To serve
2 tablespoons half-fat crème fraîche
4 sprigs of fresh parsley or dill

1 Spray four individual pieces of cooking foil, big enough
to enclose the fish entirely, with the low-fat cooking
spray. Place a salmon steak on each piece of foil. Put
a teaspoon of margarine on the top of each steak and
then divide the rest of the ingredients evenly between
the steaks.

2 Fold up the salmon in the foil to make sealed parcels,
then leave in the fridge to marinate for up to 3 hours but
for a minimum of 10 minutes.

3 Preheat the oven to Gas Mark 6/200°C/400°F and
bake the fish for 20 minutes, until cooked through.

4 To serve, open the foil and remove the fish on to
plates, reserving the juices in the foil. Remove the outer
skin and the central bone from the fish and pour over
the juices left in the foil. Top each steak with a little
crème fraîche and garnish with the herbs.

Variation This recipe works equally well with cod steaks.
The points per serving will be 3.

Thai steamed salmon

6 Points per serving	Points per recipe 12½

Serves 2 ● Preparation and cooking time 30 minutes ●
Calories per serving 310 ● Freezing not recommended
*Steaming times for fish are totally dependent on
the thickness rather than the weight, so measure
your fish carefully. This Thai-influenced recipe is
light yet flavoursome.*

low-fat cooking spray
4 medium shallots, sliced finely
2.5 cm (1-inch) piece of fresh root ginger, sliced into fine
  matchsticks
2 garlic cloves, sliced into fine slivers
25 g (1 oz) soft brown sugar
2 tablespoons fish sauce
2 salmon steaks, each about 3 cm (1¼-inch) thick and
  weighing approximately 150 g (5½ oz) each
fresh coriander, to garnish

1 Heat a frying-pan and spray with the low-fat cooking
spray. Fry the shallots, ginger and garlic for 1 minute
until aromatic, then add the sugar and fish sauce. Stir
then set aside.

2 Place each piece of salmon on the middle of a piece
of baking paper, at least four times its size. Pile the
ginger mixture on top of each and then fold up the
baking paper around the fish to make an air-tight parcel.

3 Place both parcels in a steamer, cover and steam for
10 minutes or until the steaks are opaque and cooked
through. Serve immediately with the juices poured over
and fresh coriander sprigs.

Top tips Steam fish either in a fish kettle, bamboo
steamer or a saucepan with a steaming basket.

Skate with capers and garlic

3 Points per serving   Points per recipe **6½**

Serves 2 ● Preparation and cooking time 15 minutes ●
Calories per serving 190 ● Freezing not recommended
If you have not eaten skate before then do try it –
it is easy to cook and eat. It is available in the
supermarket, has no bones, is delicately flavoured
and has a meaty texture. Serve with 200 g (7 oz)
new potatoes per person and steamed spinach or
broccoli adding 2 points per serving.

2 skate wings, weighing approximately
    225 g (8 oz) each
1 bay leaf
6 peppercorns
a sprig of parsley
For the sauce
1 garlic clove, sliced in fine slivers
1 tablespoon olive oil
2 tablespoons white wine vinegar
2 tablespoons capers
2 tablespoons chopped fresh parsley

1 Put the skate wings in a large frying-pan with the bay
leaf, peppercorns and parsley. Pour in boiling water to
cover and bring back to the boil. Simmer for 6 minutes
until the fish is cooked through, then drain.
2 In another pan fry the garlic in the olive oil until just
golden then carefully add the vinegar (the oil may spit).
Add the capers and parsley and stir in. Place the skate
on plates then pour over the sauce over.

Variation Skate is also very good grilled under a medium
heat for 3–4 minutes on each side, then served with
this sauce.

Grilled trout with fennel

2½ Points per serving   Points per recipe **9½**

Serves 4 ● Preparation and cooking time 20 minutes ●
Calories per serving 235 ● Freezing not recommended
This recipe calls for bulb fennel which is now
available in most supermarkets. It has a crisp
aniseed flavour that complements the oily trout.
This is a light dish best served with a medium
slice of crusty bread to mop up the juices, adding
on 1 point per serving.

2 large fennel bulbs, each sliced into 6 lengthways
low-fat cooking spray
4 trout fillets, weighing approximately 150 g (5½ oz) each
juice of 1 lemon
2 teaspoons olive oil
salt and freshly ground black pepper
lemon wedges, to serve

1 Preheat the grill to medium. Boil or steam the fennel
pieces for 5 minutes. Spray an ovenproof dish with the
low-fat cooking spray and lay the fennel in it.
2 Season the trout fillets and place them on top of the
fennel. Pour the lemon juice over and spray with the
low-fat cooking spray.
3 Grill for 8 minutes then serve drizzled with the olive oil
and accompanied by the lemon wedges.

Trout with red pepper sauce

2 Points per serving	Points per recipe **8**

Serves 4 ● Preparation and cooking time 25 minutes ●
Calories per serving 230 ● Freezing not recommended

A delicious, bright red sauce perfectly complements the strong trout flavour.

2 medium red peppers, de-seeded and halved
4 garlic cloves, unpeeled
1 tablespoon balsamic vinegar
low-fat cooking spray
4 trout fillets, weighing approximately
   150 g (5½ oz) each, unskinned
salt and freshly ground black pepper

1 Preheat the grill to hot and put the peppers, skin side-up on the grill pan with the garlic cloves. Grill for 10 minutes until blistered and blackened all over. Transfer into a plastic bag, wrap up and leave to cool and 'sweat'.
2 When cool enough to handle remove the skin from the peppers and the garlic and place in a food processor with the vinegar and seasoning. Blend to a purée.
3 Cover the grill pan with a piece of foil, spray with the low-fat cooking spray then place the trout fillets on it skin side-up and spread with some of the red pepper paste. Grill for 4–5 minutes until cooked through and the skin crispy. Serve with more of the sauce.

Variations The purée is also good as a sauce for grilled meats, especially chicken, and for baked potatoes.

Pesto tuna

3½ Points per serving	Points per recipe **14½**

Serves 4 ● Preparation and cooking time 15 minutes ●
Calories per serving 285 ● Freezing not recommended

Pesto infuses fresh tuna steaks with a delicious basil flavour, perfectly complemented by a cherry tomato salsa for a touch of the 'Olé'. Serve with 150 g (5½ oz) pasta ribbons tossed in lemon juice adding 3 points per serving.

4 tuna steaks, weighing approximately
   150 g (5½ oz) each
30 g (1¼ oz) pesto sauce
lemon wedges, to serve
For the salsa
250 g pack cherry tomatoes, quartered
1 medium red onion, chopped finely
a bunch of fresh basil, chopped roughly
1 tablespoon balsamic vinegar
2 teaspoons olive oil
salt and freshly ground black pepper

1 Mix all the salsa ingredients together in a bowl then set aside. Preheat the grill to medium.
2 Spread each tuna steak with a little pesto on one side, place pesto-side-up on a piece of foil on the grill pan and grill for 4 minutes. Turn the steaks over, spread the other side with more of the pesto and grill for another 4 minutes until cooked through.
3 Serve immediately with the salsa and lemon wedges to squeeze over.

Variation For a fiery alternative, try spreading each tuna steak with a teaspoon of sweet chilli sauce instead. It's available in some supermarkets or in Asian food stores. 2 tablespoons are a ½ point.

Learn to really savour your food – make it look visually stimulating, slow the pace and separate eating from other activities such as watching television

Spicy crab cakes

3 Points per serving	Points per recipe **11½**

Serves 4 ● Preparation time 40 minutes + 30 minutes chilling (optional) ● Calories per serving 265 ● Freezing not recommended *Crab cakes make a special brunch dish and if you're using canned crab they needn't be expensive at all. Serve with a soy dipping sauce or sweet chilli sauce (2 tablespoons are a ½ point) and a crisp salad.*

2 medium red peppers, de-seeded and halved
1 medium egg, beaten
2 × 120 g cans white crab meat, drained
250 g (9 oz) cooked potatoes, peeled and diced
2 spring onions, chopped finely
½ teaspoon chilli powder or 1 small red chilli,
   de-seeded and chopped finely
a bunch of fresh coriander, chopped
1 tablespoon Worcestershire sauce
juice and zest of 2 limes
4 drops Tabasco sauce
1 teaspoon English mustard
4 medium slices bread, made into breadcrumbs
low-fat cooking spray
salt and freshly ground black pepper

1 Place the peppers cut-side down on the grill pan and grill them under a high heat until the skins are blackened and blistered. Place them in a plastic bag and leave to cool.

2 Meanwhile, mix together all the other ingredients, except the low-fat cooking spray in a bowl. When the peppers are cool enough to handle, peel away the skins and chop the flesh finely then add to the crab cake mixture and mix in.

3 Make the mixture into eight patties and, if you have time, place on a tray in the fridge to firm up for 30 minutes. Otherwise cook them immediately in a frying-pan sprayed with the low-fat cooking spray and fry for 4–5 minutes on either side until golden brown and cooked through. You may need to do this in two batches.

Top tip Handle the crab cakes carefully if they have not been chilled as they will break up easily.

Moules Provençales

½ Point per serving	Points per recipe **2½**

Serves 4 ● Preparation and cooking time 20 minutes ● Calories per serving 100 ● Freezing not recommended *A very quick and simple recipe for one of the British Isles' most common and most delectable shellfish. Serve with a medium slice of crusty fresh bread to mop up the juices, adding 1 point per slice.*

low-fat cooking spray
2 garlic cloves, chopped finely
1 medium onion, chopped finely
150 ml (5 fl oz) stock
400 g can chopped tomatoes
a bunch of fresh basil or thyme, chopped
1 kg (2 lb 4 oz) mussels, soaked, rinsed and drained
salt and freshly ground black pepper

1 Heat a large saucepan and spray with the low-fat cooking spray then sauté the garlic and onion for 5 minutes until soft, adding a little water if necessary to prevent them from sticking.

2 Add the stock, tomatoes, herbs and seasoning and cook briskly for 5 minutes. Then add the mussels and cover the pan with a lid. Continue to cook for another 5 minutes, shaking the pan vigorously a few times.

3 When you remove the lid the mussels should have fully opened. Discard any that have not.

4 Spoon into serving bowls and serve.

Top tip Care must be taken to avoid eating a bad mussel (which includes soaking them, changing the water twice, then rinsing well in fresh tap water to thoroughly clean them). To check that each is alive, before cooking gently try and close it with your fingers, it should snap shut at your touch. If it remains open, or fails to shut completely it is safest to assume that it is dead so discard it.

Spicy Thai mussels

Serves 2 as a main course ● Preparation and cooking time 35 minutes ● Calories per serving 170 ● Freezing not recommended *These mussels are cooked in a soupy mixture of chilli, coconut and lime. Fragrant Thai rice, or noodles make good accompaniments, adding the extra points as necessary.*

2 teaspoons Thai green curry paste
100 ml (3½ fl oz) 88% fat-free coconut milk
5 cm (2-inch) piece of fresh root ginger, grated
1 medium fresh red chilli, de-seeded and chopped finely
850 ml (1½ pints) vegetable or chicken stock
2 kg (4½ lb) mussels, soaked, rinsed and drained
juice and zest of 2 limes
a small bunch of fresh basil or coriander, chopped roughly

1 Heat a large saucepan, add the curry paste and fry for 1 minute then add the coconut milk. Cook for another minute then add the ginger, chilli and the stock. Cook for about 10 minutes.

2 Add the mussels and cover with a lid. Shake the pan vigorously and cook for 3 minutes. Add the lime juice and zest and coriander or basil, shake again and cook another 3 minutes. Discard any mussels that have not opened and serve. (scc Top tip for Moules Provençales on page 124).

Variations Serve as a starter for 4 and the points per serving will be 2½.

Prawn and lime cocktail

Serves 2 ● Preparation time 5 minutes ● Calories per serving 210 ● Freezing not recommended *A classic dish given a new twist with the addition of lime.*

200 g (7 oz) cooked, peeled prawns, defrosted if frozen
4 tablespoons low-fat mayonnaise
1 tablespoon tomato purée
juice and zest of 2 limes
2 celery sticks, chopped finely
2 spring onions, chopped finely
2 Little Gem lettuces, shredded
salt and freshly ground black pepper

1 Mix together the prawns, mayonnaise, tomato purée and lime juice, then stir in the celery, spring onions and season to taste.

2 Divide the shredded lettuce between two serving plates or glasses and top with the prawn mixture, garnishing with the lime zest and a little freshly ground black pepper.

Sip a glass of water or have a cup of tea while you prepare food. It will stop you nibbling!

Seafood and parsley tart: Enjoy delicious seafood in a savoury egg custard on a crisp, golden pastry base for only 5½ points per serving

Seafood and parsley tart

5½ Points per serving	Points per recipe **21½**

Serves 4 ● Preparation time 40 minutes + 30 minutes chilling ● Cooking time 30 minutes ● Calories per serving 290 ● Freezing not recommended *A low-point version of a classic French tart.*

For the pastry
50 g (1¾ oz) polyunsaturated margarine
100 g (3½ oz) plain flour
a pinch of salt
1 medium egg white, beaten
For the filling
low-fat cooking spray
4 medium shallots, chopped (or 1 large onion)
4 garlic cloves, chopped
200 g bag frozen mixed seafood, defrosted
50 ml (2 fl oz) dry white wine
a small bunch of fresh parsley, chopped
2 medium eggs, beaten
150 ml (5 fl oz) skimmed milk
salt and freshly ground black pepper

1 Make the pastry by rubbing the margarine into the flour and salt until the mixture resembles fresh breadcrumbs then add 1 tablespoon of water and quickly bring together into a ball with your hand. Wrap in clingfilm and chill for 30 minutes.

2 Preheat the oven to Gas Mark 6/200°C/400°F. Roll out the pastry to a circle about 5 mm (¼-inch) thick and use to line a 19 cm (7½-inch) loose-bottomed flan tin. Line with foil or baking paper and fill with baking beans.

3 Bake blind for 15 minutes then remove the beans and lining, brush the case with the beaten egg white and bake for a further 10 minutes or until evenly golden brown.

4 Lower the oven temperature to Gas Mark 5/190°C/375°F. Heat a saucepan and spray with the low-fat cooking spray then fry the shallots and garlic for about 4 minutes until softened then add the seafood with the white wine and parsley.

5 Remove from the heat and stir in the eggs, milk and seasoning. Pour into the pastry case and bake for 25 to 30 minutes, until just set and lightly browned.

Top tip To save time you could use ready-made shortcrust pastry.

Prawns in garlic and ginger

1 Point per serving	Points per recipe **4½**

Serves 4 ● Preparation and cooking time 15 minutes ● Calories per serving 80 ● Freezing not recommended *A very simple dish that is cooked in minutes. Serve with 200 g (7 oz) cooked egg noodles and steamed broccoli, adding 3 points per serving.*

low-fat cooking spray
1 teaspoon sesame oil
2.5 cm (1-inch) piece of fresh root ginger, grated finely
2 garlic cloves, cut into thin slivers
juice of 2 limes
2 tablespoons light soy sauce
250 g (9 oz) peeled, raw prawns
a small bunch of fresh coriander, chopped

1 Heat a wok or large frying-pan and spray with the low-fat cooking spray, add the sesame oil and heat until hot then add the ginger and garlic and stir-fry for 1 minute.

2 Add the lime juice, soy and the prawns and stir-fry for a 3–4 minutes more until the prawns are pink. Sprinkle with fresh coriander and serve.

Top tip The larger tiger or king prawns are the best to use in this recipe.

Chilli seafood

| ½ Point per serving | Points per recipe **3** |

Serves 4 ● Preparation and cooking time 15 minutes ●
Calories per serving 100 ● Freezing not recommended

You could just use prawns for this recipe, but I've chosen the bags of frozen mixed seafood for their ease and convenience. The sauce gives the dish a good, spicy kick. Serve with steamed bok choy and 3 tablespoons cooked rice adding 3 points per serving.

2 tablespoons hoisin sauce
2 tablespoons chilli sauce
1 teaspoon soy sauce
1 teaspoon fish sauce
½ teaspoon caster sugar
½ teaspoon sesame oil
low-fat cooking spray
5 cm (2-inch) piece of fresh root ginger, peeled and
  chopped finely
6 spring onions, chopped, plus extra to garnish
2 garlic cloves, crushed
250 g (9 oz) frozen mixed seafood, defrosted
½ teaspoon dried chilli flakes

1 Mix together the first six ingredients in a bowl then set aside.
2 Heat a wok or large frying-pan and spray with the low-fat cooking spray, then fry the ginger, chopped spring onions and garlic for 1 minute. Add the seafood and chilli and toss well to mix.
3 Pour the sauce mixture over and toss again. Serve immediately, scattered with spring onion.

Variation This recipe is also very good made with 4 medium, skinless, sliced raw chicken breasts instead of the seafood. The points per serving will be 2½.

Grilled snapper with mango salsa

| 2 Points per serving | Points per recipe **7½** |

Serves 4 ● Preparation and cooking time 20 minutes ●
Calories per serving 130 ● Freezing not recommended

The fillets are grilled until the skin is crisp and charred then served with salsa for a New World taste experience.

low-fat cooking spray
4 × 100 g (3½ oz) unskinned snapper fillets
salt and freshly ground black pepper
coriander, to garnish (optional)
For the salsa
1 large red chilli
4 spring onions, chopped finely
1 medium ripe but firm mango, skinned and diced finely
200 g (7 oz) cherry tomatoes, quartered
juice of 1 lime

1 Heat the grill to high and spray a baking sheet with the low-fat cooking spray. Cut each fillet into three slightly on the diagonal and place skin-side-up on the baking sheet. Spray with the low-fat cooking spray and season well. Grill for 3–4 minutes until cooked through.
2 Meanwhile, mix all the salsa ingredients together, season, and spoon on to plates. Arrange the grilled fish on top and serve, garnished with coriander, if using.

Top tip To prepare a mango, stand it on its stalk end and slice two thick slices from each side. Place these skin-side down on the board and with the tip of the knife cross-hatch the flesh down as far as the skin. Pick up the piece and push the skin upwards to make a 'hedgehog'. Slice off the cubes and eat or use.
Variation Try papaya instead of the mango for another interesting flavour.

Success seems to be largely a matter
of hanging on after others have let go

Goan prawn curry

Serves 4 ● Preparation and cooking time 30 minutes ●
Calories per serving 140 ● Freezing not recommended

*Goa is on the west coast of India, famous for it's
fantastic seafood cooking. Freshly caught fish,
prawns, lobsters etc. are combined with the usual
Indian curry spices of cumin, coriander and
turmeric but with the more usually South East
Asian addition of coconut and fresh ginger. Serve
with 4 tablespoons cooked basmati rice adding
3 points per serving.*

400 g (14 oz) frozen uncooked prawns, defrosted and
    peeled, tails left on
2 tablespoons white wine vinegar
1 teaspoon tumeric powder
1 tablespoon coriander seeds
1 teaspoon cumin seeds
low-fat cooking spray
1 medium onion, sliced finely
4 garlic cloves, cut into slivers
2.5 cm (1-inch) piece of fresh root ginger, peeled and
    chopped finely
100 ml (3½ fl oz) 88%-fat-free coconut milk
juice of 1 lemon
300 ml (½ pint) stock
1 large green chilli, de-seeded and sliced thinly
1 bunch fresh coriander
salt

1 Place the prawns in a bowl with the vinegar and ½ a
teaspoon of salt and soak for 5 minutes to enhance their
flavour. Meanwhile, grind the turmeric, coriander and
cumin seeds together in a pestle and mortar or spice
mill, until they are a fine powder.
2 Heat a large frying-pan and spray with the low-fat
cooking spray, add the onion, garlic and ginger and fry
gently for 5 minutes until softened. Stir in the ground
spices and fry for 2 minutes more.
3 Add the coconut milk, lemon juice and stock, bring
to the boil then simmer for 5 minutes. Add the prawns
and cook for 3–4 minutes until they have all turned pink.
Finally, stir in the chilli and coriander just before serving.

Variation Use 2 tablespoons of curry paste for
convenience instead of all or some of the spices.
Add a ½ point per serving.

American shrimp

Serves 4 ● Preparation and cooking time 35 minutes ●
Calories per serving 435 ● Freezing not recommended

*This is a distinctively spicy stew, popular in the
southern states of America. Delicious served with
a glass of chilled lager (1 point per half pint).*

800 g (1 lb 11 oz) potatoes, peeled and cut into large chunks
4 medium rashers lean back bacon, fat and rind removed
    and cut into thin strips
450 g (1 lb) frozen sweetcorn
400 g (14 oz) frozen, cooked, peeled prawns
For the seasoning
2 tablespoons yellow mustard seeds
½ tablespoon black peppercorns
½ tablespoon dried chilli flakes
1 dried bay leaf
½ tablespoon coriander seeds
½ tablespoon ground ginger
1 tablespoon ground mace
1 tablespoon salt

1 Bring 1.2 litres (2 pints) of water to the boil in a large
pan. Meanwhile, put all the seasoning ingredients except
the salt into a spice mill or pestle and mortar and grind
to a fine powder. Add the salt and blend very quickly.
2 Add all but 2 tablespoons of the seasoning mixture to
the boiling water, then add the potatoes and simmer for
15 minutes.
3 Add the bacon and sweetcorn and simmer for 5 minutes
more. Add the prawns and cook for 5 minutes without
boiling then drain.
4 Serve piled on to plates with the reserved seasoning
mix sprinkled over the top.

All the recipes have been carefully chosen and developed to minimise points, while maximising flavour and satisfaction. The chapter called Oodles of Noodles, Rice and Beans on page 70 has more tasty meat dishes.

mouthwatering
meat

Steak, mushroom and Guinness pie

7½ Points per serving	Points per recipe **30½**

Serves 4 ● Preparation time 35 minutes ● Cooking time 2½ hours ● Calories per serving 330 ● Freezing recommended *A nostalgic and delicious pie.*

low-fat cooking spray
2 medium onions, diced finely
1 medium carrot, sliced finely
2 celery sticks, sliced finely
2 sprigs fresh sage, chopped
200 g (7 oz) button mushrooms
4 tablespoons plain flour
400 g (14 oz) lean stewing steak, cubed
150 ml (5 fl oz) stock
150 ml (5 fl oz) Guinness
salt and freshly ground black pepper
For the pastry
100 g (3½ oz) shop-bought ready-rolled puff pastry

1 Preheat the oven to Gas Mark 2/150°C/300°F. Heat a non-stick frying-pan with the low-fat cooking spray and fry the onions, carrot, celery and sage until softened, then remove from the heat and put into an ovenproof casserole dish.

2 In the same pan fry the mushrooms until softened and add them to the casserole dish.

3 Sprinkle the flour on a plate, season then roll the meat in it until completely covered. Spray the pan with low-fat cooking spray again and fry the meat until browned all over. Add to the casserole dish. Pour the stock and Guinness over and put in the oven, covered, for 2 hours, stirring occasionally.

4 Meanwhile, place a 20 cm (8-inch) pie dish upside-down on the rolled-out pastry and cut out a circle slightly larger than the dish.

5 When the meat mixture is cooked, carefully transfer to the pie dish and increase the oven temperature to Gas Mark 7/220°C/425°F.

6 Place the pastry on top of the dish, using any trimmings to make leaves for the top. Push down the pastry on to the edge of the dish to seal and 'knock up' the sides. Brush with a little skimmed milk and make a slit in the middle for the steam to escape.

7 Bake for 15–20 minutes or until risen and golden.

Rich beef stew

5 Points per serving — Points per recipe **19½**

Serves 4 ● Preparation time 35 minutes ● Cooking time 1 hour ● Calories per serving 340 ● Freezing recommended
A dark, thick stew with a tang of fruit and tomato. Served here with floury boiled potatoes but baked potatoes would also be lovely.

> 400 g (14 oz) extra-lean beef, cubed
> low-fat cooking spray
> 2 large onions, chopped
> 2 garlic cloves, peeled
> 100 g (3½ oz) dried apricots, chopped
> 8 sun-dried tomato halves, sliced
> 400 g can chopped tomatoes
> 600 g (1 lb 5 oz) floury potatoes, peeled and cubed e.g.
>   Maris Piper, King Edward
> a bunch of fresh parsley, chopped, to serve (optional)
> salt and freshly ground black pepper

1 Heat a non-stick frying pan and dry-fry the beef over high heat until it is browned all over. Remove from the heat and set aside.

2 Spray the frying-pan with the low-fat cooking spray and reduce the heat to medium. Fry the onions and garlic for 4 minutes until softened. Put the meat back in the pan, scatter the apricots and sun-dried tomatoes over and season well.

3 Add the canned tomatoes and 600 ml (1 pint) water and bring to the boil. Reduce the heat and simmer for 1 hour until thick and rich, stirring occasionally.

4 Meanwhile, boil the potatoes in plenty of boiling salted water, drain and serve with the stew, scattered with parsley, if using.

Variations You could use dried prunes (4½ points per serving), raisins (5 points per serving) or dates (5 points per serving) instead of the apricots.

Steak sandwich with onion jam

6 Points per serving — Points per recipe **12**

Serves 2 ● Preparation and cooking time 25 minutes ● Calories per serving 365 ● Freezing not recommended
This is one of the best lunches I know. Usually you have to pay a fortune for it in a flashy restaurant, but it is quick and easy and altogether more satisfying to take the trouble to make and eat at home.

> 1 French bread baton, weighing approximately 150 g (5½ oz)
> 1 small beef steak, weighing approximately 140 g (5 oz)
> low-fat cooking spray
> 2 medium red onions, sliced thinly
> 2 teaspoons caster sugar
> 2 teaspoons Dijon mustard
> about 4–6 lettuce leaves
> salt and freshly ground black pepper

1 Halve the bread baton lengthways and then cut into two and place on two serving plates. Cut the steak in half and place both halves between two sheets of polythene or baking paper. Beat with a rolling pin until thin, but be careful not to break up the meat.

2 Heat a non-stick frying-pan and spray with the low-fat cooking spray and fry the onions for about 5 minutes until softened. Sprinkle with sugar and 2 tablespoons of water and continue to cook for about 5 minutes until all the water has evaporated and the onions have caramelised.

3 Remove the onions from the pan and set aside.

4 Spray the pan with low-fat cooking spray again and when it is very hot, fry the thin steaks for 1 minute on each side, seasoning before they go into the pan.

5 Meanwhile, spread the bread with the mustard and top with some lettuce leaves. Place the cooked steaks on top and cover with onion jam. Replace the top halves and serve.

Variations If you are not a fan of beef, then try the same recipe with a 140 g (5 oz) skinless chicken breast (5 points per serving) or 140 g (5 oz) turkey breast steak (4½ points per serving).

Beef Provençal

4	Points per serving	Points per recipe	17

Serves 4 ● Preparation time 25 minutes ● Cooking time 2½ hours ● Calories per serving 295 ● Freezing recommended *A robust, earthy stew from Provence in Southern France. Serve with a Green Bean and Shallot Salad (page 43).*

    1½ tablespoons seasoned flour
    400 g (14 oz) lean stewing steak, fat removed and sliced
    3 teaspoons olive oil
    4 medium carrots, sliced
    3 medium onions, chopped
    2 garlic cloves, crushed
    150 g (5½ oz) mushrooms, sliced thickly
    200 ml (7 fl oz) red wine
    200 ml (7 fl oz) stock
    10 stoned olives in brine, chopped
    salt and freshly ground black pepper

1 Preheat the oven to Gas Mark 2/150°C/300°F. Put the flour on a plate then roll the meat in it to coat. Heat the oil in a non-stick frying-pan, add the meat and brown all over. Transfer to an ovenproof casserole dish.

2 Cook the carrots, onions and garlic for 5 minutes in the same frying-pan until beginning to brown and soften. Add the mushrooms, wine and stock and bring to the boil, scraping up any juices stuck on the bottom of the pan and stirring in.

3 Pour over the meat in the casserole dish, cover and cook for 2½ hours. Just before serving, check the seasoning and sprinkle the olives over.

Steak au poivre

8	Points per serving	Points per recipe	16

Serves 2 ● Preparation and cooking time 15 minutes + up to 3 hours marinating ● Calories per serving 345 ● Freezing recommended *This classic recipe is still the all-time-favourite way of eating steak for many people. It is delicious with boiled, minted new potatoes (2 points per 200 g/7 oz serving) and a fresh, peppery watercress salad.*

    2 rump or entrecote steaks, each 2.5 cm (1-inch) thick
        and weighing approximately 175 g (6 oz)
    1 heaped teaspoon mixed black, white and pink
        peppercorns
    2 teaspoons olive oil
    2 shallots, chopped
    5 tablespoons meat or vegetable stock
    30 ml (1 fl oz) brandy
    2 tablespoons half-fat crème fraîche
    salt

1 Trim the steaks of any fat, crush the peppercorns in a pestle and mortar or spice mill then rub into both sides of the steaks, pressing them in with your hand. Cover with foil and leave as long as possible for up to 3 hours.

2 Heat a non-stick pan, add the olive oil and fry the steaks for 4–5 minutes for medium done. Season with salt, remove from the pan and set aside, keeping warm, while you make the sauce.

3 Fry the shallots for 2 minutes in the oil and meat juices remaining in the pan then add the stock and brandy and cook rapidly, scraping up the juices from the bottom of the pan and stirring in. Add the crème fraîche and bring to the boil then pour over the steak and serve.

Variation This recipe is also absolutely delicious made with fresh tuna steaks rather than the beef. The points per serving will be 4½.

Try to limit alcohol to 14 points a week

Beef goulash

4½ Points per serving   Points per recipe **19**

Serves 4 ● Preparation time 20 minutes ● Cooking time 2½ hours ● Calories per serving 335 ● Freezing recommended *A very slow-cooked casserole that requires a little planning but can then be left to transform into a satisfying dinner.*

400 g (14 oz) stewing steak, cubed
450 g (1 lb) onions, chopped
2 garlic cloves, crushed
2 tablespoons plain flour
2 tablespoons paprika
a bunch of parsley or a few sprigs of thyme
600 ml (1 pint) tomato juice
450 g (1 lb) potatoes, peeled and cut into cubes but
    not washed
2 teaspoons tomato purée
2 tablespoons low-fat plain yogurt
1 medium green pepper, chopped finely, to garnish (optional)
salt and freshly ground black pepper

1 Preheat the oven to Gas Mark 2/150°C/300°F.

2 Dry-fry the beef in a non-stick casserole dish until browned all over, then remove and set aside. Add the onions and garlic to the pan and cook for 5 minutes until soft.

3 Return the meat to the pan and blend in the flour and paprika. Add the herbs, season and add tomato juice to cover. Cover with a lid and put in the oven for 1½ hours.

4 Add the potatoes to the goulash and return to the oven for 1 hour.

5 Remove from the oven and stir in the tomato purée and yogurt, sprinkle with the chopped pepper, if using, and serve.

Roast beef with Yorkshire pudding

5½ Points per serving	Points per recipe 33

Serves 6 ● Preparation time 1 hour ● Cooking time 1½ hours ● Calories per serving 310 ● Freezing not recommended *Serve with the Perfect roast potatoes on page 69.*

2 tablespoons English mustard powder
1 beef joint e.g. sirloin, rib or topside, weighing
  approximately 1 kg (2 lb 4 oz), boned and rolled
For the Yorkshire pudding
1 medium egg
150 ml (5 fl oz) skimmed milk
a pinch of salt
50 g (1¾ oz) plain flour
low-fat cooking spray
For the gravy
1 tablespoon plain flour
300 ml (½ pint) stock

1 Preheat the oven to Gas Mark 7/220°C/425°F. Rub the mustard powder all over the outside of the meat and place in a roasting tin, cut-side down. For a medium-cooked joint, roast for 20 minutes then reduce the oven temperature to Gas Mark 4/180°C/350°F and cook for another hour.

2 Meanwhile, make the Yorkshire pudding batter by whisking the egg with the milk and salt in a bowl then leave to stand for 15 minutes. Add the flour, whisk again until thoroughly mixed and leave to stand until ready to cook.

3 Remove the meat from the roasting tray, and place on a carving board, cover with foil and leave to stand. Do not wash the tray.

4 Increase the oven temperature to Gas Mark 7/220°C/425°F. Spray a 10–12 cup non-stick Yorkshire pudding tin with the low-fat cooking spray and place in the oven to get hot. After 10 minutes remove using an oven glove, pour in the prepared batter and return to the oven for 15–20 minutes until risen and golden.

5 Meanwhile, make the gravy in the roasting tray. Place the tray on the hob over a high heat (use an oven glove as it will still be very hot). Sprinkle in the flour then pour in the stock. Scrape up all the juices stuck to the bottom of the tray with a wooden spoon and bring to the boil. Boil for 1 minute then strain into a serving jug.

6 Carve the beef and serve 3 medium slices (35 g/1¼ oz each) with the Yorkshire puddings and gravy.

Kebabs with mint and yogurt dip

5½ Points per serving	Points per recipe 22

Serves 4 ● Preparation and cooking time 30 minutes + 1–12 hours marinating ● Calories per serving 265 ● Freezing recommended *Cooked either on a BBQ or under the grill this hot, cumin and garlic-flavoured beef stays moist and tender. Best served with a medium pitta bread and green salad, adding on 2½ points each.*

400 g (14 oz) lean beef steak, cubed
200 g (7 oz) mushrooms
8 fresh bay leaves
For the marinade
2 tablespoons olive oil
1 tablespoon red wine
1 large red chilli, de-seeded and chopped finely
1 tablespoon ground cumin
2 garlic cloves, crushed
salt and freshly ground black pepper
For the dip
300 ml (½ pint) low-fat plain yogurt
a bunch of fresh mint, chopped finely
½ cucumber, peeled, de-seeded and chopped finely

1 Mix all the marinade ingredients together in a shallow bowl then mix in the beef, mushrooms and bay leaves. Cover and marinate in the refrigerator for at least 1 hour, preferably overnight.

2 Make the dip by mixing together all the ingredients and turning into a serving bowl. Refrigerate before serving.

3 To cook the kebabs, heat the BBQ or grill, thread the meat, mushrooms and bay leaves alternately on to soaked wooden or metal skewers then grill for 5–10 minutes, turning once, until cooked through.

4 Serve the kebabs, pushed off the skewers, with the dip.

Top tip Soak wooden skewers in water for 10 minutes before using to prevent them from burning.

Szechuan beef stir-fry

| 2 | Points per serving | Points per recipe | 9 |

Serves 4 ● Preparation time 35 minutes + 4 hours marinating ● Calories per serving 160 ● Freezing recommended *A tasty stir-fry with the most tender beef.*

250 g (9 oz) lean beef braising steak, cut into thin strips
1 teaspoon bicarbonate of soda
For the sauce
1 teaspoon cornflour
2 tablespoons tomato purée
1 tablespoon of rice or wine vinegar
1 teaspoon chilli powder
1 teaspoon caster sugar
2 teaspoons soy sauce
For the stir-fry
2 teaspoons peanut oil
2 garlic cloves, sliced into slivers
2.5 cm (1-inch) piece of fresh root ginger, peeled and sliced into fine matchsticks
1 bunch of spring onions, sliced finely
200 g (7 oz) mushrooms, preferably oyster, sliced finely
125 g can water chestnuts, drained

1 Put the beef in a bowl with the bicarbonate of soda and just enough water to cover. Leave to marinate in the refrigerator for about 4 hours.
2 Mix the cornflour into a paste with 2 tablespoons water and then mix in all the other sauce ingredients.
3 When ready to cook, drain the beef and pat dry on kitchen paper. Heat the oil in a large frying-pan or wok until just smoking then add the beef and toss around the pan for 2 minutes. Add the garlic and ginger and stir-fry for another minute.
4 Add all the other ingredients, toss and stir-fry over high heat for 2 minutes. Give the sauce ingredients a stir and pour over. Bring to the boil, stir and serve.

Variation For a quick and convenient alternative, buy ready-made Szechuan sauce from a supermarket and use instead of all the sauce ingredients. With 4 tablespoons the points will stay the same.

Lazy lasagne

| 6½ | Points per serving | Points per recipe | 27 |

Serves 4 ● Preparation time 35 minutes ● Cooking time 40 minutes ● Calories per serving 585 ● Freezing recommended *As delicious as lasagne can be, it is still fairly time-consuming to make. For this recipe, labour-saving products have been used to produce a satisfying lasagne in minutes. Serve with a crisp green salad for no extra points.*

low-fat cooking spray
400 g (14 oz) lean minced beef
1 tablespoon Worcestershire sauce
520 g jar low-fat ragu Bolognese sauce
200 g (7 oz) button mushrooms, sliced in half
250 g (9 oz) no-precook lasagne sheets
For the sauce
300 ml (½ pint) skimmed milk
1 bouquet garni sachet
3 tablespoons cornflour
50 g (1¾ oz) mature, reduced-fat Cheddar cheese
2 teaspoons French mustard
salt and freshly ground black pepper

1 Preheat the oven to Gas Mark 5/190°C/375°F. Heat a large, non-stick frying-pan and spray with the low-fat cooking spray. Fry the meat until it is not longer pink and the grains are separated, stirring, then season and add the Worcestershire sauce, ragu and mushrooms. Bring to the boil. Simmer for a few minutes.
2 Meanwhile, make the cheese sauce by simmering all but 2 tablespoons of the milk with the bouquet garni for 5 minutes. Remove the bouquet garni and blend the cornflour with the remaining milk and add to the hot milk. Bring back to the boil and cook for a further 2 minutes until thickened, stirring. Season, then add the cheese and mustard and stir again.
3 Put a layer of mince in the base of an ovenproof dish, cover with a layer of lasagne sheets, then a layer of mince. Repeat until you have used up all the lasagne and mince. Pour the cheese sauce over and bake for 40 minutes until golden and tender when tested with the point of a sharp knife.

Menu plan

Fast Family Feast

~

Tomato, Mozzarella and Basil Salad, page 42
1 serving . . . 2 points

~

Lazy Lasagne, page 136
(pictured here)
1 serving . . . 6½ points

~

Peach Brûlée, page 180
1 serving . . . 2 points

Total points per meal 10½ points

Beef hotpot

Serves 4 ● Preparation time 30 minutes ● Cooking time 1 hour ● Calories per serving 325 ● Freezing recommended *A comforting casserole full of flavoursome root vegetables with a warming hint of wine.*

>   low-fat cooking spray
>   400 g (14 oz) lean stewing steak, cubed
>   4 medium onions, chopped
>   4 garlic cloves, chopped
>   4 medium carrots, chopped into semi-circles
>   4 medium parsnips, chopped into semi-circles
>   4 small swedes or turnips, chopped
>   leaves of a bunch of fresh thyme or from 4 sprigs fresh
>   rosemary, chopped
>   400 g can chopped tomatoes
>   2 tablespoons tomato purée
>   100 ml (3½ fl oz) red wine (optional)
>   salt and freshly ground black pepper

1 Heat a large casserole dish and spray with the low-fat cooking spray then brown and season the beef. Remove and set aside. Add the onions and garlic to the pan and cook for 4 minutes until softened.

2 Return the beef to the casserole dish with the carrots, parsnips, swede or turnips, herbs, tomatoes, tomato purée, red wine, if using, season and add enough water to cover.

3 Bring to the boil, cover and simmer for 1 hour or until thick and rich.

Burgers with spicy salsa

Serves 4 ● Preparation and cooking time 30 minutes ● Calories per serving 275 ● Freezing recommended *Tasting these burgers you would never guess that they are packed full of vegetables, giving you lots of nutrients and fewer points than other types of burger. Serve in medium burger buns (2 points each) with lots of crisp lettuce.*

>   250 g (9 oz) lean minced beef
>   2 medium courgettes, grated
>   2 medium carrots, grated
>   1 large onion, chopped finely
>   2 garlic cloves, crushed
>   1 medium red pepper, de-seeded and chopped
>   2 teaspoons English mustard
>   2 medium slices bread, made into breadcrumbs
>   1 medium egg
>   salt and freshly ground black pepper
>   low-fat cooking spray
>   **For the spicy salsa**
>   6 medium plum tomatoes, quartered, de-seeded and
>   diced finely
>   1 small red onion, diced finely
>   1 small red chilli, de-seeded and diced finely
>   juice of 1 lime
>   2 teaspoons balsamic vinegar

1 Mix together all the ingredients for the burgers, except the cooking spray, then take tablespoonfuls of the mixture and roll into eight patties. Heat a frying-pan and spray with the low-fat cooking spray and fry the patties in batches for 3–4 minutes on each side until cooked through. Remove from the pan and set aside, covered with foil to keep warm while you cook the remainder.

2 Make the salsa by mixing all the ingredients together.

Top tip Burgers can also be cooked on a char-grill or BBQ for a smokey flavour.

Remember that it's natural for

your weight to fluctuate now and again

Honey and mustard pork skewers

4½ Points per serving	Points per recipe 18½

Serves 4 ● Preparation and cooking time 30 minutes ●
Calories per serving 255 ● Freezing not recommended
*Tender pieces of pork and wedges of apple threaded
on to skewers and grilled with a honey and
mustard glaze and served with a tangy crème
fraîche sauce.*

    400 g (14 oz) lean pork, cut into 16 cubes
    4 medium dessert apples, cored and quartered
    2 tablespoons clear honey
    2 tablespoons whole-grain mustard
    100 ml (3½ fl oz) half-fat crème fraîche

1 Preheat the grill to high and lay a piece of foil on top
of the grill pan. Alternately thread pieces of pork and
apple wedges on to eight metal or wooden skewers
(see Top tips).
2 Gently heat the honey and mustard together in a small
pan then brush over the meat and apples.
3 Grill on one side and then turn over, brush again and
grill the other side for a few minutes until they are
golden brown and cooked through.
4 Add the crème fraîche to the remaining honey and
mustard in the pan and bring to the boil. Place the
skewers on serving plates, pour the sauce over and
serve.

Top tips If using wooden skewers then soak them in
water for 10 minutes before use to prevent them from
burning under the grill. If you have a rosemary bush in
your garden then pick some old, woody, thick stalks as
these can be used as a fragrant alternative skewer.

Sweet, sticky, peppered pork

3½ Points per serving	Points per recipe 14

Serves 4 ● Preparation and cooking time 25 minutes ●
Calories per serving 260 ● Freezing not recommended
*A quick and easy recipe with vibrant flavours.
Serve with 4 tablespoons cooked rice and a salad,
adding on 3 points per serving.*

    2 tablespoons reduced-sugar marmalade
    4 pork escalopes, weighing approximately 150 g
        (5½ oz) each
    2 tablespoons peppercorns, crushed
    low-fat cooking spray
    For the sauce
    2 tablespoons balsamic vinegar
    150 ml (5 fl oz) orange juice
    1 tablespoon whole-grain mustard
    1 teaspoon cornflour, made into a paste with a
        tablespoon of water

1 Gently heat the marmalade in a pan with 2 tablespoons
of water, then brush over the pork escalopes. Place the
crushed peppercorns on a plate and press the escalopes
down on to them so that they become covered.
2 Heat a non-stick pan and spray with the low-fat
cooking spray. Fry the escalopes in 2 batches for 2–3
minutes on each side until cooked through, then set
aside and keep them warm while you make the sauce.
3 With the pan still on the heat pour in the vinegar and
scrape up all the left over juices and bits left from the
pork with a wooden spatula or spoon. Pour in the orange
juice and stir in the mustard and cornflour and bring to
the boil. Boil for 1 minute, stirring, until the sauce has
thickened.
4 Serve the pork with the sauce poured over.

Top tip For a more attractive dish, buy mixed peppercorns
which include red, white and black ones.

Italian pork-stuffed courgettes

| 3½ | Points per serving | Points per recipe | 15 |

Serves 4 ● Preparation time 30 minutes ● Cooking time 20 minutes ● Calories per serving 295 ● Freezing recommended *A wonderfully evocative recipe that is simple to make. Serve with a point-free salad.*

> 8 medium courgettes
> low-fat cooking spray
> 1 small onion, chopped finely
> 2 garlic cloves, chopped finely
> 400 g (14 oz) lean pork mince
> leaves from 4 fresh rosemary sprigs, chopped finely
> juice and zest of 1 lemon
> 2 tablespoons Worcestershire sauce
> 2 medium slices of bread, made into fresh breadcrumbs
> a bunch of fresh parsley, chopped
> salt and freshly ground black pepper

1 Preheat the oven to Gas Mark 4/180°C/350°F. Cut the courgettes in half lengthways and scrape out the seeds with a teaspoon but reserve. Heat a frying-pan and spray with the low-fat cooking spray. Fry the onion and garlic for 4 minutes until softened.

2 Add the mince and season well. Stir until browned all over then add the courgette seeds, rosemary, lemon juice and zest and Worcestershire sauce. Cook for 2–3 minutes.

3 Put the courgettes on a baking tray sprayed with the low-fat cooking spray with their hollowed-out sides up. Spoon in the mince mixture and press down with the back of the spoon. Mix together the breadcrumbs and parsley and season then sprinkle over the top of the mince.

4 Bake for 20 minutes or until golden brown and crispy.

Pork curry with lime

| 4 | Points per serving | Points per recipe | 16½ |

Serves 4 ● Preparation time 20 minutes ● Cooking time 2 hours ● Calories per serving 260 ● Freezing not recommended *Don't be put off by the long cooking time of this very easy and unique-tasting curry; all the ingredients are just put in a pot and left to cook. Serve with 4 tablespoons cooked rice per person but don't forget to add 3 points per serving.*

> 1 tablespoon Thai green curry paste
> 400 g (14 oz) lean pork, cubed
> 2 tablespoons plain flour
> 4 garlic cloves, chopped
> juice and zest of 1 lime
> 3 medium potatoes, peeled and diced
> 4 medium tomatoes, chopped
> leaves from 1 sprig rosemary, chopped
> 300 ml (½ pint) stock
> 2 tablespoons Worcestershire sauce
> 150 ml (5 fl oz) virtually fat-free fromage frais
> salt and freshly ground black pepper

1 Preheat the oven to Gas Mark 4/180°C/350°F. Heat the curry paste in a flame-proof casserole dish then add the pork and toss until browned all over and covered in the curry paste. Add the flour and seasoning and toss again.

2 Add all the other ingredients except the fromage frais and put in the oven, covered, for 2 hours.

3 When cooked, take out of the oven and stir in the fromage frais.

Bangelloni

4½ Points per serving	Points per recipe 19

Serves 4 ● Preparation time 55 minutes ● Cooking time 25 minutes ● Calories per serving 440 ● Freezing recommended *So-called as it is sausages inside cannelloni. A very satisfying and tasty dish which is delicious served with a point-free salad.*

>   450 g (1 lb) thin 95% fat-free sausages
>   low-fat cooking spray
>   1 medium onion, chopped
>   2 garlic cloves, chopped
>   400 g can chopped tomatoes
>   100 ml (3½ fl oz) white or red wine
>   1 tablespoon Worcestershire sauce
>   1 tablespoon honey
>   a bunch of fresh basil or parsley, chopped
>   250 g (9 oz) no-precook cannelloni tubes (approximately 12)
>   40 g (1½ oz) reduced-fat mature Cheddar cheese, grated
>   salt and freshly ground black pepper

1 Grill the sausages for 10–15 minutes or until cooked through and brown. Meanwhile spray a frying-pan with the low-fat cooking spray and fry the onion and garlic for 5 minutes until softened.

2 Add the tomatoes, wine, Worcestershire sauce, honey and seasoning and bring to the boil. Simmer for 20 minutes or until reduced and thickened then stir in the fresh herbs.

3 Preheat the oven to Gas Mark 6/200°C/400°F. Push the cooked sausages into the cannelloni tubes and arrange in layers in an ovenproof dish that has been sprayed with cooking spray.

4 Pour the tomato sauce over and scatter with the grated cheese. Cover with foil and bake for 20 minutes until bubbling, then remove the foil and cook for a further 4 minutes until golden.

Sizzling sausage hotpot

2½ Points per serving	Points per recipe 9½

Serves 4 ● Preparation time 15 minutes ● Cooking time 20 minutes ● Calories per serving 205 ● Freezing not recommended *A sausage hotpot with peppers and paprika to warm you up. Serve with 4 tablespoons cooked rice (3 points per serving) or a medium jacket potato (2½ points per serving).*

>   low-fat cooking spray
>   450 g (1lb) 95% fat-free pork sausages, chopped
>   200 g (7 oz) button mushrooms
>   2 medium red peppers, de-seeded and diced finely
>   400 g can chopped tomatoes
>   2 teaspoons paprika
>   leaves of a bunch of fresh oregano, chopped
>   1 tablespoon French mustard
>   150 ml (5 fl oz) stock or water
>   150 ml (5 fl oz) low-fat plain yogurt

1 Heat a large saucepan and spray with the low-fat cooking spray, add the sausages and fry until browned all over. Add all the other ingredients except the yogurt and bring to the boil.

2 Simmer for 20 minutes then remove from the heat and stir in the yogurt.

Malaysian BBQ pork

4½ Points per serving   Points per recipe **25½**

Serves 6 ● Preparation time 25 minutes + a minimum of 2 hours marinating ● Cooking time 45 minutes ● Calories per serving 225 ● Freezing not recommended *Serve with very lightly steamed pak choy or spinach.*

900 g (2 lb) lean pork fillet, trimmed of all fat
2 spring onions, chopped, to garnish

For the marinade
1 tablespoon clear honey
150 ml (5 fl oz) dark soy sauce
50 ml (2 fl oz) medium-dry sherry
150 ml (5 fl oz) stock
1 tablespoon soft brown sugar
1 cm (½-inch) piece of fresh root ginger, peeled and sliced finely
1 small onion, chopped

1 Mix all the marinade ingredients together in a pan. Bring to the boil then simmer for 15 minutes. Let cool.

2 Put the pork fillets in a shallow dish that is large enough to hold them side by side. Pour the marinade over. Cover and chill in the refrigerator for at least 2 hours, preferably overnight, turning the meat several times.

3 Preheat the oven to Gas Mark 6/200°C/400°F. Drain the pork, reserving the marinade. Place the meat with the marinated onion and ginger bits on top of it on a rack over a roasting tin and pour water into the tin to a depth of 1 cm (½-inch).

4 Place the tin in the oven and roast for 20 minutes. Remove the meat from the oven and brush with the marinade again then put back and roast for another 20 minutes or until cooked through.

5 Meanwhile, put the marinade liquid into a saucepan, bring to the boil then simmer for 5 minutes. Serve the pork in slices either hot or cold with the marinade as a sauce and garnished with chopped spring onions.

Toad-in-the-hole

| **4** | Points per serving | Points per recipe **16½** |

Serves 4 ● Preparation time 10 minutes ● Cooking time
45 minutes ● Calories per serving 275 ● Freezing
recommended *This dish brings back childhood
memories for so many people - and is child's play
itself to make.*

125 g (4½ oz) plain flour
½ teaspoon salt
1 medium egg
300 ml (½ pint) skimmed milk
low-fat cooking spray
450 g (1 lb) 95% fat-free pork sausages

1 Preheat the oven to Gas Mark 7/220°C/425°F. Sift the
flour and salt into a large bowl then add the egg and half
the milk.
2 Gradually stir in the flour and beat until smooth then
stir in the rest of the milk.
3 Spray a shallow ovenproof dish with the low-fat
cooking spray and arrange the sausages in it with a little
space between each. Pour in the batter and bake for
40–45 minutes or until the batter is well-risen and
brown.

Grilled pork with caramelised apples and mash

| **5½** | Points per serving | Points per recipe **22½** |

Serves 4 ● Preparation and cooking time 1 hour 20
minutes ● Calories per serving 420 ● Freezing not
recommended *A very British supper.*

For the mash
1 kg (2 lb 4 oz) floury potatoes
4 tablespoons skimmed milk
4 fresh sage leaves, chopped
salt and freshly ground black pepper
For the pork and apples
2 large cooking apples
juice of 1 lemon
4 lean pork escalopes, weighing 100 g (3½ oz) each
low-fat cooking spray
1 tablespoon honey
2 tablespoons soy sauce
150 ml (5 fl oz) apple juice
2 tablespoons half-fat crème fraîche

1 Peel and core the apples, cut into rings then place in a
large bowl and squeeze the lemon juice over to prevent
them becoming brown.
2 Boil the potatoes in a large pan of salted water for
30 minutes or until tender. Drain and using a tea towel
to protect your hands, peel them with a knife. (The skins
should come away very easily, the knife is used as a
lever as the potatoes are too hot to handle.)
3 Put the peeled potatoes back into the pan and mash.
Stir through the milk and sage and season to taste.
Cover to keep warm, and set aside.
4 Heat the grill. Place the escalopes on the grill tray.
Season and grill for 4 minutes, turn, season again and grill
for 4 minutes more or until cooked through and golden.
5 Heat a frying-pan and spray with the low-fat cooking
spray. Add the apples slices and their juice and honey
and cook over a high heat until golden brown and the
liquid has evaporated then remove to a plate. Cover to
keep warm and set aside.
6 Pour the soy sauce and apple juice into the pan and
bring to the boil. Boil until the liquid is reduced by half,
remove from the heat and stir in the crème fraîche.
7 Serve the pork escalopes with the caramelised apple
and sauce accompanied by a spoonful of the mash
and sage mixture.

Lamb chops with redcurrant sauce

5½	Points per serving	Points per recipe	22

Serves 4 ● Preparation and cooking time 20 minutes + 1–12 hours marinating ● Calories per serving 335 ● Freezing not recommended This recipe requires a little forethought since it needs to be marinated but thereafter is especially quick and easy. Serve with 200 g (7 oz) minted new potatoes, adding 3 extra points per serving.

8 lamb leg chops, weighing approximately 75 g
(2¾ oz) each
150 ml (5 fl oz) orange juice
2 garlic cloves, crushed
2 teaspoons hazelnut oil
salt and freshly ground black pepper
For the sauce
4 tablespoons redcurrant jelly
150 ml (5 fl oz) orange juice
1 fresh rosemary sprig

1 Place the chops on a tray and season. Mix the orange juice, garlic and hazelnut oil together in a jug then pour over the chops. Turn the chops once or twice until completely coated in the marinade and then refrigerate for at least 1 hour but preferably overnight.
2 To make the sauce, put the ingredients in a saucepan and bring to the boil. Boil rapidly for 2 minutes then remove the rosemary sprig and pour the sauce into a serving jug.
3 Heat the grill or griddle and transfer the chops on to it pouring over any juices left in the tray. Grill for 3 minutes on each side until golden brown but still very slightly pink in the middle. Serve with the sauce poured over.

Braised lamb chops

5	Points per serving	Points per recipe	20

Serves 4 ● Preparation time 30 minutes ● Cooking time 1 hour ● Calories per serving 355 ● Freezing recommended This makes a traditional and satisfying midweek dinner with a minimum of hassle.

2 tablespoons plain flour
4 lamb leg chops trimmed of all fat, weighing
approximately 450 g (1 lb) in total
low-fat cooking spray
1 large onion, sliced
a small bunch of fresh thyme or marjoram
150 ml (5 fl oz) stock
450 g (1lb) sweet potatoes, peeled and sliced thickly
100 g (3½ oz) mushrooms, sliced
4 medium beef tomatoes, sliced thickly
salt and freshly ground black pepper

1 Put the flour on a plate, season, then roll the chops in it. Heat a large frying-pan and spray with the low-fat cooking spray. Brown the lamb for a few minutes on each side then remove from the pan to a plate and set aside.
2 Spray the pan with the low-fat cooking spray again and fry the onion for 4 minutes until softened. Add the herbs and the stock, scraping up any juices stuck to the bottom of the pan.
3 Arrange a layer of the sweet potato slices on the bottom of the pan and then top with the lamb. Cover and cook gently for 45 minutes.
4 Add the mushrooms and then a layer of tomato slices. Season and cook for another 15 minutes then serve.

Variation Use ordinary potatoes rather than sweet ones for a more traditional dish. The points per serving will be 4½.

Lamb dhansak

4 Points per serving	Points per recipe 15½

Serves 4 ● Preparation time 30 minutes ● Cooking time 1 hour ● Calories per serving 270 ● Freezing recommended
A mild, fragrant curry of lamb cooked with pumpkin, tomatoes and lentils. Serve with flatbreads (page 187) or 4 tablespoons of cooked rice and a tablespoon of very low-fat plain yogurt, adding on 3 points.

2 large onions, chopped finely
150 g can chopped tomatoes
225 g (8 oz) pumpkin or squash, peeled and chopped finely
a bunch of fresh coriander, chopped
a bunch of fresh mint, chopped
150 g (5½ oz) split yellow lentils
300 g (10½ oz) lean lamb, cubed
1 teaspoon turmeric
1 teaspoon chilli powder
1 teaspoon caster sugar
450 ml (16 fl oz) water
4 tablespoons vinegar
1 teaspoon cumin seeds, crushed in a mill or pestle and mortar
salt and freshly ground black pepper

1 Put all the ingredients in a large pan, bring to the boil and then simmer for 1 hour or until the lentils and lamb are soft and tender.
2 Mash the lentils with a wooden spoon, taking care not to break up the meat, then serve.

Irish stew

7½ Points per serving	Points per recipe 30

Serves 4 ● Preparation time 30 minutes ● Cooking time 1½ hours ● Calories per serving 550 ● Freezing recommended *This stew has all the elements of a meal within it so needs no accompaniments. It is a thick and rich combination of lamb, root vegetables and pearl barley.*

8 lamb leg chops trimmed of fat, weighing approximately 600 g (1 lb 5 oz) in total
4 medium onions, chopped
4 medium carrots, chopped
4 medium parsnips, chopped
100 g (3½ oz) pearl barley, pre-cooked for 20 minutes in boiling salted water, then drained
leaves from 2 rosemary sprigs, chopped finely
4 sage leaves, chopped finely
600 ml (1 pint) stock
4 medium potatoes, peeled and sliced thinly
1 bunch fresh parsley, chopped (optional)
salt and freshly ground black pepper

1 Preheat the oven to Gas Mark 3/170°C/325°F. Heat a large flameproof casserole dish and brown the meat all over then remove to a plate and set aside. Add the vegetables to the dish and cook for 5 minutes, turning with a wooden spoon, then remove to a plate and set aside.
2 Layer the meat, vegetables and par-boiled barley in the casserole dish, sprinkling with herbs and seasoning.
3 Pour the stock over and cover with a layer of potatoes overlapping like fish scales and season again. Put the lid on the casserole and bake for 1 hour. Remove the lid and increase the oven temperature to Gas Mark 6/200°C/400°F and continue to cook for 30 minutes or until the potatoes have browned. Serve sprinkled with the chopped parsley, if using.

For each negative thought that pops into your mind, immediately counteract it with two positive ones

Lancashire hotpot:
    Ideal for Sunday lunch with friends or family
        when you want something that looks great
    and satisfies everyone

Lancashire hotpot

| **8** | Points per serving | Points per recipe | **32½** |

Serves 4 ● Preparation time 15 minutes ● Cooking time 2½ hours ● Calories per serving 480 ● Freezing recommended *A traditional stew of lamb cutlets with thyme and a crisp and golden potato topping.*

low-fat cooking spray
800 g (1 lb 11oz) potatoes, peeled and sliced thinly
600 g (1 lb 5 oz) lamb cutlets, fat removed and bones cleaned
3 medium onions, chopped finely
2 medium carrots, sliced
4 sprigs fresh thyme, chopped
1 bay leaf
a pinch of sugar
300 ml (½ pint) stock
25 g (1 oz) polyunsaturated margarine, melted
salt and freshly ground black pepper

1 Preheat the oven to Gas Mark 3/170°C/325°F. Spray a casserole or oven-proof dish with the low-fat cooking spray then put a layer of potatoes in the bottom. Lay the cutlets on top.
2 Sprinkle in the onions, carrots and herbs and season well then sprinkle with sugar. Finish with the rest of the potatoes arranged over the top so that the slices overlap one another.
3 Pour in the stock and brush the top with the melted margarine. Cover and bake for 2½ hours, removing the cover for the last 40 minutes so that the potatoes crisp up and brown.

Moussaka

| **5** | Points per serving | Points per recipe | **21** |

Serves 4 ● Preparation time 40 minutes ● Cooking time 40 minutes ● Calories per serving 305 ● Freezing recommended *This version of the Greek casserole contains different vegetables and has a low-point tangy yogurt topping.*

2 medium aubergines, sliced thinly
2 medium courgettes, sliced thinly
low-fat cooking spray
350 g (12 oz) minced lamb
1 medium onion, chopped
2 garlic cloves, chopped
1 teaspoon ground cinnamon
a bunch of fresh marjoram, chopped
400 g can chopped tomatoes
1 tablespoon honey
1 medium egg
150 ml (5 fl oz) low-fat plain yogurt
2 tablespoons grated mature, low-fat Cheddar cheese
salt and freshly ground black pepper

1 Preheat the oven to Gas Mark 5/190°C/375°F and heat the grill. Arrange the aubergine and courgette slices over a baking tray, season and grill for 4 minutes or until just browning at the edges.
2 Meanwhile, heat a frying-pan and spray with the low-fat cooking spray then brown the mince with the onion and the garlic. Season and add the cinnamon, marjoram, canned tomatoes and honey. Stir together and cook for 5 minutes.
3 In an ovenproof dish layer the mince with the grilled aubergine and courgette finishing with a layer of mince.
4 Beat together the egg and yogurt and pour over the top then sprinkle with the cheese and bake for 40 minutes or until bubbling around the edges and the top is set and golden brown.

Top tip Moussaka is also very good left overnight in the fridge and reheated the next day.

Lamb tagine

3½ Points per serving	Points per recipe 14½

Serves 4 ● Preparation time 10 minutes ● Cooking time 2 hours ● Calories per serving 200 ● Freezing recommended This speciality dish from Fez is a sweet and savoury combination of slow-cooked lamb with dried apricots, honey, cinnamon and coriander that blends together into a fragrant dish. It is lovely served with 200 g (7 oz) plain boiled potatoes (2 points per serving) or 4 tablespoons cooked rice (3 points per serving).

> 400 g (14 oz) lean lamb leg steaks, cubed
> ¼ teaspoon ground ginger
> ½ teaspoon ground coriander
> 1 teaspoon ground cinnamon
> 1 medium onion, chopped finely
> 400 g can apricots in juice, drained and chopped, juice reserved
> 1 tablespoon clear honey
> 1 teaspoon orange blossom water (optional)
> salt and freshly ground black pepper

1 Put the first five ingredients in a pan, season then pour in the apricot juice and just enough water to cover. Bring to the boil and then turn down to a simmer for 1½ hours or until you have a rich sauce.

2 Add the apricots and cook for a further 20 minutes. Finally, stir in the honey and sprinkle over the orange blossom water, if using, then serve.

Variations A tagine can be made with any meat, from chicken and turkey breast to beef or pork fillet. Adjust the points accordingly.

Moroccan lamb couscous

8 Points per serving	Points per recipe 31½

Serves 4 ● Preparation time 30 minutes ● Cooking time 1½ hours ● Calories per serving 555 ● Freezing not recommended A staple dish of Morocco, couscous is often cooked with lamb and vegetables, as in this version. It combines a heady mixture of saffron, ginger and cinnamon.

> low-fat cooking spray
> 400 g (14 oz) lean lamb, cubed
> 1 large onion, chopped
> 600 ml (1 pint) stock
> ½ small pumpkin, peeled and cubed
> 2 medium carrots, chopped roughly
> 2 medium tomatoes, chopped roughly
> 1 teaspoon ground ginger
> 1 teaspoon ground cinnamon or 1 cinnamon stick
> a pinch of saffron strands
> 50 g (1¾ oz) raisins
> 3 medium courgettes, sliced
> 400 g can chick-peas, rinsed and drained
> 250 g (9 oz) couscous
> a bunch of fresh parsley or coriander, chopped
> salt and freshly ground black pepper

1 Heat a large saucepan and spray with the low-fat cooking spray then brown the meat for a few minutes, seasoning well.

2 Remove the meat from the heat and set aside and add the onion to the pan with a few tablespoons of the stock. Cook for 4 minutes until the onion is softened, stirring frequently.

3 Add the lamb, pumpkin, carrots, tomatoes, ginger, cinnamon, saffron and stock and bring to the boil then simmer for about 1 hour, uncovered, stirring every now and then.

4 Add the raisins, courgettes and chick-peas and simmer a further 30 minutes.

5 Meanwhile, put the couscous in a bowl and pour enough boiling water over to cover with 2.5 cm (1-inch) extra. Cover the bowl with a plate and leave the couscous to steam for at least 5 minutes.

6 Just before serving stir the parsley or coriander into the lamb stew and fluff up the couscous with a fork.

Lamb brochettes with honey and lemon

3 Points per serving	Points per recipe **12**

Serves 4 ● Preparation and cooking time 30 minutes + 1–12 hours marinating ● Calories per serving 225 ● Freezing not recommended *Serve in medium pitta breads (2½ points each) or with 4 tablespoons cooked rice per person (3 points per serving).*

- 400 g (14 oz) lean lamb leg steaks, trimmed of fat and cut into 8 strips
- 2 lemons, each cut into quarter wedges
- 1 tablespoon clear honey, heated
- salt and freshly ground black pepper

For the marinade
- 150 ml (5 fl oz) low-fat plain yogurt
- 4 garlic cloves, crushed
- a small bunch of fresh mint, chopped

1 Thread the lamb strips on to eight pre-soaked wooden skewers. In a tray long enough to accommodate the skewers lying down, mix together the marinade of yogurt, garlic, mint and seasoning.

2 Put the meat in the marinade and turn until well coated. Cover and leave to marinate for at least 1 hour but preferably overnight in the refrigerator.

3 Heat the grill to high and transfer the skewers on to the grill tray. Arrange the lemon wedges around the meat and brush the brochettes with the warm honey.

4 Grill for 4 minutes then turn the brochettes and lemon. Spoon any remaining marinade over the lamb and brush the lemon with honey again. Grill again for another 4 minutes or until the lamb is just cooked through.

Top tip The skewers are soaked in water for 10 minutes before use to prevent them from burning.

Roast lamb with mint sauce

5½ Points per serving	Points per recipe **32½**

Serves 6 ● Preparation time 15 minutes ● Cooking time approximately 1½ hours + 15 minutes resting ● Calories per serving 200 ● Freezing not recommended *A roast is easy to prepare and cannot be beaten for Sunday lunch with family and friends. Serve with a selection of point-free vegetables, and Roast potatoes (see page 69) for 4¼ extra points per serving.*

- 1 small leg of lamb, weighing about 1.5 kg (3 lb 5 oz)
- 6 sprigs of rosemary, nipped into small sprigs
- 4 garlic cloves, sliced
- 2 tablespoons half-fat crème fraîche
- salt and freshly ground black pepper

For the mint sauce
- a bunch of fresh mint, leaves chopped
- 2 teaspoons caster sugar
- 2 tablespoons boiling water
- 3 tablespoons cider vinegar

1 Preheat the oven to Gas Mark 7/220°C/425°F. Put the lamb in a roasting tin and using a sharp knife make little slits all over the surface of the lamb joint. Push the sprigs of rosemary and pieces of garlic into the slits.

2 Season the joint well and roast for 15 minutes. Reduce oven temperature to Gas Mark 5/190°C/375°F and roast for a further 20 minutes per 450 g (1 lb). Meanwhile, make the mint sauce by mixing together all the ingredients. Keep in the refrigerator until ready to serve.

3 Spoon the juices over the joint every 15 minutes or so to baste. When the roast is cooked, lift off the roasting pan and put on a carving board. Cover with foil and leave to rest for 15 minutes before carving.

4 Meanwhile, make the gravy in the roasting tin. Place the tin on the hob and heat. When hot pour in 200 ml (7 fl oz) water and scrape up all the stuck on bits with a wooden spoon or spatula and stir well. Allow to bubble for a few minutes then add the crème fraîche. Heat through and strain into a serving jug. Serve 125 g (4½ oz) lamb per person.

Variation You could use wine instead of water for the gravy for 6 points per serving.

Most weight-loss programmes spell the end to dessert eating, but not at Weight Watchers. The beauty of *pure points*™ is that nothing is banned or forbidden; all you need to think about is the number of points that you eat in a day!

delicious desserts

Little chocolate pots

3½ Points per serving	Points per recipe **14½**

Ⓥ if using free-range eggs ● Serves 4 ● Preparation time 20 minutes + about 30 minutes chilling ● Calories per serving 180 ● Freezing not recommended These are very light and fluffy mousses that look great served in espresso cups or little pots.

2 medium eggs, separated
50 g (1¾ oz) caster sugar
50 g (1¾ oz) plain chocolate (70% cocoa solids),
    broken into pieces
150 ml (5 fl oz) 0%-fat Greek-style plain yogurt

1 Put the egg yolks and sugar into a bowl and whisk with an electric whisk or by hand with a balloon whisk, until really thick and mousse-like.
2 Melt the chocolate in a bowl set over a pan of simmering water. Remove from the heat and allow to cool slightly, then whisk into the egg mixture.
3 Fold the yogurt into the chocolate mixture until smooth. Whisk the egg whites until stiff then gently fold into the mixture.
4 Spoon into four little cups or pots and refrigerate until chilled and set.

Banana split

3 Points per serving   Points per recipe **3**

v Serves 1 ● Preparation time 5 minutes ● Calories per serving 250 ● Freezing not recommended *A quick and easy sweet treat for you to enjoy.*

1 small banana, peeled and split lengthways
60 g (2 oz) scoop low-fat ice cream
150 g (5½ oz) fresh strawberries, rinsed, drained and hulled
1 teaspoon icing sugar

1 Arrange the banana halves in a sundae boat or on a plate then divide the ice cream between them.
2 Halve the strawberries and scatter over the ice cream, sprinkle with sugar and serve.

Black Forest gateau

4½ Points per serving   Points per recipe **34½**

v if using free-range eggs and vegetarian fromage frais ● Serves 8 ● Preparation time 20 minutes + approximately 1 hour cooling time ● Cooking time 25 minutes ● Calories per serving 240 ● Freezing recommended *A low-fat version of this classic chocolate cake.*

For the chocolate cake
low-fat cooking spray
100 g (3½ oz) polyunsaturated margarine
50 g (1¾ oz) soft brown sugar
1 teaspoon vanilla essence
25 g (1 oz) low-fat drinking chocolate
2 medium eggs
100 g (3½ oz) self-raising flour
For the filling
1 tablespoon icing sugar
200 g (7 oz) virtually fat-free fromage frais
425 g can stoned cherries in syrup, drained with
    2 tablespoons syrup reserved, and cut in half
2 tablespoons kirsch (optional)
1 tablespoon cocoa powder, to dust

1 Preheat the oven to Gas Mark 4/180°C/350°F and spray an18 cm (7-inch) cake tin with the low-fat cooking spray.
2 Cream together the margarine and sugar then add the vanilla and chocolate and then the eggs, one at a time and beat well together. Sieve in the flour, fold into the mixture and spoon into the prepared tin. Bake for 25 minutes or until springy to the touch and a skewer inserted into the centre comes out clean.
3 Turn the cake out on to a cooling rack and allow to cool completely (about 1 hour) then slice in half to make 2 thinner cakes.
4 For the filling, stir the icing sugar into the fromage frais. Spoon 2 tablespoons of the juice from the cherries over one of the sponges with the kirsch, if using.
5 Thickly spread the fromage frais on the sponge and top with the drained cherries. Put the other sponge cake on top and gently press down. Dust the top with cocoa powder and serve, or chill then serve.

Black Forest gateau: Only 4½ points
for a delicious slice of chocolate,
cream and cherry heaven

Chocolate roulade

3½ Points per serving	Points per recipe **20½**

Ⓥ if using free-range eggs ● Serves 6 ● Preparation time 30 minutes ● Cooking time 30 minutes ● Calories per serving 200 ● Freezing recommended *A moist and gooey dark chocolate roulade filled with a white chocolate orange cream – sounds too good to be true!*

low-fat cooking spray
8 medium egg whites
a pinch of cream of tartar
150 g (5½ oz) caster sugar
50 g (1¾ oz) cocoa powder, plus extra for dusting
For the filling
100 ml (3½ fl oz) low-fat plain yogurt
50 g (1¾ oz) white chocolate, melted
zest and juice of 1 medium orange

1 Preheat the oven to Gas Mark 4/180°C/350°F. Spray a 30 × 23 cm (12 × 9-inch) Swiss roll tin with the low-fat cooking spray.

2 Whisk egg whites in a bowl with the cream of tartar until they form peaks. Add the sugar in two lots, whisking well between additions. Fold in the cocoa and then scrape the mixture into the prepared tin. Push gently up to the edges and into the corners and bake for 30 minutes.

3 Meanwhile, place a piece of baking paper just larger than the Swiss roll tin on a work surface. When the roulade is cooked, turn it out on to the paper and roll up immediately. Place on a wire rack to cool.

4 To make the filling, mix all the ingredients together then carefully unroll the cool sponge. Spread the filling over and roll up again, dust with cocoa powder and serve.

Variations Try adding a teaspoon of orange flower water or rose water to the filling for a fragrant twist.

White chocolate mocha creams

4 Points per serving	Points per recipe **16**

Ⓥ if using vegetarian cheese ● Serves 4 ● Preparation time 15 minutes + minimum ½ hour chilling ● Calories per serving 180 ● Freezing not recommended *This is a simple-to-make, pretty, swirled, mousse-like dessert that is great after dinner with coffee.*

200 g (7 oz) virtually fat-free plain fromage frais
25 g (1 oz) icing sugar
1 tablespoon instant coffee, mixed to a paste with
  2 tablespoons boiling water
100 g (3½ oz) Quark cheese
100 g (3½ oz) ricotta cheese
50 g (1¾ oz) white chocolate, melted
cocoa powder, to dust

1 Mix together the fromage frais, sugar and coffee until smooth. In a separate bowl beat together the Quark, ricotta and white chocolate until smooth.

2 Stir the two mixtures together lightly to give a swirly pattern then spoon into serving glasses. Chill for at least ½ hour before serving with a dusting of cocoa powder.

Top tip Use the best quality white cooking chocolate you can find for the best results.

White chocolate and redcurrant pavlovas

3 Points per serving	Points per recipe **22**

Ⓥ if using free-range eggs and vegetarian cheese ● Serves 8 ● Preparation time 20 minutes + cooling ● Cooking time 1 hour ● Calories per serving 150 ● Freezing not recommended *Individual pavlova cases filled with a sweet white chocolate cream and crowned with tart little redcurrants to provide the perfect balance.*

> 4 medium egg whites
> a pinch of cream of tartar
> 100 g (3½ oz) caster sugar
> **For the filling**
> 75 g (2¾ oz) white chocolate, melted
> 2 tablespoons condensed skimmed milk
> 200 g (7 oz) low-fat soft cheese
> 100 g (3½ oz) sprigs of fresh redcurrants

1 Preheat the oven to Gas Mark ½/130°C/250°F. Whisk the egg whites with the cream of tartar until they form soft peaks then whisk in half the sugar, then the other half and whisk again until stiff and glossy.

2 Line two baking sheets with non-stick baking paper and pencil on eight 15 cm (3-inch) circles. Either pipe or spoon the meringue to cover the circles, building up the edges slightly to make shallow nests. Bake for 1 hour.

3 Leave to cool on the paper and then peel off carefully.

4 To make the filling, beat together all the ingredients except the redcurrants, until smooth then spoon into the pavlovas. Top with the redcurrants and serve.

Top tip For a quick dessert use the shop-bought meringue nests. The points will remain the same.

Cherry meringue sundaes

6 Points per serving	Points per recipe **11½**

Ⓥ if using vegetarian crème fraîche ● Serves 2 ● Preparation time 5 minutes ● Calories per serving 345 ● Freezing not recommended *A quick but delicious dessert that will satisfy sweet cravings. It is stunning when made in tall glasses and you will need long sundae spoons!*

> 400 g can cherries in syrup, drained
> 2 × 150 g tubs low-fat black cherry yogurt
> 2 meringue nests, crumbled
> 2 tablespoons half-fat crème fraîche
> 2 fresh cherries or 1 glacé cherry, halved, to decorate

1 In a tall sundae glass or glass bowl, layer the cherries with the yogurt and crumbled meringue. Finish with a tablespoon of crème fraîche and a cherry on top and serve immediately.

Variations Also good made with strawberries or raspberries.

If you know you've got a special occasion coming up, cut back on treats for a few days beforehand or do some extra exercise

White chocolate and raspberry dreamcake

4½ Points per serving	Points per recipe **35**

Serves 8 ● Preparation and cooking time 20 minutes + chilling time + 2 hours setting ● Calories per serving 205 ● Freezing recommended *A sumptuously creamy, beautiful pink mousse.*

100 g (3½ oz) reduced-fat digestive biscuits
50 g (1¾ oz) polyunsaturated margarine, melted
For the topping
100 g (3½ oz) white chocolate, broken into pieces
400 ml (14 fl oz) low-fat plain yogurt
11 g sachet powdered gelatine
300 g can raspberries in syrup
To garnish (optional)
a few fresh raspberries
fresh mint leaves

1 Pulverise the biscuits in a food processor, add the melted margarine then press into a 20 cm (8-inch) loose-bottomed flan tin and chill.

2 Melt the chocolate in a bowl set over a pan of simmering water. Put the yogurt in a bowl and stir in the chocolate. Sprinkle the gelatine over 6 tablespoons of boiling water in a small pan then heat gently and stir until dissolved. Cool a little and then stir into the yogurt mixture.

3 Drain 6 tablespoons of the syrup from the raspberries and discard, then add the rest of the syrup along with the berries to the yogurt mixture. Pour into the biscuit base and chill for at least 2 hours until set.

4 Serve decorated with whole raspberries and mint leaves, if using.

Tropical fruit pavlova

2 Points per serving	Points per recipe **17½**

V if using free-range eggs and vegetarian fromage frais
● Serves 8 ● Preparation time 35 minutes + cooling ●
Cooking time 1¼ hours ● Calories per serving 165 ●
Freezing not recommended *This is a great show-stopper of a pavlova with the all-important marshmallow-like texture within a crisp exterior.*

4 medium egg whites
175 g (6 oz) caster sugar
For the topping
6 medium passion fruit, flesh and seeds scooped out
300 ml (½ pint) virtually fat-free fromage frais
1 medium pomegranate, flesh and seeds scooped out
6 medium kiwi fruit, peeled and sliced
1 medium mango, peeled and sliced

1 Preheat the oven to Gas Mark 2/150°C/300°F. Line a baking sheet with a piece of non-stick baking paper and pencil a circle about 25 cm (10 inches) in diameter on to it.
2 In a scrupulously clean and dry bowl, whisk the egg whites until holding peaks, then whisk in the sugar in two halves. Whisk well until stiff and glossy.
3 Spoon the meringue on to the circle, smoothing and shaping into a nest and making sweeping scalloped edges with a damp tablespoon.
4 Place in the oven and immediately turn the heat down to Gas Mark 1/140°C/275°F. Bake on the middle shelf of the oven for 1¼ hours then turn the oven off and allow the meringue to cool until the oven is completely cold. Peel off the baking paper and transfer to a serving plate.
5 Just before serving, stir the passion fruit into the fromage frais then spoon this on to the meringue and top with the other fruits.

Top tips If your baking paper keeps curling up on the baking sheet, try dampening it with a little water.
   See page 128 for advice on preparing mangoes.
Variations Top with fruits of your choice – soft summer berries are especially good.

Peach melba

2 Points per serving	Points per recipe **4½**

V Serves 2 ● Preparation and cooking time 35 minutes
● Calories per serving 145 ● Freezing not recommended
Fresh peaches make this a very special dish. The peaches do not need to be perfectly ripe, as they are poached. If you can find them, white peaches look stunning.

2 medium peaches
1 tablespoon caster sugar
1 vanilla pod
125 g (4½ oz) fresh or frozen raspberries
2 × 60 g (2 oz) scoops of low-fat vanilla ice cream

1 Place two individual glass serving bowls in the freezer to chill. Place the whole peaches, sugar and vanilla in a saucepan with just enough water to cover them. Bring to the boil and simmer for 10 minutes then remove with a slotted spoon.
2 Leave until cool enough to handle and then carefully peel off the skins. If it does not come off easily then put back into the water and simmer for a further couple of minutes.
3 Cut the peaches in half and gently ease out the stone and discard. Set aside.
4 To make the sauce purée the raspberries in a food processor (if you don't like pips then sieve purée at this point).
5 Remove the bowls from the freezer and place a ball of ice cream in each. Place two halves of peach on each side of the ice cream, then drizzle over some of the raspberry purée.

Top tip If you do not have a blender then gently heat the raspberries for a few minutes until they start to break down and then sieve.

Menu plan

Zest for Life

~

Vitality Rice Salad, page 38
1 serving ... 3½ points

~

Grilled Snapper with Mango Salsa, page 128
1 serving ... 2 points

~

Cold Lemon Soufflé Mousse, page 159
(pictured here)
1 serving ... 1½ points

Total points per meal 7 points

Cold lemon soufflé mousse

1½ Points per serving   Points per recipe **12**

Serves 8 ● Preparation and cooking time 30 minutes
+ cooling + minimum 3½ hours chilling ● Calories per
serving 100 ● Freezing recommended *You can trust
this soufflé not to sink in the middle!*

grated zest and juice of 3 lemons
75 g (2¾ oz) caster sugar
4 medium eggs, separated
1 tablespoon powdered gelatine
150 ml (5 fl oz) low-fat plain yogurt

1 Prepare a 14 cm (5½-inch) diameter, 850 ml (1½ pint)
soufflé dish. Cut a strip of non-stick greaseproof paper
long enough to go right around the dish with a slight
overlap and deep enough to reach from the bottom of
the dish to about 6 cm (2½ inches) above the rim. Tie
the paper around the outside of the dish with string, or
stick it with sticky tape so that it fits closely to the rim
and will stop any mixture escaping.

2 To make the mousse, put the lemon zest (reserving
a little to garnish), juice, sugar and egg yolks in a bowl
and set over a pan of simmering water. Whisk with an
electric whisk or with a hand whisk, until very pale and
fluffy. This may take 10 minutes.

3 Remove the bowl from the heat and allow to cool,
whisking again occasionally.

4 Meanwhile, put 3 tablespoons cold water into a bowl.
Sprinkle over the gelatine. Stand the bowl over boiling
water. Stir until the gelatine has dissolved.

5 Add a few tablespoons of the cooling, but not cold,
egg mixture to the gelatine (they should be the same
temperature) and whisk together, then put the whole lot
back into the egg mixture and whisk.

6 Chill for about 30 minutes until the mixture has begun
to set at the edges. Scrape down the sides with a
spatula and stir to keep an even texture.

7 Fold in the yogurt carefully to keep the mixture as full
of air as possible. Whisk the egg whites until stiff.

8 Turn the mixture into the prepared dish and put in the
fridge to set for at least 3 hours, preferably overnight.

9 To serve, remove from the fridge 1 hour before and
take off the paper collar by undoing the fastening and
sliding a knife around to detach the paper from the
soufflé. Decorate with some lemon zest.

Apple snow

2½ Points per serving   Points per recipe **9½**

ⓥ if using free-range eggs ● Serves 4 ● Preparation and
cooking time 20 minutes + cooling ● Calories per serving
130 ● Freezing not recommended *This recipe was
another favourite my mother used to give me in
my childhood. It is very simple to make and tastes
just like it sounds – a light, fluffy apple froth.*

450 g (1 lb) cooking apples, peeled, cored and chopped
zest and juice of 1 lemon
25 g (1 oz) caster sugar
2 medium eggs, separated
25 g (1 oz) dark chocolate, grated

1 Place the apples with the lemon zest and juice, sugar
and 2 tablespoons of water in a saucepan and cook,
covered, over a low heat for 5 minutes until the fruit
is pulpy.

2 Combine the apple with the egg yolks in a bowl then
set aside and leave to cool.

3 Beat the egg whites until stiff then fold them into the
apple mixture. Spoon into individual serving glasses and
grate a little chocolate over each. Serve at once.

Summer pudding

2½ Points per serving   Points per recipe 16

Ⓥ Serves 6 ● Preparation and cooking time 30 minutes
+ chilling overnight ● Calories per serving 245 ● Freezing
not recommended *A traditional English pudding
that never fails to excite the taste buds. Serve with
half-fat crème fraîche, adding the extra points.*

    500 g bag mixed frozen summer berries, defrosted
    100 g (3½ oz) caster sugar
    8 medium slices white bread, crusts removed
    2 teaspoons rose water (optional)

1 Place the fruit in a pan with the sugar and cook gently
for 10–15 minutes or until just tender.
2 Cut a circle of bread to fit into the bottom of a 900 ml
(1½-pint) pudding basin and one the same diameter as
the top.
3 Arrange bread slices around the inside of the bowl so
that the bowl is completely covered. Overlap the bread
slightly but bear in a mind what the bread will look like
when the pudding is turned out.
4 Pour in the fruit (see Top tip) then sprinkle the rose
water over, if using, and put the other circle of bread
on the top to cover it. Cover with a saucer that's small
enough to fit inside the bowl. Put in the fridge and weigh
down by placing something heavy (such as a can) on the
saucer. Leave overnight.
5 Remove the weight and saucer and turn the pudding
out on to a serving plate.

Top tip Reserve 2 tablespoons of the juice from the fruit
and use to 'colour in' any patches of bread that may
have remained white which would spoil the pudding's
appearance.
Variations Summer pudding can also be made with
rhubarb and plums.

Moist chocolate cake

4½ Points per serving   Points per recipe 46½

Ⓥ if using free-range eggs ● Serves 10 ● Preparation
time 25 minutes + cooling ● Cooking time 20 minutes ●
Calories per serving 235 ● Freezing recommended *For
chocolate lovers this must be the ultimate dessert –
it is moist and gooey with a slightly crunchy
outside and it oozes chocolate.*

    low-fat cooking spray
    50 g (1¾ oz) dark chocolate (70% cocoa solids)
    100 g (3½ oz) cocoa powder
    100 g (3½ oz) polyunsaturated margarine
    4 medium eggs
    100 g (3½ oz) caster sugar
    2 drops vanilla essence
    50 g (1¾ oz) plain flour
    25 g (1 oz) ground almonds
    icing sugar or cocoa powder, to dust

1 Preheat the oven to Gas Mark 3/170°C/325°F. Spray
an 18 cm (7-inch) cake tin with the low-fat cooking spray.
2 In a large bowl heat the chocolate, cocoa, margarine
and 100 ml (3½ fl oz) water together over a pan of
simmering water, but do not stir. When they are all
melted, stir gently together and remove from the heat.
3 Meanwhile, with an electric whisk or in a food
processor with the whisk attachment, whisk together
the eggs, sugar and vanilla for at least 2 minutes until
very light and fluffy.
4 Using a metal spoon, gently fold the creamed mixture
into the chocolate mixture. Then very gently fold in the
flour and almonds, trying not to lose any of the air in
the mixture. Pour into the prepared tin and bake for
20 minutes.
5 Remove from the tin and place on a cooling rack.
To serve, dust with icing sugar or cocoa powder.

Top tip The cake is supposed to be slightly undercooked
in the middle to retain its moist texture so do not worry
that it sinks as you remove it from the oven.

Panna cotta

| **1** Point per serving | Points per recipe **6½** |

Serves 6 ● Preparation and cooking time 15 minutes + minimum 1 hour chilling ● Calories per serving 85 ● Freezing not recommended *Panna cotta is like a vanilla mousse. This is a light version which tastes wonderful.*

> 600 ml (1 pint) skimmed milk
> 1 vanilla pod, split
> pared zest of 1 lemon
> 50 g (1¾ oz) caster sugar
> 2 tablespoons orange juice
> 1 tablespoon powdered gelatine
> fresh fruit e.g. strawberries, raspberries and mango slices, to serve

1 Place the milk in a pan with the vanilla, lemon zest and sugar and bring to the boil. Strain and set aside.
2 Put the orange juice in a bowl and sprinkle the gelatine over. Leave for 5 minutes until spongy, then stand over a bowl of simmering water and stir until the gelatine dissolves completely.
3 Whisk the gelatine mixture into the warm milk and pour into six individual timbale moulds or ramekins lined with clingfilm. Chill for at least 1 hour until set, then turn out on to plates and decorate with the fresh fruit.

Top tip See page 128 for advice on preparing mangoes.
Variations Instead of orange juice, use 2 tablespoons amaretto or a liqueur of your choice for 1½ points per serving.

Rhubarb and custard fool

| **2½** Points per serving | Points per recipe **9½** |

Ⓥ Serves 4 ● Preparation and cooking time 20 minutes ● Calories per serving 165 ● Freezing not recommended *An old-fashioned rhubarb fool is still a delicious way to round off a meal.*

> 900 g (2 lb) rhubarb, trimmed and cut into 5 cm (2-inch) lengths
> 100 g (3½ oz) demerara sugar
> zest of 1 orange
> 2 × 150 g pots ready-to-serve low-fat custard

1 Put the rhubarb in a saucepan with the sugar, orange zest and 2 tablespoons of water. Cover and simmer over a gentle heat for 5 minutes or until just tender.
2 Drain, reserving a little of the liquid, and purée in a blender or put through a sieve. Add some of the cooking liquid if too thick but take care not to make it too wet. Set aside to cool.
3 Stir in the custard, pour into serving glasses and chill before serving.

Variation For a fast and convenient version use canned rhubarb in light syrup. The points per serving will be 3½.

Choose fruit instead of cheese after a meal

Tiramisu

2 Points per serving   Points per recipe **16½**

Ⓥ if using vegetarian cheese • Serves 8 • Preparation time 20 minutes + minimum 1 hour chilling • Calories per serving 125 • Freezing recommended Perhaps this dessert has been somewhat over-done but that's only because it is so delicious. Here is a low-Point version.

18 sponge fingers
300 ml (½ pint) strong black coffee
200 g (7 oz) virtually fat-free fromage frais
150 g (5½ oz) Quark cheese
50 g (1¾ oz) icing sugar
1 teaspoon vanilla essence
25 g (1 oz) cocoa powder
25 g (1 oz) dark chocolate, grated finely

1 Line the base and sides of a 450 g (1 lb) loaf tin with clingfilm. Place a layer of sponge fingers in the bottom and pour a third of the coffee over.
2 Put the rest of the fingers in a separate bowl and pour over the rest of the coffee. Beat half the fromage frais with the Quark, icing sugar and vanilla until smooth. Spread half of this mixture over the sponge fingers in the tin.
3 Sprinkle with a little cocoa powder then top with a layer of the soaked sponge fingers. Spread the remaining half of the cheese mixture over and sprinkle again with cocoa powder.
4 Top with the remaining sponge fingers, cover with clingfilm and chill for at least 1 hour. Turn out on to a serving plate and remove the clingfilm. Spread with the remaining fromage frais and sprinkle with the grated chocolate.

Cream hearts

2 Points per serving   Points per recipe **3½**

Ⓥ if using free-range eggs and vegetarian cheese • Serves 2 • Preparation time 15 minutes + overnight draining • Calories per serving 125 • Freezing not recommended These little cream hearts are perfect to finish off a romantic dinner for two.

110 g tub diet cottage cheese
125 ml tub low-fat plain yogurt
1 tablespoon clear honey
1 medium egg white
To decorate
a few mint leaves
100 g (3½ oz) fresh raspberries

1 Press the cottage cheese through a sieve then mix with the yogurt and honey. Whisk the egg white and fold into the cheese mixture.
2 Line two moulds (see Top tips) with muslin and spoon in the mixture. Smooth the top and place on a plate in the fridge for 12 hours, preferably overnight.
3 Turn out on to individual serving plates and decorate with the raspberries and mint leaves to serve.

Top tips These look lovely made in special heart-shaped moulds which have holes in the bottom to allow the cheese to drain and which are readily available in kitchen shops. Alternatively use your initiative and recycle the cheese or yogurt carton, punch holes in the bottom and use as a mould.

Instant boozy-fruit trifle

4 Points per serving   Points per recipe **8**

ⓥ if using vegetarian fromage frais ● Serves 2 ●
Preparation time 10 minutes ● Calories per serving 235 ●
Freezing not recommended *For instant satisfaction
this punchy berry trifle is a winner. It can be
thrown together in minutes and can be boozy or
not, as you like. This recipe is for two but there's
nothing to stop you from increasing the
quantities to make more.*

> 1 trifle sponge or 2 sponge fingers
> 210 g can raspberries in natural juice
> 35 ml (1½ fl oz) sherry
> 2 × 150 g pot low-fat ready-to-serve custard
> 2 tablespoons virtually fat-free plain fromage frais
> 10 g (¼ oz) flaked almonds, toasted

1 Crush the trifle sponge or fingers and divide between
two glass serving bowls then spoon the raspberries,
their juice and the sherry, if using, over the top.
2 Pour the pots of custard over then top with a
tablespoon of fromage frais and a scattering of
toasted almonds.

Top tip Leave out the sherry and save a ½ point per
serving.
Variation You could use any of your favourite fruits
instead of the raspberries.

Summer berry mousse cake

1½ Points per serving   Points per recipe **16½**

ⓥ if using vegetarian fromage frais ● Serves 10 ●
Preparation time 20 minutes + cooling + minimum
3 hours chilling ● Calories per serving 110 ● Freezing
recommended *A gorgeous deep pink, strawberry-
flavoured mousse on a base that you may
remember from your childhood... chewy rice
crispy cakes?*

> 150 g (5½ oz) marshmallows
> 3 tablespoons skimmed milk
> 75 g (2¾ oz) Rice Krispies
> 1 sachet strawberry sugar-free jelly
> 300 g can strawberries or raspberries in natural juice,
>   drained
> 200 ml (7 fl oz) virtually fat-free fromage frais
> fresh strawberries, raspberries or blackberries and/or
>   orange segments, to decorate
> icing sugar, to dust

1 Put the marshmallows in a saucepan with the milk
and heat very gently, stirring, until the marshmallows
have melted. Remove from the heat and stir in the
Rice Krispies until well coated.
2 Line a 25 cm (10-inch) loose-bottomed cake tin with
non-stick baking paper and press the mixture into it.
Leave for 30 minutes or until set.
3 Dissolve the jelly crystals in 300 ml (½ pint) of boiling
water. Set aside and leave to cool.
4 Mix the berries with the fromage frais in a bowl.
5 When the jelly is lukewarm, stir into the berry mixture,
then pour over the Rice Krispie base and chill for at least
3 hours or until set.
6 Remove the mousse cake from the tin on to a serving
plate and decorate with fresh berries. Dust the plate
with icing sugar and serve.

Honey 'ice cream'

4 Points per serving	Points per recipe **16½**

ⓥ Serves 4 ● Preparation time 10 minutes + cooling + minimum 4 hours freezing ● Calories per serving 210 ● Freezing recommended *This is not really an ice cream as it has no cream in it, but it is so creamy and delicious that no other name fully describes it.*

> 300 ml (½ pint) low-fat custard made with 2 tablespoons reduced-sugar custard powder and 300 ml (½ pint) skimmed milk
> 100 g (3½ oz) clear honey
> 410 g can 'Light' evaporated milk, chilled

1 Make up the custard according to the pack instructions but using the honey as the sweetener instead of sugar. Leave to cool.

2 Whisk the evaporated milk until thick and doubled in volume then fold into the cool custard mixture with a metal spoon.

3 Turn into a freezer-proof container and freeze until firm around the edges. Whisk with a fork to break up the ice crystals, then freeze again until firm.

Top tip If you have an ice cream maker then put the mixture into it to freeze; there is no need to whisk to break up the crystals as the machine will do it for you.

Variations To make a vanilla ice, just leave out the honey and use the same amount of sugar instead. For a raspberry, strawberry, or mixed summer berry ice, purée 225 g (8 oz) of your chosen berries, fresh, frozen or canned and then fold into the custard. For a ripple effect, only partially fold the berries in at the end to give a swirled pattern. The points per serving will be 5.

Frozen chocolate oranges

3½ Points per serving	Points per recipe **20**

ⓥ if using free-range eggs ● Serves 6 ● Preparation and cooking time 30 minutes + minimum 2 hours freezing ● Calories per serving 190 ● Freezing recommended *A creamy, chocolate-orange mousse frozen in an orange shell.*

> 6 medium oranges
> 100 g (3½ oz) plain chocolate
> 1 tablespoon cocoa powder, plus extra to dust
> 1 teaspoon coffee powder, dissolved in 1 tablespoon boiling water
> 3 medium egg whites
> 50 g (1¾ oz) caster sugar

1 Remove the tops from the oranges and scoop out the flesh and discard the pith. Chop the flesh and set aside.

2 Melt the chocolate over a pan of simmering water. Meanwhile, mix the cocoa powder with the coffee paste then stir into the chocolate.

3 Whisk the egg whites to stiff peaks then gradually whisk in the sugar. Fold in the chocolate mixture until thoroughly blended then add the chopped orange.

4 Spoon into the orange shells, replace the lids but do not push down, and freeze until firm. Serve dusted with cocoa powder.

Top tip These oranges will keep in the freezer for up to 10 days.

Pear and almond tart

4½ Points per serving   Points per recipe **25½**

V if using free-range eggs ● Serves 6 ● Preparation time
40 minutes + chilling ● Cooking time 30 minutes ●
Calories per serving 220 ● Freezing recommended

A light version of a classic French tart.

For the pastry
50 g (1¾ oz) polyunsaturated margarine
100 g (3½ oz) plain flour
a pinch of salt

For the filling
410 g can pears in juice, drained with 2 tablespoons
   of the juice reserved
2 medium eggs, beaten
175 ml (6 fl oz) low-fat plain yogurt
½ teaspoon almond essence
50 g (1¾ oz) ground almonds
1 tablespoon reduced-sugar jam, melted with
   1 tablespoon water

1 Make the pastry by rubbing the margarine into the flour
and salt until the mixture resembles fresh breadcrumbs
then add about 1 tablespoon of water and bring together
quickly with your hand into a ball. Wrap in clingfilm and
chill for 30 minutes.

2 Preheat the oven to Gas Mark 6/200°C/400°F. Roll out
the pastry in a circle about 5 mm (½-inch) thick and use
to line a 19 cm (7½-inch) loose-bottomed flan tin. Line
with foil or baking paper and fill with baking beans.

3 Bake blind for 15 minutes then remove the beans and
lining and bake for a further 10 minutes or until evenly
golden brown.

4 Arrange the pear halves cut-side-down in the pastry
case. Beat together the eggs, yogurt, almond essence,
almonds and pear juice. Pour around the pears. Brush
the bits of pear still showing with the melted jam and
bake for 30 minutes or until the top is firm and golden
brown.

Instant raspberry yogurt ice cream

1½	Points per serving	Points per recipe	**6**

 Serves 4 ● Preparation time 20 minutes ● Calories per serving 100 ● Freezing recommended This is the perfect frozen yogurt to refresh you on a hot summer's day or use as a quick accompaniment to fresh fruit.

> 500 g (1 lb 2 oz) 0% fat Greek-style yogurt
> 275 g (9½ oz) frozen raspberries
> 1 tablespoon icing sugar

1 Chill four glass serving cups in the freezer. Blend all the ingredients in a food processor until pink and thick. Pour into the chilled glasses and serve.

Alternatively, pour into a plastic freezer container and freeze until you need it but remove from the freezer 30 minutes before you want to eat it.

Tropical mango creams

2	Points per serving	Points per recipe	**3½**

 if using vegetarian cheese and vegetarian fromage frais ● Serves 2 ● Preparation time 5 minutes + chilling ● Calories per serving 145 ● Freezing not recommended A simple recipe that takes only a little more effort than an instant whip to make, contains far less points and is delicious.

> 210 g can mango pieces in juice, drained
> 100 g (3½ oz) Quark cheese
> pared zest and juice of 1 lime
> 4 tablespoons virtually fat-free fromage frais

1 Purée the mango in a food processor then beat into the Quark, lime juice and fromage frais. Spoon into serving dishes and decorate with pared lime zest.
2 Chill then serve.

Variation Replace the mango with canned papaya in light syrup.

**Instead of cream, use low-fat plain yogurt, low-fat crème fraîche
or virtually fat-free fromage frais in sauces, soups and puddings**

Blueberry chocolate cups

| 2 | Points per serving | Points per recipe | 8 |

🅥 Serves 4 ● Preparation and cooking time 20 minutes + minimum 30 minutes chilling ● Calories per serving 110 ● Freezing not recommended *Elegant plain chocolate cups that can be filled with any number of alternatives. Here blueberries and a blackberry yogurt have been used – a combination which is sure to tempt your tastebuds.*

50 g (1¾ oz) white chocolate
2 × 120 g pots of fat-free blackberry yogurts
100 g (3½ oz) fresh blueberries

1 Melt the chocolate in a bowl over simmering water then brush it over the insides of four paper cup cases using a pastry brush. Place each cup into a different section of a Yorkshire pudding tin and refrigerate until set. Repeat this, building up layers of chocolate until you have used all the chocolate.
2 When the chocolate has set, very carefully peel the paper away and place the cups on a serving plate.
3 Fill the cups with yogurt then top with the berries and serve, or chill until serving.

Top tips It is quick and easy to melt cooking chocolate in the microwave. Just break it up into a glass or plastic bowl and put it on High for about 30 seconds. Stir and use or, if not quite melted, heat in the microwave on High for another 10 seconds, and so on until melted.

When handling chocolate, try to keep your hands as cool as possible or wear cotton gloves if you have any.

If you have the time, also brush a few small leaves, like fresh bay leaves, with the melted chocolate on their top side. When the chocolate has set, peel the leaf away and use the chocolate leaves as decorations for your desserts.

Variations If blueberries are not in season, they may be very expensive so substitute with plums and virtually fat-free vanilla diet yogurt (3½ points per serving) or tangerine segments and virtually fat-free strawberry yogurt (2½ points per serving).

Caramel mousse

| 2 | Points per serving | Points per recipe | 11 |

Serves 6 ● Preparation and cooking time 45 minutes + minimum 1 hour cooling ● Calories per serving 135 ● Freezing not recommended *It takes a little time to prepare this recipe but it is worth it as it is seductively smooth, sweet and creamy. Delicious with summer fruit or plain poached pears.*

For the caramel
100 g (3½ oz) caster sugar
For the mousse
juice of 1 lemon
15 g (½ oz) powdered gelatine
2 medium eggs
2 tablespoons caster sugar
6 tablespoons virtually fat-free fromage frais
2 medium egg whites

1 Make the caramel by gently heating 300 ml (½ pint) water and the sugar together in a saucepan. Do not stir but very occasionally pick up the pan and swirl the water around. When all the sugar has dissolved, increase the heat and bring to the boil.
2 Boil rapidly until it turns a deep, golden brown. Meanwhile fill a sink with a few inches of cold water to plunge the base of the saucepan into to cool it rapidly and stop the caramel from darkening any further.
3 Carefully add 4 tablespoons of hot water to the caramel (it may spit), stir then pour into a bowl and set aside to cool.
4 Put the lemon juice and 3 tablespoons of boiling water in a bowl and sprinkle the gelatine over. Leave for a few minutes and then stir until the gelatine has dissolved.
5 Put the eggs in a bowl with the sugar and beat over a pan of simmering water for 10 minutes until the mixture thickens and will hold the trace of the whisk. Remove from the heat and allow to cool a little before adding the gelatine and the caramel and stirring it all together.
6 Leave the mixture in a cool place to thicken then fold in the fromage frais. Whisk the egg whites until stiff then fold them in too. Spoon into individual serving dishes and chill before serving.

Most of us have a soft spot for puddings but with *pure points*™ your indulgences don't need to spell the end to your weight loss. This chapter illustrates how desserts do not have to be a guilty treat, but instead can be part of a pleasing diet.

pleasing puddings

Chocolate profiteroles

4½	Points per serving	Points per recipe	17½

Ⓥ if using a free-range egg ● Serves 4; Makes 12 ●
Preparation time 25 minutes ● Cooking time 20 minutes
● Calories per serving 300 ● Freezing not recommended
Discover the miracle of low-point profiteroles!

25 g (1 oz) low-fat margarine
75 g (2¾ oz) plain flour
a pinch of salt
1 medium egg
1 egg yolk
500 g carton 0% fat Greek-style yogurt
2 teaspoons vanilla essence
1 tablespoon clear honey
2 tablespoons cornflour
2 tablespoons low-fat drinking chocolate
300 ml (½ pint) skimmed milk

1 Preheat the oven to Gas Mark 6 /200°C/400°F and line
a baking sheet with non-stick baking parchment.
2 Heat the margarine and 150 ml (5 fl oz) water together
in a large saucepan until the margarine has just melted.
Meanwhile put the flour on to a piece of baking paper
with the salt and mix together.
3 Take the saucepan off the heat and, working quickly,
add all the flour mix into the pan using the baking paper
as a funnel. Beat together with a wooden spoon for at
least 1 minute until well blended and the mixture comes
away from the side of the pan in one lump.
4 Allow to cool for 10 minutes. Beat together the whole
egg and the egg yolk and add to the cooled mixture, half
at a time. Beat with a wooden spoon until the mixture is
smooth, thick and glossy – this is quite hard. Place 12
heaped teaspoons well apart on the baking tray.
5 Bake for 15–20 minutes until well risen and
golden. Remove from the oven and, with a sharp
knife, slit each profiterole to let the air out. Place
back in the turned off oven, the door slightly ajar
so they dry out inside and cool.
6 Mix together the yogurt, vanilla and honey. Spoon
into the cool profiteroles. Pile them up on a serving
plate.
7 Blend the cornflour and drinking chocolate with a little
of the milk in a saucepan. Blend in the rest of the milk,
bring to the boil, stirring all the time, until thickened and
smooth. Pour over the profiteroles to serve.

Bread and butter pudding

4 Points per serving	Points per recipe 22½

Ⓥ if using a free-range egg ● Serves 6 ● Preparation time 15 minutes + 30 minutes standing ● Cooking time 1 hour ● Calories per serving 275 ● Freezing not recommended *A light version of the classic, comforting bread-and-butter pudding and a great way to use up older bread.*

low-fat cooking spray
6 medium slices white or brown bread
50 g (1¾ oz) polyunsaturated margarine
2 tablespoons reduced-sugar apricot jam, or
    reduced-sugar marmalade
25 g (1 oz) golden granulated sugar
50 g (1¾ oz) raisins or sultanas
1 medium egg
600 ml (1 pint) skimmed milk
freshly grated nutmeg, for dusting
1 teaspoon cinnamon

1 Spray a 1.2 litre (2-pint) oven dish with the low-fat cooking spray and preheat the oven to Gas Mark 4/ 180°C/350°F.
2 Lightly spread each slice of bread with the margarine and then the jam or marmalade. Cut diagonally into triangles and layer in the oven dish, sprinkling a little sugar and some raisins or sultanas between each layer.
3 Beat the egg and milk together and then pour over the bread. Sprinkle with nutmeg and cinnamon and, if possible, leave to stand for 30 minutes. Cover with foil and bake for 45 minutes then remove the foil and continue to cook for 15 minutes or until just set and golden brown.

Jam roly poly

5½ Points per serving	Points per recipe 31½

Ⓥ Serves 6 ● Preparation time 25 minutes ● Cooking time 1½ hours ● Calories per serving 270 ● Freezing not recommended *This recipe will take you back to your childhood ... it's a proper stodgy, steamed version but made with healthier polyunsaturated margarine rather than suet. The result is the same; sweet, satisfying and well worth the wait! Serve with low-fat custard (see Spotted Dick, page 182) or virtually fat-free fromage frais, adding on the extra points.*

low-fat cooking spray
200 g (7 oz) self-raising flour
½ teaspoon salt
100 g (3½ oz) polyunsaturated margarine
6 tablespoons reduced-sugar strawberry or raspberry jam

1 Half fill a steamer with water and put on to boil. Spray a piece of foil measuring 23 × 33 cm (9 × 13-inches) with the low-fat cooking spray.
2 In a large bowl, mix the flour, salt and margarine together then add about 7 tablespoons of water and mix to form a light, elastic dough. Knead this very lightly until smooth. Roll out on a floured surface to an oblong 23 × 25 cm (9 × 11-inches).
3 Spread the pastry with the jam leaving a 0.5 cm (¼-inch) clear border all round. Brush the edges with a little skimmed milk and roll the pastry up evenly starting from one of the short sides.
4 Place the roll on the foil and wrap the foil loosely around, to allow for expansion, but seal the edges very well. Place the roll in a steamer (see Top tip) and cover. Steam over rapidly boiling water for 1½ hours.
5 When it is cooked, remove from the foil and serve.

Top tip If you do not have a steamer, you can use a large pan with a close-fitting lid. You could also cover the pan with foil or baking paper and then put on the lid so that it is sealed even better. Be sure to keep an eye on the water level and top it up with boiling water if necessary.

Baked cheesecake

| **4** | Points per serving | Points per recipe **22½** |

V if using free-range eggs and vegetarian Cheese ● Serves 6 ● Preparation time 20 minutes + 30 minutes chilling ● Cooking time 1¼ hours ● Calories per serving 235 ● Freezing recommended *Scrumptious!*

For the pastry
75 g (2¾ oz) plain flour, sifted with a pinch of sugar
50 g (1¾ oz) polyunsaturated margarine
a pinch of lemon zest
low-fat cooking spray
For the filling
250 g (9 oz) Quark cheese
50 g (1¾ oz) caster sugar
1 tablespoon cornflour
½ teaspoon salt
2 medium eggs, beaten
50 g (1¾ oz) sultanas, soaked in enough hot water to cover
grated zest of 1 lemon
freshly grated nutmeg
icing sugar, to dust

1 To make the pastry, mix together 1 tablespoon of the flour, the margarine and 2 teaspoons of water with a fork. Add the rest of the flour and a pinch of zest. Mix together. Turn out on a floured board. Knead lightly just until it comes together into a ball. Put in a plastic bag. Refrigerate for 30 minutes.
2 Preheat the oven to Gas Mark 4/180°C/350°F. Remove the base from a loose-bottomed 18 cm (7-inch) cake tin. Spray with cooking spray and place on a work surface.
3 Roll out the pastry straight on to the base of the tin until it is about 5 mm (¼-inch) thick. Trim any excess and then re-assemble the tin. Cover with a sheet of tin foil and scatter with baking beans (dried beans will do).
4 Bake for 15 minutes then remove the baking beans, brush with a little beaten egg taken from the filling ingredients and return to the oven for 5–10 minutes or until a light golden colour.
5 To make the filling, beat together the Quark, sugar, cornflour and salt until well blended. Whisk in the eggs.
6 Drain the sultanas. Add to the mixture with the lemon zest. Pour into the cake tin. Grate some nutmeg over the top. Return to the oven. Bake for 45–50 minutes until just set. Turn the oven off, but leave the cheesecake inside with the door ajar. Cool completely.
7 When cold, unmould and dust with icing sugar.

Apple and apricot brown betty

| **7½** | Points per serving | Points per recipe **30** |

V Serves 4 ● Preparation time 15 minutes ● Cooking time 20 minutes ● Calories per serving 510 ● Freezing not recommended *A great pudding for autumn that you can probably make with ingredients you've already got in the storecupboard. Serve with virtually fat-free fromage frais adding on the extra points.*

175 g (6 oz) coarse fresh breadcrumbs
50 g (1¾ oz) polyunsaturated margarine, melted
100 g (3¼ oz) dried apricots, soaked overnight (although
   ½ hour soaking will do) in hot water, drained and chopped
700 g (1 lb 9 oz) cooking apples, peeled, cored and chopped
25 g (1 oz) nuts, chopped e.g. almonds, walnuts, pecans,
   hazelnuts
grated zest of 1 orange or lemon
100 g (3½ oz) soft brown sugar
25 g (1 oz) polyunsaturated margarine

1 Preheat the oven to Gas Mark 5/190°C/375°F. Toss the breadcrumbs in the melted margarine until they have absorbed it evenly. Spread a thin layer in the base of a 20 cm (8-inch) soufflé dish.
2 Mix together the chopped apricots, apples and nuts then cover the breadcrumbs with a layer of the mixture. Sprinkle with the zest and sugar. Repeat the layers until the dish is full, finishing with a layer of breadcrumbs.
3 Dot with the margarine and sprinkle with any remaining sugar. Bake for 20 minutes or until crisp and golden. Serve straight from the oven.

Lemon meringue pie

7 Points per serving   Points per recipe **27½**

v if using free-range eggs ● Serves 4 ● Preparation time 30 minutes + 30 minutes chilling ● Cooking time 30 minutes ● Calories per serving 410 ● Freezing recommended for the base only *Delicious.*

For the pastry
150 g (5½ oz) plain flour
a pinch of salt
75 g (2¾ oz) polyunsaturated margarine

For the filling
3 tablespoons cornflour
150 ml (5 fl oz) water
juice and grated zest of 2 medium lemons
50 g (1¾ oz) caster sugar

For the meringue
2 medium egg whites
50 g (1¾ oz) caster sugar

1 Mix the flour and salt together. Rub in the margarine until the mixture resembles breadcrumbs.

2 Sprinkle over 1–2 tablespoons water and mix with a palette knife until the pastry comes together into lumps. Draw it together quickly with your hand, wrap in clingfilm and place in the refrigerator for at least 30 minutes.

3 Preheat the oven to Gas Mark 7/220°C/425°F. On a floured surface, roll out the dough to fit a shallow 20 cm (8-inch) tart tin. Prick all over with a fork and line with foil or baking paper and scatter with baking beans (ordinary dried beans will do). Bake for 15 minutes.

4 Remove the beans and foil or paper and bake for a further 5 minutes.

5 Mix the cornflour with the water in a saucepan. Add the lemon juice and zest and bring to the boil, stirring, until the mixture thickens. Add the sugar and stir.

6 Pour the filling into the pastry case and make the meringue. Whisk the egg whites until they are stiff then whisk in half the sugar. Fold in the rest of the sugar and then pile the meringue on top of the lemon mixture.

7 Bake for 10 minutes or until the meringue is crisp and lightly browned. Leave to cool before serving or the centre will be runny.

Variation For Key Lime Pie, follow the same recipe but use limes instead of the lemons.

Baked lemon pudding

| 4 | Points per serving | Points per recipe | 17 |

v if using free-range eggs • Serves 4 • Preparation time 15 minutes • Cooking time 45 minutes • Calories per serving 255 • Freezing not recommended *While cooking, this zesty pudding is transformed from one mixture into two separate layers: an egg custard with a lemon sponge topping.*

low-fat cooking spray
juice and grated zest of 1 lemon
50 g (1¾ oz) polyunsaturated margarine
50 g (1¾ oz) caster sugar
2 medium eggs, separated
50 g (1¾ oz) self-raising flour
300 ml (½ pint) skimmed milk

1 Preheat the oven to Gas Mark 6/200°C/400°F and spray a 1.3 litre (2¼-pint) ovenproof dish with the low-fat cooking spray.
2 Cream together the lemon zest, margarine and sugar then add the egg yolks and flour and beat well. Stir in the milk and the lemon juice.
3 Whisk the egg whites until stiff and then carefully fold into the mixture with a metal spoon. Pour into the dish and then stand the dish in a shallow tin of water and bake for 45 minutes, or until the top is set and spongy to the touch.

Indian rice pudding

| 2½ | Points per serving | Points per recipe | 10 |

v Serves 4 • Preparation time 15 minutes • Cooking time 30 minutes • Calories per serving 85 • Freezing not recommended *A traditional pudding with low point ingredients. It is delicious served with stewed fruit, reduced-sugar jam, adding the extra points, or enjoy it on its own.*

150 g (5½ oz) pudding rice
300 ml (½ pint) skimmed milk
3 cardamom pods
1 tablespoon caster sugar, preferably vanilla sugar
2 drops vanilla extract
freshly grated nutmeg
1 tablespoon rose water (optional)

1 Place the rice in a saucepan and add the milk, 600 ml (1 pint) water and the cardamom, bring to the boil, stirring. Simmer over a very low heat, stirring frequently, for 25–30 minutes, until the rice is cooked.
2 Remove the cardamom and stir in the sugar, vanilla, grated nutmeg and the rose water, if using. Then serve.

Variations For Persian Rice Pudding add 50 g (1¾ oz) raisins or sultanas, 2 teaspoons rose water and 25 g (1 oz) pistachio nuts, chopped and add 1 point per serving. If you omit the nuts, you will save a ½ point per serving.

Lemons are packed with flavour and vitamins and their juice can be added
to recipes without adding points or add to hot water and detox and refresh

Cherry batter pudding

3½ Points per serving   Points per recipe **20**

(v) if using free-range eggs ● Serves 6 ● Preparation time 15 minutes ● Cooking time 25–30 minutes ● Calories per serving 255 ● Freezing not recommended This pudding is known in France as 'clafouti'. It is much lighter than it sounds and really easy to make - a perfect last-minute dish.

low-fat cooking spray
2 × 400 g cans stoned cherries in syrup, drained
3 medium eggs
75 g (2¾ oz) plain flour
a pinch of salt
40 g (1½ oz) caster sugar
425 ml (¾ pint) skimmed milk, warmed

1 Preheat the oven to Gas Mark 7/220°C/425°F and spray an oval 25 × 8 cm (10 × 7-inch) ovenproof dish with the low-fat cooking spray.
2 Put the cherries in the dish. In a separate bowl, beat the eggs lightly then beat in the flour, salt and sugar. Gradually pour the warmed milk over, stirring well.
3 Pour the batter over the cherries and bake for 25–30 minutes. Serve hot or cold or, and perhaps for the best taste, lukewarm.

Top tip This can be made in any ovenproof dish with a 1.2 litre (2-pint) capacity.
Variations Replace the canned cherries with canned apricots in juice. The points per serving will be 2½.

Rhubarb and ginger crumble

5½ Points per serving   Points per recipe **32**

(v) Serves 6 ● Preparation time 20 minutes ● Cooking time 20–30 minutes ● Calories per serving 320 ● Freezing recommended Everyone seems to love this pudding – it is a perfect combination of sweet and tart, juicy and crunchy and very quick and easy to make.

For the fruit
2 × 400 g cans rhubarb in light syrup
2 teaspoons rose water (optional)
2 tablespoons clear honey
For the crumble
75 g (2¾ oz) polyunsaturated margarine
100 g (3½ oz) plain flour
100 g (3½ oz) wholemeal flour
50 g (1¾ oz) golden granulated sugar
50 g (1¾ oz) stem ginger, chopped
1 teaspoon ground ginger

1 Preheat the oven to Gas Mark 6/200°C/400°F. Place all the fruit ingredients in a 1 litre (¾-pint) ovenproof dish.
2 Make the crumble in a bowl by rubbing the margarine into the flour until the mixture is the texture of fine breadcrumbs then stirring in the other ingredients.
3 Sprinkle this on top of the fruit and bake for 20–30 minutes or until the fruit is bubbling up the sides of the dish and the topping is golden and crunchy

Top tip You can use fresh rhubarb instead of canned fruit; just increase the cooking time to 30–40 minutes so the fruit becomes soft and juicy.

Make a distinction between the ideal body types

portrayed in magazines and what is attainable for you

Fluffy breakfast pancakes

5 Points per serving	Points per recipe **9½**

Ⓥ if using free-range eggs ● Serves 2; Makes 10 small pancakes ● Preparation and cooking time 25 minutes ● Calories per serving 155 ● Freezing not recommended These are like the pancakes that you get in America for breakfast in huge portions with maple syrup and bacon or sausages. This is a scrumptious low point version.

2 medium eggs, separated
100 g (3½ oz) plain flour
½ teaspoon salt
2 teaspoons baking powder
2 teaspoons caster sugar
150 ml (5 fl oz) skimmed milk
low-fat cooking spray

1 Gently heat a large frying-pan or griddle. Whisk the egg whites until stiff. In a large bowl, sift the flour, salt, baking powder and sugar and mix together.
2 In a jug, beat the egg yolks and milk together. Pour this mixture into the dry ingredients and stir until just mixed but do not beat.
3 With a metal spoon, lightly fold in the egg whites. Spray the pan with the low-fat cooking spray and drop the batter on to it in tablespoonfuls. You should be able to cook 3–4 at the same time.
4 After 1–2 minutes they should be puffed up and bubbly. Flip them over with a palette knife or fish slice and lightly brown the other side.
5 Keep them warm in a low oven on a plate covered with foil or a tea towel until they are all cooked.

Crêpes Suzette

4 Points per serving	Points per recipe **7½**

Ⓥ if using a free-range egg ● Serves 2 ● Preparation and cooking time 30 minutes + 15 minutes standing ● Calories per serving 240 ● Freezing recommended for the pancakes only Crêpes Suzette has fallen out of fashion yet it is a simple and refreshing pudding that can be as grand or as plain us you want. This recipe serves two but it doubles successfully for guests.

For the crêpes
50 g (1¾ oz) plain flour
a pinch of salt
150 ml (5 fl oz) skimmed milk
1 medium egg
low-fat cooking spray
For the sauce
juice and zest of 1 orange
1 teaspoon caster sugar
15 g (½ oz) polyunsaturated margarine
1 tablespoon orange liqueur or brandy (optional)

1 Sift the flour and salt into a bowl. Add half the milk and the egg and beat well until smooth. Stir in the rest of the milk and leave to stand for 15 minutes before cooking.
2 Heat a small non-stick frying-pan and spray with the low-fat cooking spray then ladle in enough pancake batter to just cover the base of the pan when you swirl it around.
3 Fry until golden on the underside and then either flip, by tossing or with a palette knife or fish slice, and cook the other side. Slide out of the pan on to a plate and keep warm while you cook the rest of the crêpes.
4 To make the sauce, heat the orange juice, zest and sugar in the frying-pan, stirring, until the sugar is dissolved, then add the margarine and whisk. Fold the pancakes into quarters and add to the pan one by one turning in the sauce and then pushing to one side to fit the next in. Just before serving add the liqueur, if using, and ignite.

Plum pie

4½ Points per serving	Points per recipe 27½

🅥 if using a free-range egg ● Serves 6 ● Preparation time 15 minutes ● Cooking time 30 minutes ● Calories per serving 285 ● Freezing recommended *This is not a pie in the traditional sense of the word but it has a sweet, wholemeal pastry base that is topped with plums set in a kind of cheesecake batter mix. It is delicious!*

For the base
low-fat cooking spray
75 g (2¾ oz) polyunsaturated margarine
50 g (1¾ oz) caster sugar
50 g (1¾ oz) self-raising flour
50 g (1¾ oz) wholemeal self-raising flour
1 medium egg
For the filling
570 g can plums, drained
150 ml (5 fl oz) low-fat plain yogurt
1 medium egg
½ teaspoon vanilla essence
40 g (1½ oz) caster sugar

1 Preheat the oven to Gas Mark 6/200°C/400°F and spray an 18 cm (7-inch) tin with the low-fat cooking spray.
2 Place all the base ingredients in a food processor and process until blended. If you do not have a food processor then cream the margarine and caster sugar together, mix in the flours and then the egg.
3 Spoon the mixture into the prepared tin and smooth down with the back of a spoon. Stone and halve the plums and arrange over the top of the base.
4 Beat together all the other filling ingredients. Pour over the plums and bake for 30 minutes or until the edges are a deep golden brown and the filling is just set (it becomes firmer as the pie cools). Transfer to a wire rack and cut into squares. Best served warm.

Variation Use 8 fresh plums instead of canned plums for the same points per serving.

Apple pie

3½ Points per serving	Points per recipe 20½

🅥 Serves 6 ● Preparation time 25 minutes + cooling ● Cooking time 30 minutes ● Calories per serving 200 ● Freezing recommended *Always a favourite with family and friends, this apple pie is packed with flavour and is delicious served hot or cold.*

low-fat cooking spray
700 g (1 lb 9 oz) cooking apples, peeled, cored and
    quartered
2 tablespoons honey
50 g (1¾ oz) caster sugar
1 tablespoon cornflour
2 teaspoons cinnamon
juice and zest of 1 lemon
½ teaspoon vanilla essence
For the pastry
75 g (2¾ oz) plain flour, seasoned with ½ teaspoon salt
50 g (1¾ oz) polyunsaturated margarine
a little skimmed milk, to glaze

1 Preheat the oven to Gas Mark 5/190°C/375°F and spray a 20 cm (8-inch) pie dish with the low-fat cooking spray.
2 Make the pastry by mixing together 1 tablespoon of the flour, the margarine and 2 teaspoons of water with a fork. Then add the rest of the flour and mix together. Turn out on to a floured board and knead lightly just until it comes together into a ball. Put in a plastic bag and refrigerate until needed.
3 Put the apples in a pan with 4 tablespoons of water, cover and simmer gently for 10 minutes until the apples are beginning to soften. Add the honey, sugar, cornflour, cinnamon, lemon juice, zest and vanilla and stir until thick. Leave to cool slightly.
4 Roll out the pastry to fit the top of the dish with a little to spare. Put the apple in the dish and cover with the pastry. Press the edges down on top of the sides of the dish and cut off any excess. Make short slashes in the centre with a knife to allow the steam to escape and decorate with the pastry trimmings cut into leaf shapes.
5 Brush with a little skimmed milk and bake for 30 minutes or until the pastry is golden and crisp.

Menu plan

Soothing Sunday Roast

~

Spicy Pumpkin Soup, page 8
1 serving ... 0 points

~

Lemon and Garlic Roast Chicken, page 96
1 serving ... 3 points

~

Perfect Roast Potatoes, page 69
1 serving ... 4½ points

~

Zero point vegetable of your choice

~

Apple Pie, page 176
(pictured here)
1 serving ... 3½ points

Total points per meal 11 points

Quick and easy chocolate soufflé

2½ Points per serving	Points per recipe 11

ⓥ if using free-range eggs ● Serves 4 ● Preparation time 20 minutes ● Cooking time 15 minutes ● Calories per serving 175 ● Freezing not recommended *These soufflés are cooked in ramekins to make individual dark, chocolatey puddings that are served with a simple mango sauce. The recipe can be halved to serve two.*

low-fat cooking spray
3 tablespoons cocoa powder, sifted
40 g (1½ oz) caster sugar
4 medium egg whites
400 g can mango chunks in juice
icing sugar, to dust

1 Preheat the oven to Gas Mark 5/190°C/375°F. Spray four ramekin dishes with the low-fat cooking spray.
2 Place the cocoa, half the sugar and 4 tablespoons of water in a saucepan and heat, stirring, until combined.
3 Whisk the egg whites until stiff then gradually whisk in the rest of the sugar. Gently fold these into the chocolate mixture.
4 Spoon into the ramekin dishes being careful not to knock out any air, and put them straight into the oven for 12 minutes or until risen but slightly wobbly when touched.
5 Meanwhile, make the mango sauce by puréeing the canned mango chunks and their juice until smooth. Spoon around the edge of four serving plates and when the soufflés are ready, put them in the middle of the plate, dust with icing sugar and serve immediately.

Top tip Once out of the oven, the soufflés will start to sink so make sure everyone is sitting down ready to eat so they don't miss the spectacle!

Pineapple upside-down cake

5½ Points per serving	Points per recipe 33½

ⓥ if using free-range eggs ● Serves 6 ● Preparation time 25 minutes ● Cooking time 45 minutes ● Calories per serving 340 ● Freezing not recommended *This was one of the first puddings I learned to make in Home Economics class at school and I'm grateful that I was taught such classics as my basics!*

low-fat cooking spray
2 tablespoons golden syrup
225 g (8 oz) can pineapple rings in juice, drained, juice reserved
4–5 glacé cherries, halved
100 g (3½ oz) polyunsaturated margarine
50 g (1¾ oz) soft brown sugar
2 medium eggs, beaten
175 g (6 oz) self-raising flour
1 teaspoon cornflour

1 Preheat the oven to Gas Mark 4/180°C/350°F and spray an 18 cm (7-inch) round cake tin with the low-fat cooking spray.
2 Heat the golden syrup gently in a pan until runny then pour into the base of the tin. Arrange the pineapple rings on top and place half a glacé cherry in the centre of each ring cut-side up.
3 Cream together the margarine and sugar until pale and fluffy then add the eggs a little at a time beating between each addition.
4 Fold in the flour and enough of the reserved pineapple juice to give a dropping consistency. Spoon on top of the pineapple rings and bake for 45 minutes or until risen, golden and firm to the touch.
5 Meanwhile, mix a tablespoon of the remaining pineapple juice with the teaspoon of cornflour. Put the rest of the juice in a pan and heat. Stir in the cornflour and bring to the boil, stirring, until the sauce thickens. Turn the pudding out on to a serving plate and serve with the hot pineapple sauce.

Variations Upside-down puddings can be made in the same way using canned pears or fresh, trimmed rhubarb or fresh cooking apples, peeled and cored and thinly sliced. The points per serving will remain the same for all these variations.

Baked Alaska

4 Points per serving	Points per recipe **16½**

ⓥ if using free-range eggs • Serves 4 • Preparation and cooking time 25 minutes • Calories per serving 245 • Freezing not recommended *This is an impressive dessert that can be made in minutes using shop-bought low-fat ice cream and a flan case. It's a heavenly combination of very hot and very cold with soft, chewy and crispy textures.*

18 cm (7-inch) round sponge flan case
300 g can raspberries in natural juice (or other soft fruit), drained
3 medium egg whites
75 g (2¾ oz) caster sugar
480 ml (17½ fl oz) low-fat vanilla ice cream

1 Preheat the oven to Gas Mark 8/230°C/450°F and remove all the shelves except for one in the middle.
2 Place the flan case on an ovenproof plate and spoon over the fruit.
3 Whisk the egg white until stiff then add the sugar and whisk again until glossy.
4 Scoop the ice cream quickly on top of the fruit. Pile the meringue mixture over the whole lot taking it down to the dish and making little peaks all over the surface by dabbing it with the back of a spoon or with a spatula.
5 Place in the oven immediately and cook for 2–3 minutes, watching carefully and removing immediately once the tips of the peaks turn golden brown. Serve straight away.

Honey banana pudding

6½ Points per serving	Points per recipe **40**

ⓥ if using free-range eggs • Serves 6 • Preparation time 25 minutes • Cooking time 45 minutes • Calories per serving 390 • Freezing not recommended *Like pineapple upside-down cake, this pudding is also made the wrong-way-up and then turned out, but this one has a banana-flavoured, light sponge base and bananas glazed with honey on top.*

low-fat cooking spray
4 medium bananas
2 tablespoons low-fat plain yogurt
1 teaspoon vanilla essence
75 g (2¾ oz) polyunsaturated margarine
100 g (3½ oz) caster sugar
2 medium eggs, beaten
175 g (6 oz) self-raising flour
½ teaspoon salt
2 tablespoons clear honey

1 Preheat the oven to Gas Mark 4/180°C/350°F and spray a 25 cm (10-inch) diameter, 5 cm (2-inch) deep ovenproof dish with the low-fat cooking spray.
2 Mash 1 banana with the yogurt and vanilla. In a separate bowl, cream the margarine and sugar together until light and fluffy, then beat in the eggs a little at a time.
3 Fold in the flour, salt and the banana mixture until thoroughly combined.
4 Gently heat the honey in a small saucepan until very runny then pour into the base of the dish. Slice 3 bananas and arrange over the base then spoon in the cake mixture and smooth the top.
5 Bake for 45 minutes or until golden brown on top and springy to the touch. Leave to cool in the dish for about 10 minutes before turning out on to a serving plate.

Peach brûlée

2 Points per serving   Points per recipe **2**

ⓥ Serves 1 ● Preparation and cooking time 5 minutes + cooling ● Calories per serving 105 ● Freezing not recommended *A very simple but tantalising pudding that you can make for yourself in a just few minutes.*

   1 medium fresh, ripe peach or 2 canned peach halves
   2 tablespoons low-fat plain yogurt
   1 tablespoon golden granulated or demarara sugar

1 Preheat the grill to high. Place the peaches in a shallow serving bowl or plate and spoon on the yogurt. Sprinkle over the sugar and grill until the sugar is melted. Cool for a minute or two until the sugar crisps up then serve.

Variation Use virtually fat-free fromage frais instead of yogurt for 1½ points per serving.

Fail-safe St. Clement's soufflé

3½ Points per serving   Points per recipe **14½**

ⓥ if using free-range eggs ● Serves 4 ● Preparation time 25 minutes ● Cooking time 40 minutes ● Calories per serving 225 ● Freezing recommended *This is a delicious lemon soufflé that's easy to make and served with an orange sauce.*

   low-fat cooking spray
   4 medium eggs, separated
   100 g (3½ oz) caster sugar
   grated zest and juice of 1 lemon
   For the sauce
   grated zest and juice of 2 medium oranges
   2 teaspoons caster sugar
   2 teaspoons cornflour

1 Preheat the oven to Gas Mark 4/180°C/350°F and spray a 1.2 litre (2-pint) soufflé dish with the low-fat cooking spray.
2 With an electric or balloon whisk, whisk the egg yolks until thick and pale in colour. Then whisk in half the sugar and the lemon juice and zest.
3 In a clean, dry bowl and with a clean, dry whisk, whisk the egg whites until stiff then whisk in the rest of the sugar. Fold into the lemon mixture and spoon carefully into the dish. Bake for 40 minutes or until risen and slightly wobbly to the touch.
4 Meanwhile, make the sauce by putting the orange juice and zest and sugar in a pan and heating. In a small bowl, mix the cornflour with a tablespoon of water then add to the juice with another 2 tablespoons of water. Bring to the boil stirring continuously, then pour into a serving jug. Serve hot poured over the soufflé.

If you comfort-eat when you're upset or tired, talk to a friend instead or enjoy a relaxing bath

Christmas pudding with brandy sauce

| **5½** Points per serving | Points per recipe **54** |

🆅 if using free-range eggs ● Serves 10 ● Preparation time 30 minutes ● Cooking time 4½ hours ● Calories per serving 360 ● Freezing not recommended *Delicious and light but still full of flavour!*

low-fat cooking spray
100 g (3½ oz) plain flour
1 teaspoon baking powder
100 g (3½ oz) polyunsaturated margarine
100 g (3½ oz) raisins
100 g (3½ oz) sultanas
100 g (3½ oz) currants
100 g (3½ oz) dried apricots, chopped
100 g (3½ oz) caster sugar
100 g (3½ oz) fresh breadcrumbs
1 teaspoon ground cinnamon
1 teaspoon ground ginger
½ teaspoon ground cloves
½ teaspoon ground nutmeg
1 medium egg
150 ml (5 fl oz) skimmed milk
2 tablespoons brandy

For the brandy sauce
40 g (1½ oz) cornflour
50 g (1¾ oz) dark brown sugar
600 ml (1 pint) skimmed milk
2 tablespoons brandy

1 Spray a 1.2 litre (2-pint) pudding basin with the low-fat cooking spray and line the base with a disc of non-stick baking parchment. Sift the flour and baking powder into a bowl, add the margarine and rub in with your fingertips.

2 Stir in the fruit, sugar, breadcrumbs and spices then mix in the egg, milk and brandy. Spoon into the prepared pudding basin and level the surface with the back of a spoon.

3 Cover with a double thickness of greaseproof paper with a pleat in the middle to allow for rising, and tie with string under the rim to secure. Place in a steamer or large saucepan a quarter full of boiling water and with a close-fitting lid. Steam for 4½ hours. Turn out on to a serving plate.

4 Make the sauce in a saucepan, blending the cornflour with the sugar and a little of the milk. Add the rest of the milk, bring to the boil stirring constantly and cook for 2 minutes, still stirring, until thickened then add the brandy, pour into a jug and serve.

Top tips You may feel there's enough brandy already in the pudding and sauce and prefer not to flame the pudding.

Decorate it with a dusting of icing sugar and a sprig of holly.

Variation If you want to flame the pudding to serve, after making the sauce place 2 tablespoons of brandy into a ladle and heat gently over a flame or electric ring. When it is warmed, pour over the pudding and ignite with a match.

Spotted dick

8 Points per serving	Points per recipe 33

Ⓥ if using free-range eggs ● Serves 4 ● Preparation time 20 minutes ● Cooking time 2½ hours ● Calories per serving 540 ● Freezing not recommended This pudding never fails to please. It's a real comforter on those long, dark winter nights with smells that permeate the whole house and make everyone feel cosy.

low-fat cooking spray
100 g (3½ oz) self-raising flour
1 teaspoon baking powder
75 g (2¾ oz) polyunsaturated margarine
100 g (3½ oz) fresh breadcrumbs
½ teaspoon ground cinnamon
50 g (1¾ oz) soft brown sugar
150 g (5½ oz) raisins, sultanas, currants, or mixed peel or a combination of all four
2 medium egg whites, beaten lightly
100 ml (3½ fl oz) skimmed milk
For the low-fat custard
2 tablespoons cornflour
300 ml (½ pint) skimmed milk
1 teaspoon vanilla essence
1 tablespoon caster sugar

1 Spray a 1.2 litre (2-pint) pudding basin with the low-fat cooking spray and put a steamer on to boil or quarter fill a large saucepan cover with a lid and put on to boil.
2 Mix together the flour and baking powder then rub in the margarine until the mixture resembles fresh breadcrumbs.
3 Add the breadcrumbs, cinnamon, sugar and fruit and mix well. Add the egg whites and enough milk to make a soft dropping consistency.
4 Spoon into the prepared pudding basin and wrap in a double thickness of non-stick greaseproof paper with a double fold to allow for rising and twisted and folded around the rim to secure. Steam for 2½ hours topping up the water level in the steamer every now and then.
5 Meanwhile, make the custard by blending the cornflour with a little milk in a saucepan. Stir in the rest of the milk, the vanilla essence and sugar. Bring to the boil, stirring all the time, and heat until thickened and smooth. Serve hot with the turned out pudding.

Queen of puddings

4 Points per serving	Points per recipe 15½

Ⓥ if using free-range eggs ● Serves 4 ● Preparation time 20 minutes + 15 minutes standing ● Cooking time 45 minutes ● Calories per serving 255 ● Freezing not recommended Another favourite childhood pudding although you hardly ever come across it anymore. Make it at home to ensure you still get to taste it. It can be rather sickly so this is a toned-down version that will still satisfy a sweet tooth.

low-fat cooking spray
400 ml (14 fl oz) skimmed milk
25 g (1 oz) polyunsaturated margarine
grated zest of 1 lemon
2 medium eggs, separated
50 g (1¾ oz) caster sugar
75 g (2¾ oz) fresh breadcrumbs
2 tablespoons reduced-sugar jam

1 Preheat the oven to Gas Mark 4/180°C/350°F and spray a 1.1 litre (2-pint) ovenproof dish with the low-fat cooking spray. Warm the milk in a small saucepan with the margarine and lemon zest.
2 Whisk the egg yolks with half the sugar and then pour on the warmed milk mixture, stirring as you pour. Put the breadcrumbs into the base of the dish and strain the custard mixture over. Leave to stand for 15 minutes.
3 Bake in the oven for 30 minutes or until lightly set. Meanwhile, gently warm the jam then spread it over the baked pudding. Whisk the egg whites stiffly and add the other half of the sugar. Whisk again and pile on top of the pudding covering it completely.
4 Bake for a further 15 minutes or until the meringue is lightly browned and crisp then serve immediately.

Summer berry cobbler

| 4 | Points per serving | Points per recipe | 23½ |

ⓥ Serves 6 ● Preparation time 25 minutes + cooling ●
Cooking time 25 minutes ● Calories per serving 240 ●
Freezing not recommended *This makes a delicious
dessert and deserves a revival. Serve with a
tablespoon of virtually fat-free fromage frais for
no extra points.*

> 500 g pack frozen summer fruit, defrosted
> 40 g (1½ oz) caster sugar
> **For the topping**
> 150 g (5½ oz) self-raising flour
> 1 teaspoon baking powder
> 50 g (1¾ oz) caster sugar
> grated zest and juice of 1 large orange
> 50 g (1¾ oz) polyunsaturated margarine

1 Preheat the oven to Gas Mark 6/200°C/400°F. Place the
fruit in an 18 cm (7-inch) round oven dish and sprinkle with
sugar.

2 To make the topping, sift the flour and baking powder
together into a bowl. Stir in the sugar, zest and juice of
the orange. Melt the margarine and pour into the centre
while still hot. Using a wooden spoon quickly but gently
stir everything together thoroughly but do not beat.

3 Using 2 dessertspoons, spoon the mixture into six
moulds on top of the fruit. Place the mounds around the
edge of the dish so you leave a gap with the fruit below
showing in the middle of the dish.

4 Immediately place in the oven and bake for 25 minutes
or until the fruit is bubbling around the sides of the cobbles
which should be well-risen and golden-crusted. Remove
from the oven and allow to cool for 4–5 minutes before
serving.

Spiced apple torte

| 4½ | Points per serving | Points per recipe | 36½ |

ⓥ if using free-range eggs ● Serves 8 ● Preparation time
25 minutes ● Cooking time 30 minutes ● Calories per
serving 290 ● Freezing recommended *This apple cake
was a great hit when I was growing up. I still love
to make it as it is so versatile and goes down well
with friends of all ages.*

> 450 g (1 lb) apples, peeled and cored cubed roughly
> 2 teaspoons caster sugar (if using cooking apples)
> low-fat cooking spray
> 100 g (3½ oz) polyunsaturated margarine
> 225 g (8 oz) plain flour
> 100 g (3½ oz) soft brown sugar
> 2 teaspoons mixed spice
> 2 teaspoons cinnamon
> 2 teaspoons baking powder
> 2 medium eggs

1 Put the apples in a pan with 2 tablespoons of water
and, if using cooking apples, 2 teaspoons of sugar,
cover and heat gently until they become mushy.

2 Spray a 23 × 30 cm (9 × 12-inch) tin with the low-fat
cooking spray and preheat the oven to Gas Mark
4/180°C/350°F.

3 Rub the margarine into the flour until the mixture
resembles fresh breadcrumbs then mix in the other
dry ingredients. Beat the eggs and then stir into the
mixture.

4 Put half the mixture into the bottom of the tin and
spread evenly. Spoon in half the apple and then
sandwich it with the other half of the spice mixture.
Bake for 30 minutes or until golden brown and firm to
the touch. Cut into squares and keep in the tin.

It is far more satisfying to spend some of an evening baking than it is to sit in front of the television! But remember, the secret to successful dieting while enjoying tasty treats is to count the points per portion size and resist eating more portions than you should!

heavenly cakes and bakes

Chocolate brownies

2½ Points per brownie Points per recipe **30½**

Ⓥ Makes 12 ● Preparation time 15 minutes ● Cooking time 25 minutes ● Calories per brownie 150 ● Freezing not recommended It is possible to have a low-fat brownie! These are 2¹/₂ points each, that's much less than a shop-bought brownie and they are still soft and chewy, light and nutty. It is a fantastic recipe as you make the whole thing in the baking tin so there is very little washing up!

low-fat cooking spray
175 g (6 oz) self-raising flour
a pinch of salt
2 sachets low-fat drinking chocolate
100 g (3½ oz) soft brown sugar
100 g (3½ oz) polyunsaturated margarine, melted
1 tablespoon clear, distilled vinegar
1 teaspoon vanilla essence

1 Preheat the oven to Gas Mark 4/180°C/350°F. Spray a 20 cm (8-inch) square baking tin with the low-fat cooking spray.
2 Sift the flour, salt and drinking chocolate into the tin, add the sugar and stir to combine.
3 Mark three grooves down the middle of the tin. Pour the margarine into one, the vinegar into the second and the vanilla and walnuts, if using (see Variation) into the third. Then pour 200 ml (7 fl oz) water over and stir really well to make sure there are no lumps of flour left.
4 Bake for 25 minutes, then cool in the tin for 15 minutes before transferring to a wire rack and allowing to cool further before eating.

Top tip Brownies are best crusty on the outside but gooey and chewy in the middle so test after they have been in the oven 20 minutes or so by inserting a skewer into the centre. It should come out with just a little of the mixture on it whilst the top should be dark and crusty.
Variation Add 50 g (1¾ oz) chopped walnuts with the vanilla in Step 3 if you wish. The points per brownie will be 3.

Quick and easy wholemeal bread

1½	Points per slice	Points per loaf	20

Ⓥ Makes 2 medium loaves which cut into about 16 slices each ● Preparation time 15 minutes + 45 minutes–1 hour rising ● Cooking time 35–40 minutes ● Calories per slice 95 ● Freezing recommended *Home-made bread has many advantages over its shop-bought equivalents including being less expensive and containing fewer additives. It is tasty, satisfying and, most importantly, you know exactly how many points are in it.*

This bread is delicious served with one of the scrumptious soups in the first chapter or toasted and spread with reduced-sugar jam or marmalade for an extra ½ point per heaped teaspoon.

    900 g (2 lb) plain wholemeal flour
    10 g (¼ oz) salt
    15 g (½ oz) soft brown sugar
    15 g (½ oz) fresh yeast or 10 g/¼ oz dried yeast
    600 ml (1 pint) warm water
    low-fat cooking spray

1 Mix the flour, salt and sugar together in a large bowl. Make a well in the centre.

2 Mix the yeast into a wet paste with a little warm water and pour into the well with a little more of the water.

3 Mix together with your hands, adding more water if it is too dry, until you have a slippery dough that comes away from the bowl in a smooth ball. Different flours vary in their absorbency so add the water a bit at a time in case the dough becomes too wet and sticky.

4 Divide the dough between two 13 × 23 cm (9 × 5-inch) bread tins which have been warmed and sprayed with low-fat cooking spray. Cover with a clean, floured tea towel and leave in a warm place until the dough has risen by more than a half, usually around 45 minutes–1 hour.

5 Preheat the oven to Gas Mark 6/200°C/400°F. Sprinkle the loaves with flour and bake for 35–40 minutes. Check that they are cooked by tapping the bottom – they should sound hollow.

Top tips This recipe makes two medium loaves – one to eat and one to wrap in a plastic bag and freeze for up to 3 months.

Uncooked bread will rise if you leave it in the fridge but it will take 24 hours, so it is not absolutely necessary to put it in a warm place but it does speed up the process. If you put it in an airing cupboard, on top of the boiler or on top of the oven, then the dough will rise quickly giving a more open texture than if left in the kitchen for, say, 1½ hours, when it rises very gently.

Variations Your bread will vary greatly depending on the flour that you use so try different brands and types or try mixing types, for example use half white and half wholemeal flour, or half white and half rye flour. Organic and stone-ground flours are well worth a try as most give a lovely texture and flavour. Always use a 'strong' bread flour, as this means that it has a high gluten content which will make it rise better.

Always eat a healthy breakfast and then there'll be less chance of you giving in to unhealthy snacks mid-morning

Spiced scone round

3	Points per slice	Points per recipe	26

V Serves 8 ● Preparation time 30 minutes + 10 minutes cooling before you can eat it! ● Cooking time 30 minutes ● Calories per slice 205 ● Freezing not recommended This is a slightly sweet, thick, potato scone round with raisins and cinnamon which is baked in the oven until it is crusty on the outside but is still soft in the middle. It is delicious plain or spread with reduced-sugar jams or marmalade for an extra ½ point per heaped teaspoon.

> 450 g (1 lb) peeled potatoes, cut into chunks
> 50 g (1¾ oz) polyunsaturated margarine, melted
> 50 g (1¾ oz) caster sugar
> 50 g (1¾ oz) raisins
> a pinch of salt
> ½ teaspoon ground cinnamon
> 175 g (6 oz) self-raising flour, sifted
> low-fat cooking spray
> icing sugar, to dust

1 Preheat the oven to Gas Mark 7/220°C/425°F. Boil the potatoes in plenty of unsalted water until tender. Drain and mash with the melted margarine, then stir in the sugar, raisins, salt and cinnamon while the potatoes are still hot.

2 Using a wooden spoon, add the flour a little at a time until you have a stiff dough. Shape into a round about 5 cm (2-inches) thick on a baking tray sprayed with low-fat cooking spray.

3 Mark into eight segments lightly with a knife and bake for 30 minutes or until golden and crusty on top.

4 Transfer to a wire rack to cool for at least 10 minutes before dusting with icing sugar and serving.

Top tip This scone's light texture relies on being made with hot mashed potato so yesterday's left-overs will not do.

Variations The spice can be varied from cinnamon to ground ginger or use orange zest instead.

Fast flatbreads

2	Points per flatbread	Points per recipe	20½

V Makes 12 ● Preparation time 20 minutes ● Cooking time 4 minutes for each flatbread ● Calories per flatbread 125 ● Freezing recommended These flatbreads are a great stand-by recipe for when you run out of bread and you need a filling snack fast. They are the everyday bread of India, and are called 'chappati' or 'roti' and could not be easier to make. Eat them warm with a light lunch of soup or with reduced-fat hummous or guacamole (page 27), adding on the extra points.

> 450 g (1 lb) plain wholemeal flour
> 1 teaspoon salt
> 1 teaspoon sunflower oil

1 Blend the flour, salt and oil and bind to a pliable dough with about 350 ml (12 fl oz) warm water. Knead for 5 minutes or longer if you can as it will make the flatbreads softer in the end.

2 Divide the dough into twelve golf-ball-sized portions. Lightly coat with flour, shape into a ball in your palm and flatten slightly.

3 Roll out into flat discs, as thin as possible, flouring the work surface if necessary to stop them sticking.

4 Heat a frying-pan or griddle and cook one disc until the surface bubbles (about 2 minutes). Turn over and press the surface down with a clean cloth to cook the other side evenly. As soon as brown spots appear, the flatbread is cooked.

5 Remove and keep warm wrapped in a tea towel or foil whilst you cook the others.

Top tip If the flatbreads stick whilst cooking, dust with a little flour. Be careful not to let the flour burn or it will give a bitter taste to the breads.

Variations Add a teaspoon of ground cumin and/or coriander for an Indian flavour or fresh chopped herbs like thyme, rosemary, oregano and/or parsley for a Mediterranean twist.

Hot cross buns

2½ Points per bun   Points per recipe **39½**

Ⓥ if using a free-range egg ● Makes 16 ● Preparation time 30 minutes + 2–2½ hours rising ● Cooking time 15 minutes ● Calories per bun 165 ● Freezing recommended

Traditionally eaten on Good Friday. You can start making these hot cross buns the day before and keep the dough in the fridge to bake in the morning. They are much more substantial and satisfying than most of the shop-bought ones, not to mention tastier and lower in points.

350 g (12 oz) plain flour
100 g (3½ oz) plain wholemeal flour
25 g (1 oz) fresh yeast (or 15 g/½ oz dried)
½ teaspoon caster sugar
150 ml (5 fl oz) warm water
150 ml (5 fl oz) skimmed milk
1 teaspoon cinnamon
1 teaspoon ground nutmeg
1 teaspoon salt
50 g (1¾ oz) caster sugar
75 g (2¾ oz) currants
50 g (1¾ oz) chopped mixed peel
50 g (1¾ oz) polyunsaturated margarine, melted
1 medium egg, beaten
a little skimmed milk, to glaze

1 Sift half of the quantities of each flour into a bowl and make a well in the centre. Blend the yeast with the ½ teaspoon of sugar and a little of the warm water. Leave for 5 minutes in a warm place to froth then add the rest of the water.

2 Pour the water mixture and the milk into the well in the flour. Mix well then leave, covered, in a warm place for about 45 minutes until risen to double its size.

3 Meanwhile, sieve the rest of each flour then mix with the spices, salt, caster sugar, dried fruit and peel. Add this mixture to the risen dough with the melted margarine and egg and mix well with your hands, kneading until smooth. Leave, covered, in a warm place for about 1 hour.

4 Turn the risen dough out on to a floured surface and roll or pat it out and divide into 16 pieces. Shape them into rounds and place well apart on a baking tray that has been sprayed with low-fat cooking spray and then lightly floured.

5 Mark each round with a cross using a sharp knife. Cover and leave either in the fridge overnight ready for baking the next day, or in a warm place for 15 minutes while you preheat the oven to Gas Mark 7/220°C/425°F.

6 Brush with a little milk to glaze then bake for 15 minutes. Leave on a wire rack to cool.

Top tip If you are keeping dough overnight in the fridge, remove and leave in a warm place for 30 minutes before baking.

Tasty soda bread

| **2** Points per slice | Points per recipe **31½** |

v Makes 16 slices ● Preparation time 15 minutes ● Cooking time 35–45 minutes ● Calories per slice 135 ● Freezing not recommended This Irish soda bread recipe is made with low-fat plain Bio yogurt rather than the usual buttermilk. The process is very quick so the dough requires no kneading or rising time.

Serve the bread with soup or stews or toasted and spread with reduced-sugar jam or marmalade, adding an extra ½ point per heaped teaspoon.

350 g (12 oz) plain wholemeal flour
225 g (8 oz) plain white flour
25 g (1 oz) fine oatmeal
1 teaspoon salt
1 teaspoon bicarbonate of soda
400 g (14 oz) low-fat plain Bio yogurt

1 Preheat the oven to Gas Mark 8/230°C/450°F. In a large bowl mix together the dry ingredients and then make a well in the centre.
2 Add the yogurt and gradually work into the dry ingredients with your hand. Add a little water if necessary to make a soft, but not sticky, dough.
3 Turn out on to a floured surface and knead lightly to shape into a round. Flatten slightly until it is about 5 cm (2-inches) thick.
4 Put on to a baking sheet, mark a deep cross with a knife and bake for 15–20 minutes, then reduce the oven temperature to Gas Mark 6/200°C/400°F for 20–25 minutes or until the bread sounds hollow when tapped on the base.
5 Cool on a wire rack and enjoy when just warm or cooled.

Golden cornbread

| **5½** Points per slice | Points per recipe **33** |

v if using a free-range egg ● Serves 6 ● Preparation time 15 minutes ● Cooking time 25–30 minutes ● Calories per slice 320 ● Freezing recommended This is a New England-style cornbread made with sweetcorn and cornmeal with the optional addition of hot chilli peppers. It is tangy and moist with a lovely yellow colour. Try it with any of the soups (pages 6–21) or salads (pages 36–51) or with Roasted autumn roots (page 58) or Spring vegetable stew (page 55), adding on the extra points.

low-fat cooking spray
275 g (9½ oz) cornmeal (polenta)
75 g (2¾ oz) plain flour
2 teaspoons bicarbonate of soda
1 medium egg
150 ml (5 fl oz) skimmed milk
425 ml (15 floz) low-fat plain yogurt
400 g can sweetcorn, rinsed and drained
115 g jar chilli peppers, drained and chopped (optional)
30 g (1¼ oz) fresh parsley, chopped
salt and black pepper

1 Preheat the oven to Gas Mark 6 /200°C/400°F. Spray a shallow tin or small roasting tin, approximately 25 cm (10-inch) square, with the low-fat cooking spray.
2 In a large bowl combine the cornmeal, flour, bicarbonate of soda and seasoning.
3 In a jug combine the egg, milk and yogurt. Pour into the dry ingredients and lightly combine, being careful not to over-stir as this will cause the cornbread to be tough. Stir in the sweetcorn, chopped chillies, if using, and parsley.
4 Pour the mixture into the tray and bake for 25–30 minutes until firm and golden on top.
5 Enjoy while still warm or cool on a wire rack.

Banana cake

| **3½** Points per slice | Points per recipe **29½** |

v if using free-range eggs and vegetarian cheese ● Makes 8 slices ● Preparation time 15 minutes + cooling ● Cooking time 1¼ hours ● Calories per slice 235 ● Freezing recommended *This recipe is a great way to use up bananas that have turned brown in the fruit bowl.*

low-fat cooking spray
225 g (8 oz) white self-raising flour
¼ teaspoon bicarbonate of soda
50 g (1¾ oz) polyunsaturated margarine
2 medium eggs
2 tablespoons low-fat plain Bio yogurt
3 medium ripe bananas
2 teaspoons ground allspice
For the topping
50 g (1¾ oz) low-fat soft cheese
grated zest and juice of 1 lime or lemon
25 g (1 oz) caster sugar

1 Preheat the oven to Gas Mark 3/170°C/325°F and spray a 20 cm (8-inch) cake tin with the low-fat cooking spray and line with non-stick baking paper.
2 Place all the cake ingredients in a food processor and mix for a few minutes. Alternatively, mix together by hand, mashing the banana with a fork first.
3 Pour the mixture into the prepared tin and bake for 1¼ hours or until a thin skewer inserted into the middle comes out clean. Leave to cool in an airtight container.
4 Make the topping by gently mixing together the ingredients being careful not to over-mix or it will curdle. Spread over the cake and serve immediately.

Top tip Cooling the cake in an airtight container helps to keep it moist. The cake will keep for up to 3 days in an airtight container wrapped in clingfilm or foil.

Poppy seed bread ring

| **3** Points per slice | Points per recipe **62½** |

v if using free-range eggs ● Makes 20 slices ● Preparation time 30 minutes + 3½ hours rising ● Cooking time 25 minutes ● Calories per slice 185 ● Freezing recommended *A squishy, soft, sweet bread.*

500 g (1 lb 2 oz) strong white flour
½ teaspoon salt
1 sachet easy-blend dried yeast
50 g (1¾ oz) caster sugar
2 medium eggs, beaten
50 g (1¾ oz) polyunsaturated margarine, melted
grated zest of ½ lemon
2 tablespoons 0% fat Greek-style yogurt
150 ml (5 fl oz) warm water
low-fat cooking spray
175 g (6 oz) poppy seeds
40 g (1½ oz) ground almonds
2 tablespoons honey, plus extra to glaze the ring

1 Combine the flour, salt, yeast and sugar in a bowl. Make a well in the centre and pour in the eggs, margarine, lemon zest and yogurt. Mix with a wooden spoon adding just enough water to form a soft dough.
2 Turn out on to a floured surface and knead for 10 minutes until smooth. Place in a bowl sprayed with the low-fat cooking spray, cover with a tea towel or clingfilm and leave in a warm place for 2 hours to rise.
3 For the filling, place the poppy seeds in a bowl and cover with boiling water. Leave to stand for 1 hour then drain thoroughly and dry on kitchen paper or a clean, dry tea towel. Mix with the ground almonds and honey.
4 Once the dough has risen, knock it back with your fists and push out using the heel of your hands and then roll out to a rectangle about 46 × 25 cm (18 × 25-inches). Spread the poppy seed mixture over, leaving a 2.5 cm (1-inch) border.
5 Roll up the bread like a Swiss roll, being careful to keep it even, then bring the two ends together, and gently pinch, to form a ring. Carefully transfer to a baking sheet sprayed with the low-fat cooking spray. Melt the remaining honey and brush over the loaf then put in a warm place for 30 minutes to rise.
6 Preheat the oven to Gas Mark 6/200°C/400°F and bake for 20–25 minutes or until puffed up and golden. Gently transfer to a wire rack to cool.

Date and walnut loaf

2½ Points per slice	Points per recipe 32½

V Makes 12 slices ● Preparation time 15 minutes ● Cooking time 1 hour ● Calories per slice 175 ● Freezing recommended *This is a classic, heavenly combination.*

low-fat cooking spray
300 ml (½ pint) skimmed milk
75 g (2¾ oz) black treacle
50 g (1¾ oz) polyunsaturated margarine
200 g (7 oz) plain wholemeal flour
3 teaspoons baking powder
½ teaspoon salt
½ teaspoon bicarbonate of soda
50 g (1¾ oz) soft dark brown sugar
125 g (4½ oz) dates, chopped roughly
50 g (1¾ oz) walnuts, chopped roughly

1 Preheat the oven to Gas Mark 3/170°C/325°F. Spray a 23 × 13 cm (9 × 5-inch), 1 litre (1¾-pint) loaf tin with the low-fat cooking spray, line with baking paper and then spray again.
2 In a small saucepan, warm the milk, treacle and margarine together.
3 Sift the dry ingredients into a large bowl and stir in the sugar. Mix in the dates and walnuts.
4 Stir in the warmed liquid to make a fairly smooth, thick paste. Pour into the prepared tin, smooth the top and bake for 1 hour or until a skewer inserted into the middle comes out clean.

Top tip Use a metal measuring spoon dipped in boiling water or flour to measure out the treacle.
Variation Try using chopped soaked apricots instead of the dates and blanched almonds instead of walnuts. The points remain the same.

Coffee cup cakes

3½ Points per cake	Points per recipe 40½

V if using a free-range egg ● Makes 12 ● Preparation and cooking time 25 minutes ● Calories per cake 205 ● Freezing recommended *These little coffee-flavoured cup cakes, served with an espresso syrup, are ideal as a dinner party dessert.*

125 g (4½ oz) polyunsaturated margarine
125 g (4½ oz) caster sugar
1 teaspoon vanilla essence
1 medium egg
150 g (5½ oz) self-raising flour
2 teaspoons instant coffee granules dissolved in
    2 tablespoons boiling water
2 tablespoons skimmed milk
For the coffee syrup
100 g (3½ oz) caster sugar
200 ml (7 fl oz) strong black coffee
1 tablespoon coffee liqueur e.g. Tia Maria

1 Preheat the oven to Gas Mark 4/180°C/350°F. Place 12 cup cake cases in a Yorkshire pudding tray or muffin tray.
2 In a bowl, cream together the margarine and sugar until light and fluffy. Add the vanilla and egg and beat well.
3 Fold in the flour, coffee and milk. Place a tablespoon of the mixture into each cake case and bake for 15–20 minutes until a skewer inserted into the centre of one cake comes out clean and they are risen and golden.
4 For the coffee syrup, place the coffee, sugar, and liqueur, if using, in a saucepan over a low heat and stir until the sugar has dissolved. Allow the syrup to boil for 5 minutes until it thickens. To serve remove the cakes from their cases, put on separate plates and pour the syrup over.

Top tip These cup cakes will keep for a few days in an airtight container.

Blueberry muffins: At only 2½ points per serving, these are ideal take-to-work snacks; they taste fantastic with morning coffee!

Blueberry muffins

2½ Points per muffin	Points per recipe 29½

Ⓥ if using a free-range egg ● Makes 12 ● Preparation time 15 minutes ● Cooking time 20 minutes ● Calories per muffin 155 ● Freezing not recommended This recipe is made using dried blueberries which are now readily available in the baking section of supermarkets. These are very convenient to keep in your storecupboard.

200 g (7 oz) plain flour
½ teaspoon bicarbonate of soda
2 teaspoons baking powder
75 g (2¾ oz) caster sugar
a pinch of salt
75 g (2¾ oz) polyunsaturated margarine, melted
100 ml (3½ fl oz) low-fat plain yogurt
100 ml (3½ fl oz) skimmed milk
1 medium egg
200 g (7 oz) fresh blueberries

1 Preheat the oven to Gas Mark 6/200°C/400°F. Line a Yorkshire pudding tin or muffin tray with 12 muffin or cup cake cases.
2 Combine all the dry ingredients in a bowl. In another bowl mix the melted margarine, yogurt, milk and egg together.
3 Pour the wet ingredients into the dry and combine very gently so you don't over-work the mixture.
4 Gently stir in the blueberries, again keeping the mixing to a minimum, then quickly spoon into the muffin cases. Bake for 20 minutes, until risen and golden on top.
5 Transfer to a wire rack and cool or eat warm.

Top tip These muffins keep well for up to 3 days stored in an airtight container.
Variation Substitute the fresh blueberries with dried blueberries; just soak for 10 minutes in hot water. The points per serving will remain the same.

Tea-time apple cake

2½ Points per square	Points per recipe 28

Ⓥ if using a free-range egg ● Makes 12 squares ● Preparation time 20 minutes ● Cooking time 35 minutes ● Calories per square 135 ● Freezing not recommended This is a lovely moist cake with lots of apple slices on top.

2 medium cooking apples, peeled, cored and chopped
low-fat cooking spray
50 g (1¾ oz) brown sugar
150 g (5½ oz) plain flour
½ teaspoon baking powder
½ teaspoon baking soda
a pinch of salt
1 medium egg
50 g (1¾ oz) polyunsaturated margarine, melted
100 ml (3½ fl oz) low-fat plain yogurt
1 teaspoon vanilla essence
For the topping
3 medium eating apples, peeled, cored and sliced finely
1 teaspoon ground cinnamon
4 tablespoons reduced-sugar apricot jam

1 In a small saucepan simmer the chopped apples with 2 tablespoons of water, covered, for 5 minutes or until soft. Put in a liquidiser and whizz until a smooth purée is formed. This should make about 125 ml (4 fl oz).
2 Preheat the oven to Gas Mark 4/180°C/350°F. Spray a 25 × 15 cm (10 × 6-inch) shallow, rectangular cake tin with the low-fat cooking spray.
3 Mix all the dry ingredients together in a bowl. Beat the egg with the melted margarine, apple purée, yogurt and vanilla. Add this to the dry ingredients and stir until blended.
4 Pour the batter into the prepared tin and arrange the apple slices over. Sprinkle the cinnamon over the top and bake for 35 minutes until golden brown.
5 Heat the apricot jam with the water and stir until melted then brush over the apple cake to glaze then serve either warm or cold.

If you're always in a hurry in the mornings, prepare your breakfast and lunch the night before

Gingerbread

| **3** Points per slice | Points per recipe **37½** |

(V) if using a free-range egg ● Makes 12 slices ●
Preparation time 20 minutes ● Cooking time 1¼ hours ●
Calories per slice 200 ● Freezing recommended This is
a rich, dark and flavoursome gingerbread that is
baked as a loaf and is just the thing to enjoy on a
cold winter's day.

low-fat cooking spray
175 g (6 oz) medium oatmeal
175 g (6 oz) self-raising flour, sifted
¼ teaspoon salt
75 g (2¾ oz) polyunsaturated margarine, cut into pieces
2 teaspoons ground ginger
75 g (2¾ oz) soft light brown sugar
2 tablespoons black treacle (see Top tips)
1 medium egg
150 ml (5 fl oz) skimmed milk
½ teaspoon lemon juice or vinegar

1 Preheat the oven to Gas Mark 3/170°C/325°F and
spray a 23 × 13 cm (9 × 5-inch), 1 litre (1¾-pint) loaf tin,
line with baking paper and spray again.
2 Combine the oatmeal, flour and salt in a bowl then
rub in the margarine until the mixture resembles fine
breadcrumbs.
3 Stir in the ginger and sugar. Heat the treacle gently
in a small pan then add the egg and pour into the dry
ingredients with the milk and lemon juice or vinegar.
4 Stir well to combine then pour into the tin and bake
for 1 hour–1 hour 10 minutes or until a skewer inserted
into the centre comes out clean. Cool on a wire rack
before removing from the tin.

Top tips Gingerbread tastes just as good, if not better,
if stored in foil in a tin for a few days before eating.

To measure out tablespoons of treacle, dip a metal
measuring spoon in boiling water first.

Carrot cake with orange icing

| **3** Points per slice | Points per recipe **24** |

(V) if using free-range eggs and vegetarian cheese ●
Makes 8 slices ● Preparation time 15 minutes + cooling
● Cooking time 20 minutes ● Calories per slice 190 ●
Freezing recommended Carrot cake with its moist
texture and natural sweetness, is always popular.
This version has a zesty orange icing to really get
the tastebuds tingling.

low-fat cooking spray
2 medium eggs
100 g (3½ oz) caster sugar
50 g (1¾ oz) polyunsaturated margarine, melted
175 g (6 oz) carrots, grated
100 g (3½ oz) self-raising flour, sifted
1 teaspoon ground cinnamon
½ teaspoon ground nutmeg
For the orange icing
50 g (1¾ oz) low-fat soft cheese
25 g (1 oz) icing sugar
zest of 1 medium orange and 1 tablespoon of the juice

1 Preheat the oven to Gas Mark 5/190°C/375°F. Spray
an 18 cm (7-inch) round cake tin with the low-fat cooking
spray, line the base with baking paper then spray again.
2 Whisk the eggs and sugar together until light and
fluffy. Gradually whisk in the melted margarine then add
all the remaining cake ingredients.
3 Pour into the tin and bake for 20 minutes or until
golden brown and firm to the touch. Turn out of the tin
and leave on a wire rack to cool.
4 Make the icing by beating together the soft cheese,
sugar, orange zest and juice then spread over the
cooled cake.

Top tip Carrot cake will keep for several days in an
airtight container.

Devil's food cake

5½ Points per slice	Points per recipe **52½**

Ⓥ if using free-range eggs ● Makes 10 slices ●
Preparation time 30 minutes + cooling ● Cooking time
25 minutes ● Calories per slice 290 ● Freezing not
recommended *This full-blown chocolate cake is*
temptation indeed. It's for a special occasion when
nothing but chocolate cake will do, and it has
fewer points than the usual chocolate cake.

    low-fat cooking spray
    100 g (3½ oz) polyunsaturated margarine
    150 g (5½ oz) light brown soft sugar
    2 medium eggs
    40 g (1½ oz) plain chocolate (minimum 70% cocoa solids)
    100 ml (3½ fl oz) boiling water
    150 g (5½ oz) plain flour
    ½ teaspoon baking powder
    1 teaspoon bicarbonate of soda
    100 ml (3½ fl oz) low-fat plain yogurt
    1 teaspoon vanilla essence
    For the filling
    50 g (1¾ oz) polyunsaturated margarine
    50 g (1¾ oz) icing sugar, plus extra to dust
    1 teaspoon cocoa powder, plus extra to dust

1 Preheat the oven to Gas Mark 5/190°C/375°F. Spray
two 18 cm (7-inch) cake tins with low-fat cooking spray,
line the bases with baking paper and spray again.
2 Cream the margarine and sugar together until light
and fluffy. Add the eggs one at a time beating well
between each addition.
3 Break up the chocolate into a saucepan, pour the
boiling water over and heat gently until smooth and
thick. Cool a little and then add to the creamed mixture
and blend well.
4 Sift the flour with the baking powder and bicarbonate
of soda and add to the mixture with the yogurt and
vanilla. Mix well then pour into the prepared tins and
bake for 25 minutes or until risen and a skewer inserted
into the middle comes out clean.
5 Turn out the cakes and leave on a wire rack to cool.
Meanwhile, make the filling by beating together the
margarine, sugar and cocoa powder until fluffy then use
to sandwich together the cooled cakes. Dust the top
with cocoa powder or icing sugar and serve.

Chocolate chestnut cake

5 Points per slice	Points per recipe **49**

Ⓥ if using free-range eggs and vegetarian cheese ●
Makes 10 slices ● Preparation time 20 minutes + cooling
● Cooking time 20 minutes ● Calories per slice 250 ●
Freezing not recommended *This is the lightest*
chocolate sponge filled with a creamy chocolate
and chestnut cream that's thoroughly indulgent.

    low-fat cooking spray
    100 g (3½ oz) polyunsaturated margarine
    100 g (3½ oz) caster sugar
    2 medium eggs
    100 g (3½ oz) self-raising flour
    25 g (1 oz) unsweetened cocoa powder
    For the filling
    200 g (7 oz) unsweetened chestnut purée
    50 g (1¾ oz) plain dark chocolate (minimum 70%
        cocoa solids), melted
    200 g (7 oz) low-fat soft cheese
    1 teaspoon vanilla essence
    icing sugar, to dust

1 Preheat the oven to Gas Mark 4/180°C/350°F. Spray
two non-stick 18 cm (7-inch) cake tins with low-fat
cooking spray.
2 Cream the margarine and sugar together until fluffy,
either in a food processor or by hand, then add the eggs
one at a time beating well between each addition.
3 Sift in the flour and cocoa powder and mix thoroughly.
Spoon equal amounts into the prepared tins and bake for
20 minutes until risen and a skewer, when inserted in
the middle, comes out clean.
4 Turn out the cakes on to wire racks to cool.
5 When cool, slice each cake in half horizontally to
make four discs. Mix all the filling ingredients together
then place one cake disc on a plate and spread it with a
quarter of the filling, top with another disc, then repeat
until all four discs are used. Decorate with mounds of
the remaining filling. Refrigerate for ½ hour before serving,
then dust with icing sugar.

Top tip Chestnut pureé can be found in most
supermarkets, usually in the sauces and pickles section.

Menu plan

Boxing Day Tea

~

Turkey Frittata, page 30
1 serving ... 4½ points

~

Christmas Cake, page 197
(pictured here)
1 serving ... 6½ points

Total points per meal 11 points

Christmas cake

ⓥ if using free-range eggs ● Makes 16 slices ●
Preparation time 45 minutes + 2 hours soaking (optional)
● Cooking time 4 hours ● Calories per slice 380 ●
Freezing recommended *Friends and family alike
will love this low point Christmas cake.*

250 g (9 oz) sultanas
4 tablespoons rum or brandy (optional)
low-fat cooking spray
175 g (6 oz) candied peel, chopped
175 g (6 oz) glacé cherries, halved
100 g (3½ oz) blanched almonds, chopped
250 g (9 oz) currants
225 g (8 oz) plain flour
100 g (3½ oz) polyunsaturated margarine
100 g (3½ oz) soft brown sugar
2 tablespoons clear honey or black treacle
grated zest of 1 lemon
grated zest of 1 orange
4 medium eggs
½ teaspoon salt
½ teaspoon mixed spice
½ teaspoon grated nutmeg
2–4 tablespoons skimmed milk
For the icing
4 tablespoons reduced-sugar jam
227 g ready-to-roll royal icing

1 Soak the sultanas in the rum or brandy, if using, for up
to 2 hours before you make the cake.
2 Preheat the oven to Gas Mark 2/150°C/300°F. Spray a
20 cm (8-inch) round cake tin with the low-fat cooking
spray, line twice with baking paper that stands a good
2.5 cm (1-inch) above the top of the tin, and spray again.
Tie a band of baking paper around the outside of the tin
to give extra protection from over-browning.
3 In a large bowl, mix all the fruit and nuts with a
tablespoon of the flour to coat them. Cream the
margarine and sugar together until light and fluffy,
then mix in the honey or treacle and the lemon and
orange zest.

4 Beat the eggs with a whisk until thick and foamy and
add a little at a time to the margarine mixture beating
well after each addition. If the mixture shows signs of
curdling then mix in a tablespoon of flour and keep
beating. Sift the rest of the flour, salt and spices
together and lightly fold into the mixture.
5 Fold in the fruit and nut mixture and just enough milk,
if necessary, to make a batter moist enough to drop off
a spoon if given a good shake.
6 Spoon into the prepared tin and make a deep hollow
in the centre to ensure that the cooked cake has a flat
top for icing. Cover with a double layer of baking paper
and bake for 4 hours or until a warm skewer inserted
into the middle comes out clean.
7 Allow the cake to cool in the tin for 1 hour before
placing on a cooling rack.
8 To ice, place the cake on a board. Warm the jam in a
pan with 4 tablespoons of water until melted. Brush the
sides and the top of the cake with the jam.
9 Roll out the royal icing to a piece large enough to
cover the whole cake like a blanket. Drape over the
rolling pin to place over the cake and then press gently
on to the cake's surface and trim the edges. From any
left-over icing or trimmings, cut out decorations in the
shapes of a star, holly leaf or Christmas tree. Paint with
food colourings and place on top. Alternatively, decorate
with sprigs of holly.

Lemon drizzle cake

4 Points per slice   Points per recipe **32½**

Ⓥ if using free-range eggs ● Makes 8 slices ● Preparation time 25 minutes ● Cooking time 30–40 minutes ● Calories per slice 260 ● Freezing recommended *A sharp, lemony cake with a sweet, crystallised sugar topping.*

low-fat cooking spray
100 g (3½ oz) polyunsaturated margarine
100 g (3½ oz) caster sugar
2 medium eggs, beaten
4 tablespoons skimmed milk
1 teaspoon baking powder
grated zest and juice of 2 medium lemons
175 g (6 oz) self-raising flour
2 tablespoons caster sugar,
    for the topping

1 Preheat the oven to Gas Mark 5/190°C/375°F. Spray an 18 cm (7-inch) round tin with the low-fat cooking spray, line with baking paper and spray again.

2 Cream together the margarine and sugar until light and fluffy. Add the eggs one at a time and beat well between each addition. Add the milk, baking powder and lemon zest and beat well.

3 Sift the flour into the mixture and fold in lightly. Spoon into the prepared tin and bake for 30–40 minutes or until golden brown and a skewer inserted into the centre comes out clean.

4 Meanwhile, to make the topping heat together the sugar and lemon juice until the sugar is dissolved. When the cake is cooked place on a wire cooling rack. Pour the lemon syrup over the hot cake and leave to cool.

Cinnamon and apple muffins

| **2½** Points per muffin | Points per recipe **30** |

V if using a free-range egg ● Makes 12 ● Preparation time 15 minutes + cooling ● Cooking time 20 minutes ● Calories per muffin 145 ● Freezing not recommended

These light and healthy muffins can be made in just 30 minutes. They are perfect for breakfast, especially if you are on the go.

1 medium egg
75 g (2¾ oz) polyunsaturated margarine, melted
100 ml (3½ fl oz) low-fat plain yogurt
100 ml (3½ fl oz) apple juice
3 tablespoons clear honey, warmed
2 large dessert apples, peeled, cored and grated
200 g (7 oz) plain flour
2 teaspoons baking powder
½ teaspoon bicarbonate of soda
a pinch of salt
1 teaspoon ground cinnamon

1 Preheat the oven to Gas Mark 6/200°C/400°F. Line a Yorkshire pudding tin or muffin tray with 12 muffin cases.
2 In a large measuring jug beat together the egg, margarine, yogurt, apple juice, honey and grated apple. Mix all the other dry ingredients together in a large bowl. Add the wet ingredients to the dry and gently but quickly mix together then spoon into the muffin cases.
3 Bake for 20 minutes or until risen and the centres spring back when gently pressed. Place on a wire rack to cool and store in an airtight container for up to 3 days.

Top tip Use dessert apples (such as Cox, Gala or Spartan) for the best results.

Super speedy scones

| **1** Point per scone | Points per recipe **18** |

V Makes 20 ● Preparation time 25 minutes ● Cooking time 15 minutes ● Calories per scone 55 ● Freezing recommended *A recipe for scones is fantastic to have in your repertoire as, once you are familiar with making them, you can have them made and sitting warm on the table within ½ hour - great for when unexpected visitors drop in. Serve warm on their own (the fruit version suggested in variations is especially good like this) or cool, split and fill with a teaspoon of low-fat yogurt or virtually fat-free fromage frais for no extra points.*

low-fat cooking spray
225 g (8 oz) self-raising flour
¼ teaspoon salt
40 g (1½ oz) polyunsaturated margarine
1 teaspoon caster sugar
150 ml (5 fl oz) skimmed milk, plus extra to glaze

1 Preheat the oven to Gas Mark 7/220°C/425°F. Spray a baking tray with the low-fat cooking spray.
2 Sieve the flour into a large bowl and mix in the salt. Cut the margarine into small pieces and add, rubbing together with your fingertips until the mixture resembles fine breadcrumbs. Stir in the sugar.
3 Make a well in the centre, pour in the milk and gradually stir into the mixture. Turn out on to a floured surface and knead very quickly and lightly to form a smooth dough.
4 Roll out to 1 cm (½-inch) thick. Using a cutter, cut into 6 cm (2½-inch) diameter circles. Place on the prepared baking sheet. Press together the trimmings and repeat the rolling and cutting process until the dough is all used up.
5 Brush the tops with a little milk and bake for 12–15 minutes until risen and golden then cool on a wire rack.

Top tip Scones will keep for a day or two in an airtight container but benefit from being warmed through before serving.

Variations Add 50 g (1¾ oz) of raisins or sultanas if you like fruit scones. The points will remain the same.

Coconut and raspberry cup cakes

4½ Points per cup cake   Points per recipe **47½**

ⓥ if using free-range eggs ● Makes 10 ● Preparation time 15 minutes ● Cooking time 15 minutes ● Calories per cup cake 200 ● Freezing not recommended These golden cup cakes are very light and have a wonderful texture given by the coconut, and lovely sharp flavour from the raspberries. Serve with more fresh raspberries and virtually fat-free fromage frais for a dessert or for tea with fruit or herb teas, adding on the extra points.

> 25 g (1 oz) ground almonds
> 50 g (1¾ oz) desiccated coconut
> 225 g (8 oz) icing sugar
> 50 g (1¾ oz) plain flour
> ½ teaspoon baking powder
> 125 g (4½ oz) polyunsaturated margarine, melted
> 5 medium egg whites
> 100 g (3½ oz) raspberries, fresh or frozen

1 Preheat the oven to Gas Mark 4/180°C/350°F. Mix the ground almonds, coconut, sugar, flour and baking powder together in a bowl. Add the melted margarine and mix to combine.

2 Whisk the egg whites until they hold stiff peaks then fold gently into the almond mixture.

3 Pour the mixture into cup cake cases in a Yorkshire pudding or muffin tin. Sprinkle the raspberries over the top of each cake.

4 Bake for 12–15 minutes or until the cakes are golden and springy to the touch.

Pear tea cakes

7½ Points per tea cake   Points per recipe **31**

ⓥ if using free-range eggs ● Makes 4 individual cakes; serves 4 ● Preparation time 25 minutes ● Cooking time 25 minutes ● Calories per tea cake 440 ● Freezing not recommended These are cooked as individual upside-down cakes or can be made in one 20 cm (8-inch) round cake tin. Delicious with a lovely cup of tea.

> 4 canned pear halves, sliced, or 2 fresh pears, cored, peeled and sliced
> low-fat cooking spray
> 100 g (3½ oz) polyunsaturated margarine
> 75 g (2¾ oz) caster sugar
> 1 tablespoon clear honey
> 2 medium eggs
> 1 teaspoon vanilla essence
> 100 g (3½ oz) self-raising flour
> 1 tablespoon reduced-sugar jam, to glaze
> 1 teaspoon icing sugar, to dust

1 If using fresh, unripe pears, poach until soft in a little water. Remove from the heat and drain.

2 Preheat the oven to Gas Mark 3/170°C/325°F. Spray four 12 cm (4½-inch) individual tart tins with the low-fat cooking spray.

3 Lay the pear slices in the bottom of the tins and set aside. Make the sponge by creaming together the margarine, sugar and honey until light and fluffy.

4 Add the eggs one at a time and beating well between each addition then add the vanilla essence. Sift the flour and fold into the mixture. Pour the mixture over the pears in the tins and bake for 25 minutes or until a skewer inserted into the centre comes out clean.

5 Invert the cakes on to serving plates. Heat the jam with a tablespoon of water on a low heat until melted then brush on the cakes to glaze. Dust with a little icing sugar and serve.

**If you get tired during the day and are losing concentration –
take a short nap if you can. That might be all you need to relax and refresh you**

Ginger melting moments

| **1½** Points per biscuit | Points per recipe **24** |

V Makes 16 biscuits ● Preparation time 15 minutes + cooling ● Cooking time 15 minutes ● Calories per biscuit 90 ● Freezing not recommended *These classic biscuits are not just the easiest and quickest to make but possibly the easiest and quickest to eat!*

> low-fat cooking spray
> 100 g (3½ oz) polyunsaturated margarine
> 40 g (1½ oz) icing sugar
> 1 tablespoon finely grated fresh root ginger
>   or 1 teaspoon ground ginger
> 75 g (2¾ oz) self-raising flour
> 75 g (2¾ oz) cornflour

1 Preheat the oven to Gas Mark 5/190°C/375°F and spray two baking sheets with low-fat cooking spray.
2 Cream the margarine and sugar together and then stir in the ginger and flours to make a stiff dough.
3 Divide the dough into 16 pieces and roll into little balls. Place on the baking sheets, press down gently and bake for 15 minutes. Cool on the baking trays for a few minutes before transfering to a cooling rack.

Top tip These melting moments will keep for a week in an airtight container.

Vanilla kisses

| **1½** Points per biscuit | Points per recipe **17** |

V if using free-range eggs ● Makes 12 biscuits ● Preparation time 15 minutes + cooling ● Cooking time 10–15 minutes ● Calories per biscuit 75 ● Freezing not recommended *These little kisses make lovely presents in pretty cake cases or they are great as a dinner party dessert with coffee or for a special tea.*

> 2 medium egg whites
> 50 g (1¾ oz) caster sugar
> 50 g (1¾ oz) ground almonds
> 50 g (1¾ oz) plain flour
> ½ teaspoon almond essence (optional)
> **For the filling**
> 1 teaspoon vanilla essence
> 25 g (1 oz) polyunsaturated margarine
> 50 g (1¾ oz) icing sugar

1 Preheat the oven to Gas Mark 5/190°C/375°F. Line a baking sheet with baking paper.
2 Whisk the egg whites until stiff, then fold in the sugar, almonds, flour and almond essence if using.
3 Place teaspoons of the mixture on to the baking sheet and bake for 10–15 minutes or until the kisses are pale brown. Place on a wire rack to cool.
4 Meanwhile, make the filling by creaming together the vanilla essence, margarine and sugar. Sandwich the cooled biscuits together in pairs and then place them in paper cake cases.

Variation For coffee kisses, flavour the filling with 1 teaspoon instant coffee powder dissolved in 1 teaspoon hot water instead of the vanilla.

Festive spice cookies

2½ Points per cookie	Points per recipe **54**

Ⓥ Makes 20 cookies ● Preparation and cooking time 35 minutes ● Calories per cookie 175 ● Freezing not recommended *These cookies are made with lots of delicious spices and are especially good for cutting into shapes for Christmas decorations or party treats.*

> low-fat cooking spray
> 400 g (14 oz) plain flour
> 100 g (3½ oz) self-raising flour
> 1 teaspoon baking powder
> 1 teaspoon bicarbonate of soda
> 1 teaspoon ground ginger
> 1 teaspoon ground cinnamon
> ¼ teaspoon nutmeg
> 125 g (4½ oz) polyunsaturated margarine
> 125 g (4½ oz) soft brown sugar
> 3 tablespoons black treacle
> 2 tablespoons golden syrup

1 Preheat the oven to Gas Mark 4/180°C/350°F and lightly spray a baking tray with the low-fat cooking spray.
2 Sift the flours, baking powder, bicarbonate of soda and spices together into a large bowl and make a well in the middle. In a saucepan melt the margarine, sugar, treacle and syrup together and then pour into the well. Add 2 tablespoons of water and mix together well.
3 Turn out on to a floured surface and roll out to about ½ cm (¼-inch) thick. Cut into shapes and place on the baking sheet working quickly while the dough is still warm.
4 Bake for 10 minutes or until the cookies are slightly risen and a dark golden brown. They should still be slightly soft in the middle as they will harden on cooling. Remove from the oven and, if using as decorations, make holes to hang them whilst they are still warm and soft.
5 Transfer to a wire rack to cool then decorate if you wish.

Chewy oat biscuits

1½ Points per biscuit	Points per recipe **23½**

Ⓥ Makes 18 ● Preparation time 20 minutes ● Cooking time 15 minutes ● Calories per biscuit 80 ● Freezing not recommended *These chewy little biscuits are a great low-point snack that will stave off hunger.*

> 75 g (2¾ oz) plain flour
> ½ teaspoon bicarbonate of soda
> 75 g (2¾ oz) brown sugar
> 75 g (2¾ oz) porridge oats
> 75 g (2¾ oz) polyunsaturated margarine
> 1 tablespoon golden syrup
> low-fat cooking spray

1 Preheat the oven to Gas Mark 3/170°C/325°F. In a bowl sift together the flour and bicarbonate of soda then add the sugar and oats.
2 Melt together the margarine and syrup in saucepan over a low heat and pour into the dry mixture.
3 Mix together and then place dessertspoonfuls of the mixture well apart on a baking sheet sprayed with the low-fat cooking spray. Leave plenty of space between each biscuit to allow them to spread and then flatten each slightly with your finger tips so that you have discs about 2.5 cm (1-inch) in diameter.
4 Bake for 15 minutes or until golden brown.

Top tip Store in an airtight container to keep these biscuits crisp and fresh for 3–4 days.

Fruit and nut softies

| **2** Points per biscuit | Points per recipe **40** |

V if using a free-range egg ● Makes 20 biscuits ●
Preparation time 20 minutes ● Cooking time 15 minutes
● Calories per biscuit 125 ● Freezing not recommended
These drop cookies are made with cooked carrots
which makes them delightfully moist, chewy
and sweet.

100 g (3½ oz) polyunsaturated margarine
100 g (3½ oz) soft brown sugar
225 g (8 oz) freshly cooked carrots, drained and mashed
1 medium egg, beaten
200 g (7 oz) plain flour
1 teaspoon baking powder
½ teaspoon ground cinnamon
½ teaspoon ground ginger
¼ teaspoon ground nutmeg
75 g (2¾ oz) raisins
50 g (1¾ oz) pecans nuts
    or walnuts, chopped

1 Preheat the oven to Gas Mark 5/190°C/375°F. Line two
baking sheets with non-stick baking paper. In a bowl
cream together the margarine and sugar. Add the carrots
to the creamed mixture then add the egg.
2 Sift the flour, baking powder and spices over the
mixture and add the raisins and nuts. Beat together
thoroughly. Drop teaspoons of the mixture on to the
baking sheets and spread them out with the back of
the spoon leaving plenty of space between them.
3 Bake for 12–15 minutes or until golden brown. Leave
to cool on the baking sheet for 10 minutes before
transferring to a wire rack.

index by points

index